Daring to Care with Music Education

Daring to Care with Music Education

Pedagogies for Authentic Connection and Musical Engagement

KARIN S. HENDRICKS

OXFORD
UNIVERSITY PRESS

Oxford University Press is a department of the University of Oxford. It furthers the University's objective of excellence in research, scholarship, and education by publishing worldwide. Oxford is a registered trade mark of Oxford University Press in the UK and in certain other countries.

Published in the United States of America by Oxford University Press
198 Madison Avenue, New York, NY 10016, United States of America.

Library of Congress Cataloging-in-Publication Data
Names: Hendricks, Karin S., 1971- author.
Title: Daring to care with music education : pedagogies for authentic connection and musical engagement / Karin S. Hendricks.
Description: [1.] | New York : Oxford University Press, 2025. |
Includes bibliographical references and index. |
Identifiers: LCCN 2025000558 (print) | LCCN 2025000559 (ebook) |
ISBN 9780197777541 (hardback) | ISBN 9780197777558 (paperback) |
ISBN 9780197777572 (epub) | ISBN 9780197777589
Subjects: LCSH: Music—Instruction and study, | Caring. |
Engagement (Philosophy)
Classification: LCC MT1.H44 D37 2025 (print) | LCC MT1.H44 (ebook) |
DDC 780.71—dc23/eng/20250106
LC record available at https://lccn.loc.gov/2025000558
LC ebook record available at https://lccn.loc.gov/2025000559

DOI: 10.1093/9780197777589.001.0001

Paperback printed by Marquis Book Printing, Canada
Hardback printed by Bridgeport National Bindery, Inc., United States of America

Contents

Figures

Preface

I hope you find this book to be a rainy-day, snuggle-by-the-fire kind of read, where you rest on the sofa under a warm blanket and contemplate each page at a nice leisurely pace. Or perhaps you will take the text to the beach with you on summer vacation, where you can browse around from section to section in whatever order inspires you. But I also envision you using it as a quick professional development resource, where you sneak in a page or two here and there during those precious moments when you actually get to sit down and eat lunch uninterrupted for at least 30 seconds. My hope is that you will find places in the book that leave you feeling good, confident, and inspired to change the world—or at least make one day better for at least one student. At the same time, I won't consider my work complete unless I am also a true friend who isn't afraid to tell the truth even when it's hard, and to offer ideas that give you cause for pause.

I experienced my own varied pace and range of emotions as I wrote this book. From time to time, I would drop into the project as inspiration struck, writing as fast as my fingers would allow. Other times I would spend weeks and months contemplating a single idea that was so complex that it kept me up at night as I mulled over ways to write something that seemed much bigger than one person could possibly express. While writing, sometimes I experienced all the warm fuzzies and electric inspiration that I hope you will also enjoy—but at other times the content of the book caused me to feel deep, inexpressible distress for the state of the world.

Daring to Care with Music Education has been challenging yet rewarding to write. Much of its content is adapted from the *Oxford Handbook of Care in Music Education* (OHCME), which I edited. The OHCME is a collection of 48 chapters written by 70 authors from around the world. *Daring to Care* is intended to provide busy music teachers a small snapshot of the OHCME content, while also broadening and deepening its applications for music classrooms and studios. It covers a broad array of topics that center around the ways in which music teachers might care *for*, *about*, and *with* music students.

Throughout the book I act as a kind of emcee, introducing and celebrating the brilliant ideas of many music-teaching colleagues across the world—including and beyond those who contributed to the OHCME. My aim has been to dive deeply into these ideas, create a montage from their work, and share practical approaches through a new organizational structure based on the ways these ideas resonated with me. This writing journey has been one of deep personal learning, deep contemplation, and deep care. I hope you feel that care as you read.

The authors who contributed to the OHCME inspired me, challenged me, and taught me so much. My hope for this book is to give you a small taste of some of the ideas we shared in that volume, in ways that might be immediately applicable to your teaching context. If you connect deeply with any particular idea and want to explore it more, I invite you to use the chapter endnotes to find OHCME chapters and other sources that you'd like to read as well.

A note about names: Throughout the book I mix more personal narratives with scholarly literature, to make theoretical concepts more relatable. For these narratives I sometimes use pseudonyms and have changed identifying information to protect the identity of the person involved. Other times I use actual names and identifying information, with permission. Where I write personal narratives that involve close friends or family members I use their first name, to reflect the intimacy of these interactions. However, in instances where I cite research by these same friends or my spouse, I use their last name, to maintain consistency with how I cite the work of other scholars.

A note about writing style: You may notice that I took care with hyphens to designate "caring *with*" as a noun or verb, and "caring-*with*" as an adjective. At the same time, I break many of the scholarly research style "rules" that are taught in many music education research classes, choosing instead to use a more casual and personal tone. This stylistic approach is purposeful; the book is intended to be an informal, practical treatment of various scholarly topics in music education. My primary goal is to create the kind of caring-*with* connection that I write about throughout the book. I have tried to resist a voice of authority and instead engage as a co-learner along with the reader. I use the "editorial we" throughout to signify that I, too, am learning from each of these ideas as I share them.

A disclaimer: The ideas in this book are intended to apply to a broad audience of music teachers. I expect that there are some ideas that will align better with some readers, and other ideas with other readers. I invite you to take what is meaningful for you, while also recognizing when certain ideas are not practical or realistic to your particular context. Although I hope these ideas will encourage you to stretch out of your comfort zone, I trust that you will do so within reason and within professional boundaries as they relate to your own teaching context. As I note in Chapter 9, the process of change requires continual self-reflection and self-grounding to ensure alignment with our own best interests.

Finally, to every reader of *Daring to Care*: I assume—simply because you have picked up this book—that you already care a lot about music, students, and education. Welcome. I'm glad to have you on this journey, as we explore together what it means to care *with* music education in ways that invite us to connect even more deeply, more appropriately, more effectively, more authentically, and more expressively with our students and the music we make.

Acknowledgments

This book exists because of the generous contributions of the authors in the *Oxford Handbook of Care in Music Education.* Throughout this project I have tried to honor each of your perspectives with care, knowing how much I have learned—and have yet to learn—from each of you. Thank you for sharing your deep knowledge, dedication, and wisdom. I look forward to a lifetime of continued interactions with each of you. Thank you also to the scholars who reviewed the book proposal; your insights were invaluable for the book's format, voice, and approach.

Thank you also to the following people who offered advice, support, or inspiration that impacted the final product of *Daring to Care* in some way: Corie Benton, Louis Bergonzi, Cara Bernard, Jessica Billings-White, Jordanne Burgess, Kelly Bylica, Mary Cohen, Diana Dansereau, André de Quadros, Ruth Debrot, Cheryl Freeze, Lady Gaga, Yank'l Garcia, Matthew Garrett, Andrew Goodrich, Lucy Green, Beth Hendricks, Bob Hendricks, Rob Hendricks, Steve Hendricks, Sue Hendricks, Juliet Hess, Estelle Jorgensen, Brian Kellum, Lisa Koops, Chance Krause, Kaitlyn Leahy, Katie Le Sesne, Lily Lung-Grant, Rebecca MacLeod, Gary McPherson, Sundas Mohi-Truong, Kristen Pellegrino, Rebekah Pierson, James Ray, Becky Roesler, Lorenzo Sánchez-Gatt, Jackie Smith, Gareth Smith, Tawnya Smith, Taylor Swift, Adam Symborski, Lynn Tuttle, Kính Tiến Vũ, Bruce Walker, Tammy Yi, Iris Yob, Harvey Young, and Xianjun Yu. From small but impactful comments or suggestions during the OHCME process, to reading chapter drafts for *Daring to Care*, to picking up slack where I fell short in the last two years, to hour-long phone conversations or multiple email exchanges about this project, to impacting the world the way you do—your ideas, insights, and/or gifts of time have changed this work.

Thanks to the OUP and Newgen editorial team for their kindness, care, and professionalism throughout this project. Michelle Chen, Alex Rouch, Egle Zigaite, and Loga Veera Puviyarasi have each played an important role in bringing this book to completion, and I am grateful. Thank you to my fabulous neighbors for your friendship and genuine care; and to my family—parents, siblings, nieces and nephews, and beautiful great-niblings, for your constant support and unconditional love. You mean the world to me. Thanks also to Boston University faculty, staff, and administration for making my sabbatical possible so I could finish this work. I work with some truly amazing people who embody care for, about, and with one another. Your gifts of time, support, and inspiration made this book possible in so many different ways.

Speaking of my sabbatical, I'd like to thank everyone who encouraged me (kicking and screaming!) to take one. You were right; I needed the time to center and ground in the work. Thanks also to the folks at the public libraries of Provincetown and Truro, Massachusetts, for providing a space for me to write and reflect while staring out at the Cape Cod Bay and organic gardens, respectively. It was immensely meaningful and cathartic to stare at the ocean waves while writing about some of the more cognitively and emotionally challenging topics in this book.

Finally, I am grateful beyond words for my life partner, Tawnya—who teaches me daily, in loving ways, about compassion, empathy, trust, and unselved and ecological humility. Thank you, Tawnya, for your patience and unconditional love, and for helping me see the world from a richer and more caring perspective. I can't imagine who I would be without you. I am grateful to have discussed these ideas with you, and to be inspired by your own book ideas while we enjoyed an extended "writing retreat" together. Now, to the beach!

1

Caring and Music Education

Why Do We Need a Book about This?

Chapter Overview

In our current world, music teachers must grapple with numerous distractions that prevent music learners from being fully present, fully engaged, and fully expressive. This chapter introduces various conceptualizations of care and offers research-based strategies for caring in ways that promote deeper levels of student engagement, motivation, and musicianship. Topics include the need for care, what caring in music education looks like, definitions of care, types of caring (caring *for*, *about*, and *with*), compassion and care in music education, compassionate music teaching as caring *with*, and replacing the notion of teachers as superheroes with a recognition of every co-learner's superpowers.[1]

Introduction

You are likely familiar with the old and well-worn adage, "Students don't care how much you know, until they know how much you care." This simplistic little saying has a lot of truth behind it—and if you're reading this book, you're likely already on board with the idea. But you may also agree that it's not really as simple as the saying suggests. It is sometimes easy to care, but sometimes very challenging, for a variety of reasons.

It is important to know *how* to care. Even with the best of intentions, what we may think of as a caring act may not be received that way by someone else. Further, the ways we show care will differ with each student, class, or context. This book is intended to dive deeply into various ways of caring in music education, to provide music teachers with a space to reflect about our present practices and reconsider the effectiveness and relevance of our caring efforts. It is also intended as a resource guide and support for busy, passionate, and caring teachers who are making a tangible impact every day in the lives of music learners.

What we do in the music classroom or studio has a ripple effect in the world. Caring and compassionate practices may be more necessary than ever in this current era of global uncertainty, political division, and emotional isolation. So many

Daring to Care with Music Education. Karin S. Hendricks, Oxford University Press. © Oxford University Press 2025.
DOI: 10.1093/9780197777589.003.0001

crises and uncertainties in the world today demand that we care more deeply for our students, for music, for our communities, and for ourselves. As I explain in this chapter and the next, music has a demonstrated power for connection, and music education can serve to lift students up in times of difficulty—yet music-making and music education also have the capacity to cause further harm. It is imperative, therefore, that we focus on using music to connect authentically with co-learners in healthy, sustainable, and life-giving ways.

As the world around us continues to shift dramatically, so must our teaching. With every new technological, political, or musical development, we must revisit what we do with an openness and willingness to change. Yet change is inherently uncomfortable. When we are responsible for the learning and growth of others, it can be terrifying to recognize our vulnerabilities and admit what we don't know, or that we don't have all the answers. But if we are open to learning along with our students, the journey can be joyous and take us places we never imagined.

The Need for Care and Connection

When I wrote *Compassionate Music Teaching*[2] just a few years ago, I was concerned about our rapidly shifting world, where nearly everything around us appeared to be changing (including music education). I was interested in the unique ways in which new generations of students would need to be taught—what it meant to learn and make music together, and to learn from one another. I recognized a shift not only in what it meant to be a music learner and teacher but also what it meant to be musical. I wrote about maintaining and fostering human relationships: teacher to student, student to student, within and between musical communities, and even the relationships we nurture within ourselves. I wrote of the need for human connection, and the unique ways in which exercising compassion in music learning settings can catalyze authentic relationships and authentic expression.

The need for care and connection has only amplified since then. A composite of recent events has created what Rachel Dirks calls "a pressure cooker of stress in which today's youth are navigating their lives"[3]—including continued fallout from the COVID-19 pandemic, escalating concerns with climate change, rising racial and political tensions, and aggressive social comparison via social media. Since March 2020, approximately one in four young adults has contemplated suicide, and three in four have experienced at least one adverse symptom of poor mental health.[4] Educational institutions are facing an unprecedented need to provide students, faculty, and staff with psychological support and counseling, not only considering current crises but also due to rising awareness of sexual abuse and other traumas. Music teachers must be equipped to work with students experiencing trauma and mental health concerns—while simultaneously managing our own immense stresses.[5]

Technological advancements cannot, and should not, be the single scapegoat to blame for the current downward spiral in mental and emotional health. Throughout this book we will explore many reasons behind the sense of unrest and lack of wellbeing among students and teachers alike. Yet the unprecedented opportunity for virtual connections, combined with reports of deep loneliness and isolation among today's youth, illuminates the need for music teachers to consider how we can foster authentic connections through music learning experiences—experiences that bolster, deepen, and enrich the inner lives of the students in our care.

Music classrooms and pedagogies must change even more rapidly now, in parallel with sudden shifts in society, technology, and—perhaps most notably—the dynamism of music learners' inner worlds. What better place than music education to do this critical work? Music-making can provide a unique means for tapping into these unfamiliar, complex, and ineffable feelings that so many are experiencing. It can offer a space for healing and evoke more life-giving ways of being and seeing the world—but only when handled with care.

New Ways of Teaching and Being

Music teachers do not have to choose between kindness and quality! Throughout this book I argue that compassionate and care-filled approaches to music teaching are not only more humane but also *more effective* in fostering the highest and lasting levels of musicianship.[6] As educational care theorist Nel Noddings explains, teachers and learners "will not achieve even [. . .] meager success unless our children believe that they themselves are cared for and learn to care for others."[7]

Fear-based motivational approaches have never served us in music education. They have been a damaging survival-of-the-fittest tradition, showing no long-term benefit toward musicianship or fostering an authentic love of music.[8] It is time to remove such harmful uncaring practices from our profession forever. As the student mental health crisis will likely escalate in the future,[9] we need more affirming approaches that not only foster student confidence, competence, and wellbeing but also connect students, teachers, and communities in meaningful and authentic ways.

It is unrealistic to assume that music learning can occur in a studio, rehearsal space, or community setting that is somehow sealed off from the rest of the world. Those who attempt to teach as they have in the past may be more likely than ever to confront students with blank stares and hollow expressions, or students' blatant resistance to focus on mundane facts that do not relate to the global concerns youth find to be much more pressing.[10] Radical shifts taking place in the world, and in each learner's inner world, require radical shifts in music learning and teaching.

To forge and maintain authentic musical connections, we have no choice but to grapple with the various potential distractions that keep music learners from being fully present, fully engaged in the classroom, and fully expressive. Now is the time to meet students with deeper levels of care—not as some way of "selling out on quality," "lowering standards," or "softening" more traditional music-learning approaches. On the contrary! Notions of care, as addressed in this book, compel us as music teachers to revisit not only what we do but also who we are, and to be *fiercely demanding*—of the things that truly matter to our students within and across our shared musical communities. In so doing, it is possible that levels and pathways of musicianship will soar beyond our prior expectations as we open ourselves to learning—alongside our students—all sorts of new and previously unimagined things about music-making, about teaching, about life, and about ourselves.

Educational systems will likely continue to change rapidly, requiring music teachers to remain remarkably flexible and adaptive to new pedagogical and technical approaches while also refining our practices of compassion, human connection, and expression. In this book I draw from the wisdom of over 70 authors who contributed to the *Oxford Handbook of Care in Music Education* (OHCME), which I edited. I have curated their ideas to offer practical suggestions for how music teachers can care for, about, and with their students; act as co-learners; and facilitate spaces of authenticity, improvisation, curiosity, and community. The aim of this book is to provide a space for us to reconsider and re-envision our own positions and places in the various human interactions that are essential and ever-present in music education. It is intended as a resource for music teachers at all ages and stages as we navigate new terrain together. (See Reflection Activity 1.1.)

Defining Care in Music Education

Care is a more complicated concept than it seems at first glance. (If you care enough to read this book, you likely already know this—but I trust that you also care enough to read on.) OHCME author Liora Bresler draws on Buddhist thought to describe writings on care like a finger pointing to the moon: They are only descriptions or guides for something that is much too elusive for words and that is best understood through experience.[11] Yet care—all too often discounted or diminished in discussions of music education—is critical to understand if we are serious about striving toward human flourishing.

I don't know anyone who believes there is currently enough care in the world, yet most people disagree to some extent about how to best show care for others. For example, how many times have you heard teachers and administrators argue for vastly different educational approaches, all claiming to want "what is best for the students"? Care is similar that way—it is so personal, so subjective, so impossible to tie down, yet so critical. (See Reflection Activity 1.2.)

Music education philosopher and OHCME author Marissa Silverman proposes that there are certain actions or behaviors that "caring teachers know-to-do and feel-to-do"[12]—yet how does a music teacher become caring in the first place? Can music teachers *learn* how to care? And are all kinds of care equal? Or are some kinds of care hurtful? Throughout this book we will engage with these questions through a variety of philosophical, psychological, and sociological lenses. As OHCME author Cathy Benedict suggests, it may be a question of understanding what one means by care, because the "care" we take to conceptualize "care" drives our actions.[13]

Care may be defined as demonstrations of concern, compassion, benevolence, or even love in relation to others.[14] It has been described as a universal human need[15] and a moral imperative for music teachers.[16] However, the notion of caring is sometimes misunderstood within music education—equated simply with kindness or associated falsely with lowered expectations—and is often dismissed without consideration of its full value to music learning and teaching. Therefore, it may be helpful to begin our discussion with an overview of the different ways that we might embody care within music learning settings. Let's look at the way the meaning of care changes as it is associated with three prepositions: about, for, and with.[17]

Caring *About*

Music educators have a long history of caring *about* things. We care about getting the music just right, which requires caring about the best methods for technical instruction. We care about diction. We care about tone. We care about getting F<sharp> in tune—especially, for me, when it comes to beginning violas and cellos playing on the C string. We care about best approaches to avoid sound delay on the marching field. (Some folks even care about the physics behind those sound delays, whereas others couldn't care less about the science and just want to get everyone to play it together already.) We may care about how those choir robes look, those curved pinkies, that embouchure, that improvisation, the way the students form a line, that creative composition. We care about how everything sounds when we take it apart, and we care about what happens when we put it all back together.

We also care about students. As much as we love music, many of us chose this education profession because we care about making an impact in the lives of others. Something caused us to fall in love with music—we'll talk about those "somethings" throughout this book—and we want to share music with others as if it were the most important thing in the world. Because we care about the music, we care about the people with whom we share it. And because we care about people, we care about the music we share with them. We care about how they receive what we offer, but we also care about them as humans. We care about their wellbeing, their families, their friends, their food insecurity, their mental health, their successes, their setbacks. We care about the fact that they showed up to their lesson prepared and ready to learn, and we care when they show up unprepared. We also care about them when they don't show up at all.

Caring *about* is only the beginning, albeit a critical one. As Marissa Silverman explains, "caring *about* music and music education acknowledges there is a 'need' (or needs) to be met."[18] Yet simply recognizing those needs does not necessarily equate with caring action. For example, I will be the first among my fellow social media "share" button users to confess that there are plenty of things I care about in this world, but about which I do nothing truly impactful except to notice it, comment on it, and continue with my day. Caring action, on the other hand, requires caring *for*.

Caring *For*

If we add a dimension of caring *for* to those things we care *about*, it becomes evident that caring *for* students and *for* the music requires that we actually do something. According to Nel Noddings, caring *for* students requires an attempt to anticipate students' needs and interests, and to provide for them in ways that they perceive as being beneficial.[19] The trick here is being able to understand what acts of care may be truly right and best for students—a point we will return to later. But for the sake of definition, caring *for* students involves an action in which a teacher sees a need and responds in a way that is intended to have a positive impact.

Examples of music teachers caring *for* students abound: Offering technical instruction, offering encouragement, helping students get to the performance on time and with confidence, or giving career-related advice. Caring *for* music students very often also involves care that goes beyond their music-making, such as wiping an early childhood student's nose, providing a low-income elementary student packaged foods tucked away in a special drawer, cheering middle school students at their track meet, walking high school students down to the counseling office when they are afraid to go on their own, writing letters of recommendation for college students no matter their intended career path, or spending time listening to an older adult student who has just lost their spouse.

Caring *for* the music itself involves going beyond merely caring about that out-of-tune F<sharp> or phasing problem in the marching band and making the necessary efforts to get things right. Caring *for* music education might involve researching multiple approaches to technical instruction, seeking out new teaching strategies, and improving ourselves as teachers to be more effective. Caring *for* music education may require core reflection, which is described by OHCME author Margaret Berg as requiring five steps: (a) recognizing a situation or problem that we can improve, (b) reflection on the ideal we would like to have instead, (c) awareness of the obstacle(s) or issues that might impede that ideal, (d) using our core strengths to make an improvement, and (e) trying again with newly informed approaches.[20]

A Note about Caring for Ourselves

Caring-*for* music education necessarily involves caring for ourselves as teachers—something that we who care for others can easily forget. Bridget Sweet explains how caring people like music teachers tend to be "burnt toast eaters" who take for themselves the worst portions of a meal so others can have the best food possible.[21] But giving and giving to the point of exhaustion can only last so long before we are completely depleted. Sweet goes on: "In my work with teachers, I have found that most music educators try to prevent and/or resolve problems for students (i.e., eat the burnt toast) even if the solutions contribute significantly to their own personal burnout."[22]

Sometimes, despite our best efforts, we may not be equipped with the skills or means to fix our students' problems. There is much in our world and in the lives of our students that is beyond our control and beyond our responsibility.[23] Not only can overcaring for others lead to self-neglect but also caring for others in a trauma-filled environment can lead to what Tawnya Smith has termed "secondary traumatization," or experiences in which teachers become traumatized themselves by their engagement in the fallout from their students' often-traumatic lives.[24] I address this kind of teacher stress further in Chapter 8.

In her invitation to music educators to care *for* music education, OHCME author Estelle Jorgensen reminds us to pause for a moment in our busy, racing lives and imagine a new reality for self-care:

> [I]f we are to take care of music, *we need to take care of ourselves and those with whom we work*. Ours is a people-centered undertaking, about and for people. . . . It takes time to care about oneself and others and focusing on fewer and more crucial tasks might open more time for the most important activities that allow all of us to build the house of music education together more happily.[25]

To care for music students and the music they make most effectively, we need to find ways—no matter how difficult it may seem—to first care for ourselves. I hope you read these words not as a judgment or admonishment, but rather as a problem for *us*, as a profession, to solve together. There is already plenty of the self-care shame-game going around, which likely just makes us feel worse when we can't even care for ourselves let alone others.[26] Furthermore, for many teachers self-care is a luxury that their jobs and society do not allow.[27] Instead, I state this need for teacher self-care as a question, as a wondering of sorts, of the ways that we all might more fully and deeply engage in authentic self-care, and to make it possible for others as well. I have devoted much more space to this question in Chapter 8.

It is important to keep asking the question and trying new ways to care for ourselves as music teachers. As OHCME author Stephen Paparo suggests, "teachers who are more in touch with their own needs will be more likely to show compassion for others."[28] Caring *for* music students, for music education, and for ourselves in a new and emerging world may require us to step off the music education treadmill, reflect, and change not only our technical approaches to instruction but also who we are as people. This work can be frightening in some instances and may seem impossible at others. However, as life continues to change all around us, we may find that we have no alternative. The necessity for such new paths and new approaches elicits the concept of caring *with*.

Caring *With*

Caring-*with* music education involves teaching, learning, and caring in ways that honor the individual and unique strengths of every person in the music-making space. Although caring *about* and *for* students may be critical for understanding and meeting their needs, care can sometimes be unhealthy or unhelpful if power relationships are imbalanced or overemphasized in ways that discourage student engagement, autonomy, and growth. For example, when teachers view students through a deficit perspective and consider only the ways that the students (or the students' musical skills) need to be "fixed," they may miss out on the inherent strengths that the student brings.[29] Students are more likely to engage in and enjoy an activity in which they sense the importance of their contributions and see themselves as valued, capable participants.[30] And, as explained previously, the teacher who only "cares for" others often ends up depleted and burned out.

Finally, an attitude of caring only *for* does not fully account for the ways in which a teacher also continues to learn and develop. At the risk of sounding cliché, caring truly is sharing. Caring-*with* music education involves an empowering form of care in which music teachers and students share experience, passion, excitement, music learning goals, and humanness. In a caring-*with* musical space, teachers and students learn and grow together as they engage in dialogue about musical experiences, collectively try new things, foster trust and encourage musical risk-taking, and build a community of mutual respect.

Some of the most effective music teachers I have ever met are those who are open to learning along with their students. These teachers not only say the common phrase "I learn more from my students than I could ever teach them" but they also show it—by the ways in which they adapt their activities and instruction based on student ideas, interests, and input. These teachers understand that a caring-*with* approach does not discount the tremendous musicianship, knowledge, and authority the teacher already has; those things become apparent to the students as they interact with the teacher. The difference is that the teacher's credentials and power do not need to be displayed front and center as a way of motivating students to learn, because they are more naturally motivated by the authentic welcome they feel to bring themselves, their interests, and their passions to the music learning space.

Compassionate Music Teaching

My previous book *Compassionate Music Teaching* provides examples of caring-*with* music education. In that book I argue that overly teacher-centered approaches in our field have stymied creativity, stifled expressiveness, and interfered with possibilities for authentic connections with others, with self, and with music.[31] While writing that book, I applied research in motivation, empathy, trust, and inclusion to describe how music teachers can act as co-learners with students, welcome individual expressions, and foster a collective sense of purpose and musical engagement. The framework is centered around six qualities of teaching and learning (trust, empathy, patience, inclusion, community, authentic connection) that are demonstrated and modeled by music teachers as they practice compassion.

Compassionate music teaching involves holding students to the highest expectations, but in relation to students' identities, interests, and goals.[32] Such caring *with* involves being attuned not only to learners' feelings and needs, but to their values and worldviews as well. Caring-*with* teachers and learners are co-equals in a humanitarian sense, each bringing their own set of strengths, weaknesses, and aspirations to their collaborative music-making. I have described such collective caring-*with* learners and teachers this way:

> Although these equals may bring different . . . experiences to a music learning space (such as in the case of an adult and child), they are neither greater nor lesser than one another, and they connect through a common sense of purpose. This essence of caring about, for, *and* with, in a music learning context, is also reflective of musical meaningfulness . . . and plays a role in the pursuit of human flourishing.[33]

Figure 1.1 illustrates two very different definitions of compassion. (Spoiler alert: We are aiming for one on the right.) The figure shows how compassionate music teaching might be seen as an act of caring *with* students, not just *about* or *for* them.[34] As shown at the top of the figure, the Latin "com" means "with," whereas the word "passion" can take on very different meanings. On the left side of the figure, antiquated depictions of compassion have focused on passion as "suffering," whereas on the right side, passion refers to "excitement" or "enthusiasm." On the left side, pity-based acts of care, involve a person recognizing the pain of another and acting in ways that relieve them of that pain. Of course, we want to act in ways that help to create a world where others don't suffer, and I will address music education for social action later in this book. But we can—and I argue we should—care for others without pitying them or viewing them through a deficit mindset, as I explain below.

There are at least three problems with care from a "suffering-with" or "pity" mentality in music education. The first is obvious: The notion of suffering with students in music classrooms conjures up painful images of shared misery, such as out-of-tune passages played slowly, over and over, without improvement; or a teacher saying, "I had to learn this etude, so you do too." Surely the work of a music educator and student is demanding enough. None of us need to be miserable for the sake of misery!

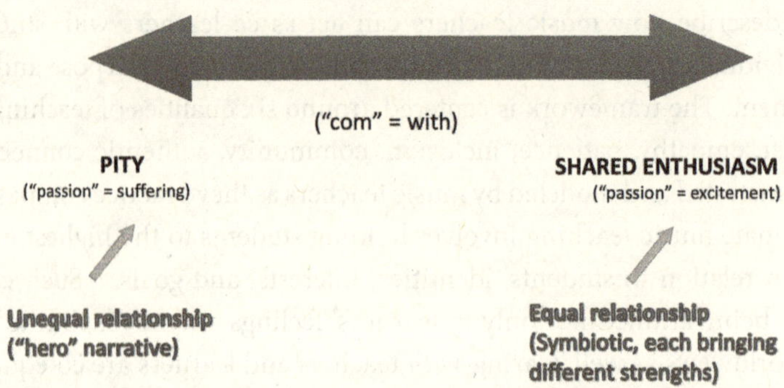

Figure 1.1 Compassion as Care: Two Definitions. Adapted from Karin S. Hendricks and Tawnya D. Smith, "Compassion, Care, Communication, and Connection in Instrumental Learning Spaces," in *Teaching Instrumental Music: Perspectives and Pedagogies for the 21st Century*, ed. Bryan Powell, Kristen Pellegrino, and Quincy Hilliard (New York: Oxford University Press, 2024), 97.

Second, students don't need to be pitied; they need to be understood. Pitying may cause a teacher to think a student needs to be "saved" somehow, rather than recognizing they have the insight and wisdom to find their own way, if supported and guided well. Pitying music students would involve thinking of them as inferior or helpless, or emphasizing what they do wrong rather than focusing on their potential and possibility. Pity often occurs when teachers and students come from different cultural backgrounds and the teacher presumes their own way of learning, behaving, or making music is superior, or the only "right" way.

Third, compassion as pity or "suffering with" might lead a teacher to give up on a student prematurely, rather than seeing them through to their full potential. This may happen because they view the student's present musicianship from a fixed mindset, or because they do not recognize the innumerable avenues a student might take toward autonomous, engaged musicianship.[35] It may also happen when "suffering with" makes everyone miserable and either student or teacher simply gives up. I think we've all been there from time to time, so I will be the first to confess that I have let plenty of students down by not envisioning a way forward before they found their way to the door. Those students have always remained in my memory and continue to teach me new and better ways of teaching and being.

Compassionate Music Teaching as Caring *With*

The right side of Figure 1.1 illustrates a more empowering approach. In contrast to the notion of compassion as pity on the left side, the right involves a more egalitarian frame of mind for caring *with*—in a music classroom or beyond—in which we recognize the dignity of the other person, see them as equals in terms of their humanity, and engage in learning and growing together in ways that draw on each person's unique strengths. Compassionate music teaching is a form of caring *with* that removes the power struggle.

When students feel caught in a power relationship with teachers, learning about music will be difficult, if not impossible. They may learn, but not about music. Instead, as I wrote in *Compassionate Music Teaching*, "what students end up learning are lessons about power, authority, embarrassment, oppression, pain, and how to 'win' or 'lose' in a system with particular rules that favor one person or idea over another."[36]

In contrast, a compassionate, caring-*with* music education celebrates and utilizes the strengths that each person brings, and allows students and teachers to expand and enhance their musicianship together. It focuses on learning and growth rather than proving one's worth according to someone else's criteria, and it evokes community and curiosity through music-making:

> Teachers act as guides, supports, and champions of students' self-selected dreams, using the students' own aspirations for musical expression as a catalyst for emphasizing the practice of diverse technical skills. Facilitating this kind of learning requires that we listen . . . and consider what learning looks like from the student's perspective. It follows, then, that we teach in the way that is best for each student or each class in each particular moment.[37]

By fostering trust and exercising healthy forms of empathy (which we will explore later in this book), teachers can create music learning environments that draw on students' strengths and make music learning more attainable, more enjoyable, and more intrinsically rewarding. (See Reflection Activity 1.3.)

What Caring *With* Might Look Like: Examples from an Early Childhood Music Class

Boxes 1a and 1b contain vignettes written by OHCME author Diana Dansereau.[38] Both vignettes depict a similar classroom scenario but with very different teaching approaches and outcomes. The first vignette shows a teaching style that might be considered only caring *about*, because Teacher Lisa appears genuinely motivated and interested in what she has prepared to share with the students. She also appears to care about the ways in which the students interact with her, and how they interact with the music and the props she has brought to the lesson. Finally, she shows some aspects of caring *for* the music (as *she* has envisioned it to be), as she reaches out to Michael to correct his musical explorations and steers him back to the activity as planned.

Box 1a Influences of Problematic Conceptualizations on Musical Engagement

Lisa sits in a circle on the carpet with eight 4-year-old children who have just arrived for music class. She begins the class by greeting the children:

LISA: Good morning!

CHILDREN: Good morning.

LISA: You can do better than that! Let me hear your enthusiasm! Good morning!

CHILDREN: (louder) Good morning!

LISA: I can't hear you!

CHILDREN: (shouting) Good morning!!!

LISA: Much better! Now, we are going to begin our class by learning a song about my favorite animal. Can anyone guess what my favorite animal might be? I'll give you a hint: It likes to jump.

MICHAEL (ONE OF THE CHILDREN): A frog?

LISA: Not a frog...

AMALIA (ANOTHER OF THE CHILDREN): A grasshopper?

LISA: No, not a grasshopper.

KAREEM: A rabbit?

LISA: Nope! Not a rabbit! Okay, I'll tell you. My favorite animal is a kangaroo and our first song is about a kangaroo.

Lisa sings the song for the children and then passes shaker eggs to each child, instructing them to keep the beat by shaking the eggs while singing the song. The children follow her instructions and appear to enjoy playing the shaker eggs. Michael explores shaking his eggs to the microbeat. Lisa pauses to correct Michael and reminds him that they are to be shaking on the macrobeat. When the song is finished, Lisa collects the eggs. Kyana holds her shaker eggs tightly, not wanting to return them. Lisa explains that it is time to move on and Kyana reluctantly, with a sad expression on her face, gives Lisa her shaker eggs.*

*Dansereau, "Compassion during Musical Engagement with Young Children," 62.

At first glance, there is much that appears to work well in the first vignette. There is a certain level of efficiency, students follow the teacher's instructions, and most students appear to be generally enjoying the shaker egg activity. The students also appear to be learning about macrobeats in ways that will likely set them up well for future lessons that expand on these ideas. However, as we look more closely, we see that Teacher Lisa sets up an unequal power relationship and student deficit mindset from the very beginning. She asks the students to match her expectations for greeting her, but without ever checking in to see how the students are feeling. She demands that they greet her louder than they did initially, without appearing to question why they may not feel like raising their voice at her (keep this instance in mind when we address trauma-informed approaches in Chapter 3).

Teacher Lisa then introduces the activity by requiring the students to guess her favorite animal, hence placing the attention on her own interests without providing room for the students to envision their own—also reinforcing the all-too-common, (non)educational practice of students having to figure out the teacher's wishes. As the music progresses, she interrupts Michael's and Kyana's attempts at musical exploration and creativity by requiring them to engage in the activity as she has planned it.

Dansereau explains how a teacher-centered approach that emphasizes teacher strengths and student deficits may discourage student musicianship:

> [D]eficit conceptualizations about childhood can permeate the environment of the music classroom, leading to an environment of protection, delayed responsibility, and dependence. Specifically, children [. . .] may be positioned as in a state of perpetual musical development—that is, viewed as musical becomings rather than musical beings. Music educators may seek to control the classroom and thus delay responsibility for children, and they may unwittingly encourage musicianship that is dependent on the educator.[39]

In sum, the vignette in Box 1a shows on-task behavior, learning about macrobeats, and some forms of caring *about* and *for* music. However, one can envision the ways in which these students are simultaneously learning about power imbalances, their failures to comply with someone else's wishes, and how their interests in musical exploration are not welcome in this space. It should not be surprising if these students were to eventually disengage with this form of teacher-centered music instruction and prefer making music on their own time, and in their own way, outside of formal music learning settings.

In contrast, the second vignette (Box 1b) illustrates ways in which Teacher Mya cares *about*, *for*, and *with* students as they make and learn music together. This second approach is an example of what Dansereau calls "co-equal interaction"[40] with students. Teacher Mya is clearly still the authority in the room; however, she uses a caring-*with* approach that affords students a sense of contribution and ownership of their musical development. This more egalitarian model is evident in the way that Mya listens and responds to students as they make music with her. She makes space in the lesson for students to volunteer their own ideas. She is also eager to learn new songs from the children, making notes of ways to incorporate their prior musical knowledge into her unit teaching plan. By connecting her learning outcomes to students' knowledge, she will likely help the lessons become more personally meaningful and easier for them to remember. She facilitates social understandings between other classmates through honoring and making space for them to share what matters to each of them.

Box 1b Children as Musical Interactors; Adults as Musical Interactors

Mya sits on the carpet as eight 4-year-old children enter the classroom. The children notice the photographs on the carpet in front of Mya which depict the songs and activities that the children have experienced in previous music classes. Some photos show props that the children have used to accompany music-making, some are images of the children moving in ways that align with particular activities, others help the children remember song characters. Each child chooses one or two photos and hands them to Mya, who adheres them to the felt board at the front of the room. The pictures will guide the content of the class and the order that the content will be experienced. Mya has also prepared a new song to share, which she will introduce toward the middle of the class.

The familiar song depicted in the first photograph involves shaker eggs, so the children and Mya move to the basket of shaker eggs which is stored on a shelf that is accessible to the children. All musicians take their two eggs and return to the carpet. Mya begins to sing the song and the children play along. At the end of the song there is a pause and James begins the song again. All musicians join James for three additional repetitions of the song. At one point, Annie chooses a scarf from a basket on the materials shelf and performs a flowing movement to accompany the singing.

After the last note, Mya sings SOL-DO and waits should a child choose to respond. Lizzie repeats Mya's pattern, so Mya sings it again to Lizzie. Ben jumps in and sings SOL-MI-DO, which Mya also repeats. Ben sings SOL-MI-DO again, and Mya sings MI-RE-DO.

HAKIM: That sounds like a song my mom sings to me!
MYA: Neat! Could you sing the song for us?
HAKIM: [sings song]
MYA: Hakim, I have never heard that song before. Would you mind singing it again so that we can all learn it?

Hakim sings and Mya makes a mental note to create a photograph depicting the song for the next class. She will work with Hakim and the other children to build on the song, perhaps adding movements or instruments.

MYA THEN SAYS: I suggest we move on to our next activity. Remember that we decided hand drums work well for this one.
Thalia grips her shaker eggs tightly, appearing unwilling to return them yet.
MYA: Thalia, do you think our next song would sound nice with some shaker eggs also?
THALIA: I want to try!

The other musicians retrieve hand drums, Mya begins the second song, and Thalia plays along with her shaker eggs. Lizzie says, "Again!" after they finish so they repeat the song.*

*Dansereau, "Compassion during Musical Engagement with Young Children," 65–66.

Teacher Mya has prepped the space with visual reminders of past lessons and invites the students to choose which aspects to review—yet after they do so, she organizes their choices in a way that will make sense musically and best support their technical development. She has also organized the room so that children can access other props if they desire, thereby encouraging movement and musical creativity along with the singing. Solfege activities are not forced but occur organically as a part of teacher–student musical interactions. Further, students' attempts at singing solfege are rewarded with more music-making. Although Thalia demonstrates resistance to Teacher Mya's instructions to put the shaker eggs away, Teacher Mya views Thalia's interest in keeping the shaker eggs as a musical curiosity rather than a distraction from her own agenda. She therefore asks Thalia follow-up questions to encourage her continued participation in the lesson, finding a way to negotiate Thalia's musical explorations with the rest of the children's interest in moving on to something new.

In this second vignette, Teacher Mya demonstrates caring *about* students and the music they bring. Her preparation with photos and props shows how she has noticed their individual activities and interests of the students. She demonstrates caring *for* the students as she has made the photos and props accessible to them, and how she organizes the photos to create a class sequence that will help the students have positive and productive learning experiences. Finally, she cares *with* the students as she makes space in the singing activity for them to contribute in ways that they choose (and with which they are comfortable), and she takes time to listen to their music and incorporate their ideas into future lessons. She also cares *with* the students as she negotiates conflict by empathizing with their needs and interests. None of us would be naive enough to imagine or expect that any music lesson will always run perfectly, but at least we can see from this second vignette how caring *with* affords room for students and teachers to make their way together toward more engaged, authentically connected, more enjoyable music-making.

Goodbye Superheroes, Hello Superpowers

Caring-*with* music education also challenges the "teacher-as-hero" narrative. Unfortunately, members of our society (including politicians and popular media) have often set up music teachers as "heroes" in ways that appear to be portrayed with gratitude and honor, but that may actually undermine student learning and teacher wellbeing. The teacher-as-hero narrative places an expectation on teachers to be "all-knowing," "masters," or "in a posture of "reaching down" to help students with alleged deficits. This problematic narrative can:

- put undue and unrealistic pressure on the teacher to be everyone and everything for students;
- create a false sense of separation between teachers and students;

- establish unhealthy or even damaging power relationships;
- create perfectionistic expectations that cause both students and teachers to conflate personal worthiness with musical performance;
- underestimate, overlook, or devalue student strengths;
- deny students opportunities to be agents their own learning; and
- disallow the teacher permission to continue learning as well.

In contrast, a caring-*with* approach recognizes that no one needs to play the role of superhero but invites everyone to contribute their own unique superpowers. The music teacher's art of alchemizing those individual superpowers together can create a music learning experience more powerful—and more empowering—than any one teacher could dream up on their own, no matter how much expertise they may already possess. Further, in an age where everything is changing so rapidly that expertise might easily become obsolete, a caring-*with* approach allows teachers to facilitate engaged, brave, and trust-filled learning spaces for music students as they also continue to learn themselves. (See Reflection Activities 1.4 and 1.5.)

Summary and Looking Forward

Although current music students are in many ways more connected with the world than any generation before them, they are exhibiting signs of isolation, fear, and deteriorating mental health that affect their lives and their ability to learn. There is a deep and pressing need to revisit music teaching practices that cause unnecessary fear, limit creativity, and breed distrust among students and teachers—and instead create learning spaces that foster community, engagement, and authentic connection. This book is a practical guide based on ideas presented in the *Oxford Handbook of Care in Music Education.* It addresses three forms of caring (for, about, with) to offer ways in which music teachers and students can interact as co-learners and forge authentic relationships with one another (and with music) through collective music-making.

Caring-*with* music education honors the individual and unique strengths of every person in the music-making space. It involves music teachers and students sharing new ideas and unique strengths, helping teachers avoid burnout while they continue to learn new things from active, engaged students. It involves holding students to the highest musical expectations but doing so in ways that align with students' values, interests, and strengths.

This chapter includes two vignettes that illustrate different forms of caring in music education. Although the first vignette shows some evidence of caring *about* students and caring *for* the music, the second vignette shows examples of how a music teacher might care *for*, *about*, and *with* students and the music they make together. Caring *with* is a form of compassionate music teaching, where teachers and students share passion and enthusiasm. Here, teachers let go of the need to be a superhero and instead facilitate every learner's unique superpowers.

The rest of this book will offer approaches to care that intersect with a broad range of topics set within music learning contexts. (See Reflection Activity 1.6.) These discussions and illustrations will extend previous conceptions of care in music education, to meet the needs of contemporary music learners and the teachers who care *for*, *about*, and *with* them. It is my hope that envisioning care as a catalyst toward connection and empowerment might inspire us as music teachers to practice persistent curiosity, and to open ourselves to a state of presence and authentic engagement with others, with music, and with ourselves.

Reflection Activities

1.1. How would you define care, without using the word?

1.2. Consider the three types of caring presented in this chapter. How have you been cared *for*? Cared *about*? Cared *with*? How have you cared for, about, and with others?

1.3. What are some of the stresses that you and your students are dealing with? In what ways have you connected with others to work through these stresses?

1.4. What are your superpowers (musical, educational, or otherwise)? What are some of your students' superpowers? How can each of these unique strengths be combined in your music learning space?

1.5. Create a playlist that illustrates the superpowers you listed above.

1.6. Go to the index of this book and choose 3–5 topics of particular interest to you. Then read the material on those pages, wherever they land in the book. If you are reading the book with others, share what insights you gained from your holistic reading of this topic.

Notes

1. Some of the material in this chapter is paraphrased, adapted, or written verbatim from my own writings in the Preface and Chapter 1 of the *Oxford Handbook of Care in Music Education*. See Karin S. Hendricks, "Preface," in *The Oxford Handbook of Care in Music Education*, ed. Karin S. Hendricks (New York: Oxford University Press, 2023), xvii–xx; and Karin S. Hendricks, "A Call for Care in Music Education," in *The Oxford Handbook of Care in Music Education*, ed. Karin S. Hendricks (New York: Oxford University Press, 2023), 5–22.
2. Karin S. Hendricks, *Compassionate Music Teaching: A Framework for Motivation and Engagement in the 21st Century* (Lanham, MD: Rowman & Littlefield, 2018).
3. Rachel L. Dirks, "Student and Teacher Mental Health: Nurturing Wellbeing within a Climate of Trust," in *The Oxford Handbook of Care in Music Education*, ed. Karin S. Hendricks (New York: Oxford University Press, 2023), 320.
4. Madeline St. Amour, "Pandemic Increasing Suicidal Ideation," *Inside Higher Ed.*, August 17, 2020, https://www.insidehighered.com/news/2020/08/17/suicidal-ideation-rise-college-aged-adults-due-covid-19-pandemic.
5. Rachel L. Dirks, Tawnya D. Smith, Patricia A. González-Moreno, and Allyn Phelps, "Mental Health and String Education: Identifying Concerns within the American String Teachers Association Community," *String Research Journal* 14, no. 1 (2024): 53–76, https://doi.org/10.1177/19484992231195013; Tawnya D. Smith, "Teaching through Trauma: Compassion Fatigue, Burnout, or Secondary Traumatic Stress?,"

in *Trauma and Resilience in Music Education*, ed. Deborah Bradley and Juliet Hess (New York: Routledge, 2022), 49–63.

6. See also Karin S. Hendricks and Tawnya D. Smith, "Compassion, Care, Communication, and Connection in Instrumental Learning Spaces," in *Teaching Instrumental Music: Perspectives and Pedagogies for the 21st Century*, ed. Bryan Powell, Kristen Pellegrino, and Quincy Hilliard (New York: Oxford University Press, 2023), 95–102.
7. Nel Noddings, "Teaching Themes of Care," *Phi Delta Kappan* 76 (1995): 675–676.
8. Randall E. Allsup and Cathy Benedict, "The Problems of Band: An Inquiry into the Future of Instrumental Music Education." *Philosophy of Music Education Review* 16, no. 2 (2008): 156–173. https://www.jstor.org/stable/40327299; Hendricks, *Compassionate Music Teaching*; Karin S. Hendricks, Tawnya D. Smith, and Jennifer Stanuch, "Creating Safe Spaces for Music Learning," *Music Educators Journal* 101, no. 1 (2014): 35–40. See also Patrick B. Forsyth, Curt M. Adams, and Wayne K. Hoy, *Collective Trust: Why Schools Can't Improve without It* (New York: Teachers College Press, 2011).
9. Dirks, "Student and Teacher Mental Health," 320; Shannan L. Hibbard and Erin E. Price, "Trauma: A Compassionate Lens for Music Teaching," in *The Oxford Handbook of Care in Music Education*, ed. Karin S. Hendricks (New York: Oxford University Press, 2023), 384–394; Tawnya D. Smith, "Caring with the Earth, Community, and Co-Learners for the Health of Biological, Social, and Musical Ecosystems," in *The Oxford Handbook of Care in Music Education*, ed. Karin S. Hendricks (New York: Oxford University Press, 2023), 141–152.
10. Karin S. Hendricks, "Contexts and Conceptualizations of Care in Music Education," in *The Routledge Companion to Creativities in Music Education*, ed. Clint Randles and Pamela Burnard (New York: Routledge, 2022), 404–415.
11. Liora Bresler, "Co-Creating Caring Relationships," in *The Oxford Handbook of Care in Music Education*, ed. Karin S. Hendricks (New York: Oxford University Press, 2023), 154–156.
12. Marissa Silverman, "Caring about Caring for Music Education," in *The Oxford Handbook of Care in Music Education*, ed. Karin S. Hendricks (New York: Oxford University Press, 2023), 31–45.
13. Cathy Benedict, "Foreword to Section Four: Care, Social Activism, and Critical Consciousness," in *The Oxford Handbook of Care in Music Education*, ed. Karin S. Hendricks (New York: Oxford University Press, 2023), 446–448.
14. Nel Noddings, *Caring: A Relational Approach to Ethics and Moral Education*, 2nd ed. (Berkeley: University of California Press, 2013); Marissa Silverman, "Virtue Ethics, Care Ethics, and the Good Life of Teaching," *Action, Criticism, and Theory for Music Education* 11, no. 2 (2012): 96–122. http://act.maydaygroup.org/articles/Silverman11_2.pdf.
15. Scott N. Edgar, "An Ethic of Care in High School Instrumental Music," *Action, Criticism, and Theory for Music Education* 13, no. 2 (2014): 111–137, http://act.maydaygroup.org/articles/Edgar13_2.pdf.
16. Randall Everett Allsup and Eric Shieh, "Social Justice and Music Education: The Call for a Public Pedagogy," *Music Educators Journal* 98, no. 4 (2012): 47–51.
17. For a more extended discussion on the various types of caring in music education (with additional prepositions), see Silverman, "Caring about Caring for Music Education."
18. Silverman, "Caring about Caring for Music Education."
19. Noddings, *Caring*, 49.
20. Margaret Berg, "Fostering Care through Core Reflection," in *The Oxford Handbook of Care in Music Education*, ed. Karin S. Hendricks (New York: Oxford University Press, 2023), 5.
21. Bridget Sweet, "Self-Care and the Music Educator," in *The Oxford Handbook of Care in Music Education*, ed. Karin S. Hendricks (New York: Oxford University Press, 2023), 3.
22. Sweet, "Self-Care and the Music Educator," 3.
23. Jessica Nápoles, "Burnout: A Review of the Literature," *Update: Applications of Research in Music Education* 40, no. 2 (2022): 24, https://doi.org/10.1177%2F87551233211037669, as cited in Sweet, "Self-Care and the Music Educator," 9.
24. Smith, "Teaching through Trauma," 49–63.
25. Estelle Jorgensen, "On Caring for Music Education in Troubled Times," in *The Oxford Handbook of Care in Music Education*, ed. Karin S. Hendricks (New York: Oxford University Press, 2023), 9.
26. Tawnya D. Smith reveals the prevalence of self-shaming in our field for the lack of self-care, which perpetuates a counterproductive cycle of self-judgment, in "Teaching through Trauma."
27. Smith, "Teaching through Trauma."
28. Stephen A. Paparo, "Somatic Self-Care for Music Educators," in *The Oxford Handbook of Care in Music Education*, ed. Karin S. Hendricks (New York: Oxford University Press, 2023), 350.
29. Diana R. Dansereau, "Compassion during Musical Engagement with Young Children," in *The Oxford Handbook of Care in Music Education*, ed. Karin S. Hendricks (New York: Oxford University Press, 2023), 56–69; Constance L. McKoy and Vicki R. Lind, *Culturally Responsive Teaching in Music Education: From Understanding to Application*, 2nd ed. (New York: Routledge, 2023); James Ray, Brian W. Kellum, and Karin S. Hendricks, "Culturally Responsive Teaching in School Orchestras," in *Teaching Instrumental Music: Perspectives and Pedagogies for the 21st Century*, ed. Bryan Powell, Kristen Pellegrino, and Quincy Hilliard (New York: Oxford University Press, 2023), 299–305.
30. Hendricks, *Compassionate Music Teaching.*

31. Hendricks, *Compassionate Music Teaching.* Others have also made similar arguments; for example, Randall E. Allsup, *Remixing the Classroom: Toward an Open Philosophy of Music Education* (Bloomington: Indiana University Press, 2016).
32. Hendricks, *Compassionate Music Teaching*; Karin S. Hendricks, "Authentic Connection in Music Education: A Chiastic Essay," in *Authentic Connection: Music, Spirituality, and Wellbeing*, ed. Karin S. Hendricks and June Boyce-Tillman (New York: Peter Lang, 2021), 237–253; Susan A. O'Neill, "Youth Empowerment and Transformative Music Engagement," in *The Oxford Handbook of Social Justice in Music Education*, ed. Cathy Benedict, Patrick Schmidt, Gary Spruce, and Paul Woodford (New York: Oxford University Press, 2015), 388–405.
33. Hendricks, "Authentic Connection in Music Education," 246.
34. Hendricks, *Compassionate Music Teaching.*
35. Carol S. Dweck, *Mindset: The New Psychology of Success* (New York: Random House, 2006); Karin S. Hendricks and Gary E. McPherson, "Reconsidering Musical Ability Development through the Lens of Diversity and Bias," in *The Oxford Handbook of Care in Music Education*, ed. Karin S. Hendricks (New York: Oxford University Press, 2023), 408–420.
36. Hendricks, *Compassionate Music Teaching.*
37. Hendricks, *Compassionate Music Teaching.*
38. For a much more in-depth discussion of these vignettes and various conceptualizations of childhood, see Dansereau, "Compassion during Musical Engagement with Young Children," 56–69.
39. Dansereau, "Compassion during Musical Engagement with Young Children."
40. Dansereau, "Compassion during Musical Engagement with Young Children."

2

Co-Creating Caring Relationships

Chapter Overview

This chapter addresses ways in which music teachers act as co-learners and facilitate authentic connections between and among students. Picking up from the elementary class vignettes presented in the previous chapter, Chapter 2 begins with descriptions of Generations Z and alpha—students whose needs, motivations, and means of connection are in many ways different from previous generations. It addresses the innate need humans have for social connections, the ways in which we connect with others, and healthful and appropriate approaches for music teachers to connect with students. The current loneliness epidemic is addressed, along with the human need for social connections and the unique potential for music to forge such connections. The social brain hypothesis is presented as a means of considering human limits for social networking. Reciprocal and responsive caring are defined, along with an explanation of the difference between reciprocal and responsive caring *for* versus caring *with*. Chapter topics include the need for connection; creating authentic connections; recognizing social limits; reciprocal and responsive care; empathy, shame, and connection; unselved or ecological humility; and trust for relationship building.

Introduction

If I were making a movie instead of writing a book, I might produce an opening scene for this chapter that starts with an aerial shot over a large city. Let's pretend, for example, that we are looking together over my home city of Boston, Massachusetts. We would see countless byways that connect to one another: tollways; freeways; highways; railways; subways; boat ways; and airways for planes, jets, and even an occasional helicopter. These byways weave and intersect, sometimes toppling over one another where multiple paths merge (sending planes over trains over cars on bridges over boats in the river—which is the case just a few hundred feet from my university office). Imagine some upbeat, James Taylor-esque acoustic guitar background music.

Next, our camera zooms closer between the streets of Boston to one public secondary school—and then inside the school walls to reveal the many hallways that

Daring to Care with Music Education. Karin S. Hendricks, Oxford University Press. © Oxford University Press 2025.
DOI: 10.1093/9780197777589.003.0002

connect within that space. As the camera zooms even closer, we see throngs of student bodies walking slowly through those hallways between classes, with heads lowered, thumbs whizzing over their phones. The hallways also weave and intersect, and students often bump into one another as they navigate the crowded space. Let's use the same background music, with a crescendo to a forte volume and the addition of some drums (I invite you to choose the beat).

Suddenly the camera angle flips upside down while everything speeds up 10 times the tempo, and we see the countless social byways connecting students to one another in a virtual space. These electronic connections are illustrated as AI-generated colored lines. They intersect and overlap one another like the city byways and school hallways, yet they also extend beyond the school space. The background music also speeds up considerably. It turns electronic and pointillistic, with a variety of rapid motifs laid over one another, and over longer bass tones. The long tones give the music a sense of groundedness that contrasts with the stochastic nature of the higher-pitched motifs. The camera pauses here for a moment, giving us a view into the connections themselves.

Inside each adolescent's mind are countless connections to a world much larger than the one inside the school's walls. Students may be watching videos, listening to tunes, sharing music, sending or receiving photos, solving a word puzzle, signing up for a climate strike. One student may be chatting with their best friend, another with their mother, another with a stranger online, another unknowingly with a chatbot. They may be searching online to decide which clothes to wear tomorrow to avoid teasing and bullying; they may be making disparaging comments online about other people's clothes, hair, abilities, or actions. They may be sharing secrets and vulnerabilities with someone they trust, whether that person is in their first-hour class or someone they wouldn't recognize if they met them on the street.

Enter the final stage of this "movie" opening: The camera zooms even further into the internal world of one adolescent who does not appear on the outside to stand out in any particular way from any other person in the scene. But as we enter that space, the world of connections is replaced with one dark gray, expansive, partially-lit hallway with no visible exit. The rapid, pointillistic music from the previous scene fades and morphs into something much slower than any other music we have heard thus far: one long bass tone overlaid by a few random vocal "oh" sounds in the soprano and alto range.

Suddenly the music stops entirely, leaving us in the near darkness of this gray and isolated hallway. Then, breaking the silence, we hear the spoken words: "Hey Sam, are you ok?"

End Scene.

Members of Generation Z, and their younger siblings in Generation alpha, are more connected with the rest of the world than any generations before them.[1] There are countless exciting ways that technological connections have expanded their perspectives and their ability to access information—including multifarious musical repertoires and capabilities for creating and producing their own music.

They are also more globally connected with one another in ways that have the potential to change the world through positive, community-based action.[2]

Despite these exciting opportunities, research tells us that today's youth are reporting deep feelings of isolation, loneliness, and deteriorating mental health.[3] They are connecting faster and more widely with more people than in any time in history, and there appears to be ample opportunity for them to be active, productive, and happy. However, they are in many ways less content and more troubled than the generations who came before them.[4]

It is not just today's youth that we should be concerned about. Over the past few decades, an epidemic of loneliness has settled into the world, spanning across generations and countries.[5] In the United States, one third of adults report having less than three close friends, while 12% report having no close friends at all.[6] In 1990, 70% of the US population claimed to have a "best friend," but in 2021 that number was down to 59%.[7] These trends of loneliness are reflected in many other countries around the world,[8] particularly, it appears, in countries with industrialized and individualistic cultures.[9]

In 2020 Vivek Murthy, who began a second term as US Surgeon General in 2021, reported on a several-decade trend showing the "rising physical and emotional toil of social disconnection."[10] He considered loneliness such a global crisis that he made it a priority in his administration, noting especially how loneliness affects physical and mental health in addition to emotional health. His book *Together: The Healing Power of Human Connection in a Sometimes Lonely World* addresses many ways that humans can overcome loneliness and isolation and support one another toward mental, emotional, and physical wellbeing.[11]

I share Murthy's concern, and I have similarly committed my life and work in music education to the study and pursuit of human connection. In this chapter I explore various ways to co-create caring relationships, social bonding, and what I call "authentic connection," through relational music learning. I first address the ways in which humans need social connection, and then describe the power of music for facilitating social bonds and authentic connection. Finally, I address how trust, mature empathy, and unselved or ecological humility work toward the co-creation of caring relationships.

Understanding Human Connection

Connection with others is literally a life-or-death matter. Research has shown that people who lack strong social connections are 50% more likely to die prematurely in comparison to people who have strong social connections.[12] How is this possible? In part, because our brains are wired to look to others for felt safety—and when we lack such a sense of safety and trust, the central nervous system responds with a threat response that increases stress hormones, blood pressure, and inflammation.[13] It is not surprising, then, that loneliness has been associated with higher risk of heart disease, stroke, dementia, anxiety, depression, poor quality sleep, weaker immune systems, poor decision-making, impulsive behavior, and substance abuse.[14]

Loneliness is different from being alone. Alone time is sometimes good for our wellbeing, and it is natural to need or crave it when we are overwhelmed and need some space to wring out our social "sponge." It is loneliness that we need to watch out for. In *Together*, Vivek Murthy clarifies the difference between isolation, solitude, and loneliness[15]—each of which will have a different impact on our physical, mental, and emotional health.

Isolation refers to being physically separated and/or out of touch with others. It can lead to loneliness, but not necessarily so, depending on how comfortable a person is with being alone. As an example, in my first school teaching job I taught at seven different rural schools, traveling to five schools per day and spending a lot of time on the road. Being a traveling teacher meant I rushed in and out of each school, eating lunch in transit and missing most faculty meetings. Because of my itinerant schedule I never had a chance to build a strong relationship with any other teachers at any school. This isolation from colleagues was accompanied by deep pangs of loneliness and a common feeling of being lost without the music teaching mentorship I desperately needed. Such feelings are common for many rural music teachers, whose sense of isolation can lead to lower teaching self-efficacy beliefs and commitment.[16] Isolation is also common among teachers who may be surrounded by colleagues in their same area, but whose approaches, values, or beliefs are in contradiction with those they work with. That kind of isolation can be similarly painful—even heart-wrenching.

Although I felt physical isolation from colleagues in my first teaching job, I nevertheless sought out daily chances to self-isolate when I arrived at the high school. My isolation from colleagues was associated with loneliness; however, at the high school I still craved and needed *solitude*, which Murthy defines as "peaceful aloneness or voluntary isolation" in which we have "an opportunity for self-reflection and a chance to connect with ourselves without distraction or disturbance."[17] I did not have a classroom at the high school and I taught on the auditorium stage, which meant I had no private place to look over my lesson plan or to regroup after a particularly busy or stressful experience earlier in the day.

Although I absolutely adored the teenagers at this school, our emotions and personalities became like oil and water if I was unable to center myself before class and prepare myself to give lightning-fast instructions and responses that matched their unbounded energy. To find that sense of peace prior to the class, I secured a key to the auditorium light booth and would regularly climb the catwalk to take a few deep breaths and count down from 10 in my head (drowning out faint sounds of teenagers asking, "Where's Ms. Hen?" in the background). Then, after climbing back down from the light booth, I was better able to care for, about, and with students in appropriate and more effective ways. Decades later, I still continue these practices of solitude through meditation, music listening, drives, hikes, and long walks along the river when I need to get away from the fast pace of my urban university position. The setting is very different now, but the need for solitude is the same.

In contrast to isolation and solitude, *loneliness* is the natural experience we feel when our bodies, minds, and emotions are telling us that we need to connect with others for the sake of our wellbeing.[18] Similar to hunger pains when we need food, loneliness is a signal that we need to do something to fill ourselves socially. Recognizing loneliness as a sign for action is power, as we can take it as an invitation for self-preserving and self-caring social outreach. The problem comes, however, when we ignore our feelings of loneliness—or misunderstand them as something being inherently wrong with us as a person, rather than recognizing loneliness for what it is: a gentle tug or note to ourselves that something is out of alignment in our social life.

Social media platforms are designed to make it easier for people to connect with others.[19] However, depending on how we engage with social media, it can also lead to even greater levels of personal dissatisfaction, distrust of others, and feelings of loneliness and isolation. Marketing algorithms work in ways that put us into camps, feeding off fear narratives that magnify differences we have with others, thereby breeding further distrust. Additionally, our "higher, faster, stronger, better" culture—in tandem with corporations that use psychological knowledge intentionally to make us feel that we're not ever enough (so they can make money by selling us things we don't need)—reinforces a socially comparative, never-good-enough climate that leaves people feeling like they're relatively worse off than other people around them who *seem* to have it all together.[20]

When we feel down about ourselves, we're less likely to share our vulnerabilities and take the risks necessary to make authentic connections.[21] And when we feel lonely, our stress response engages and causes us to withdraw.[22] Rinse and repeat, and the cycle of loneliness perpetuates itself.[23] (See Reflection Activities 2.1–2.3.)

Creating Connection through Music

There is hope—and it comes, unsurprisingly, by building positive, trusting, social connections. Murthy writes: "While loneliness has the potential to kill, connection has even more potential to heal."[24] And the good news gets even better for music teachers and learners: One of the best ways to create positive social relationships is—you guessed it—music. For example, singing in groups has been found to speed up the process of group bonding, faster than other shared group activities such as creative writing and crafts.[25] One reason for this relatively quick bonding in choral settings is because it happens at a collective (group) level through shared, synchronous music-making, and does not require that members first create individual relationships with other members in the group.[26]

Musicians understand exactly what such research is about. This experience of ineffable connection with other music-makers is known by many names—attunement, coherence, communitas, communicative musicality, effervescence, electricity, empathic creativity, entrainment, flow, and spiritual experience, to name a few.[27] In *Compassionate Music Teaching* and in other later writings I have referred to a similar experience as "authentic connection," which can include this aspect of social bonding, but—more importantly—involves practicing integrity, honesty, and vulnerability to foster self- and other-alignment. No matter what you call this kind of resonance with music, self, and others, you've likely experienced it—and I am willing to wager that it is a major reason you care enough about this topic to read this book.

Shared Music-Making for Connection

Another explanation for the uniquely rapid bonding in choir versus other activities may have to do with the process of singing itself. *Oxford Handbook of Care in Music Education* (OHCME) authors Elizabeth Parker and Jennifer Hutton explain how vocalization is an especially powerful way of connecting with others.[28] They describe how humans are born into the world already primed to connect with a caregiver's voice and heartbeat, and that we learn from the first stages of life to imitate our caregivers' vocalizations. Then, as our social circles expand, we use our voices to connect and identify with others, such that our voice "is rooted in interconnections and regular interactions with others."[29]

OHCME author Tiri Schei offers similar observations, explaining how vocal expressions from early childhood on develop in tandem with our identity. She writes: "[T]he way we use the voice, the words we choose, the tone, the sound, and the rhythm, are continually being influenced by interactions with those around us."[30] It is no surprise, then, that singing with others would lead so relatively easily and quickly to group bonding, as mutual vocalization for the sake of connection is one of our primal instincts.

Of course, all kinds of music participation can promote strong social bonds. Anyone who has performed in an instrumental ensemble can join their choir-singing colleagues and bear witness to the chilling experience of being part of something bigger than oneself when harmonizing and moving synchronously together (that said, we should not underestimate the power of singing together in any music learning setting, no matter the instrumentation or what the class objectives entail). As one of my former students wrote about his HBCU band experiences, his ensemble's principles to "love one another in fellowship" while striving together for "musicianship, scholarship, and morals" reflects the spiritual essence that is possible through such musical unity.[31] At this very instant, music classrooms across the world are acting as a "home away from home"[32] for many students because of the ways that students come together, through music, and develop ineffable bonds with one another.

Caring connections through music are meaningful and critical at all ages. They begin from the earliest mother–child musical interactions that help forge identity and a sense of security, to the connections that are forged and maintained in older adulthood. As OHCME authors Kevin Shorner-Johnson and colleagues describe, in today's world full of distractions, "to be near one another and sharing of one's undivided attention to create music is a radical act of care."[33] (See Reflection Activities 2.4–2.5.)

A Note of Caution

Lest we celebrate too naively about the potential for social bonding through music, let us remember that it is our responsibility to create communal musical experiences that are indeed positive, caring, and life-giving. The research about singing and social bonding cited above does not tell the whole story: There are plenty of instances where people have been harmed when music learning settings were uncaring spaces, and where students have been hurt physically, mentally, and emotionally by teachers, peers, and/or audience members.[34] Furthermore, although collective music-making can increase connection and build positive relationships, group musical experiences can be so powerful as to sway people to act collectively in ways that can cause disconnection from, or even harm to, others outside the group. For example, our global histories are rich with instances of political leaders using music to motivate people to engage in collective destruction of others.[35]

As we celebrate the power of music, it is important to also notice the various ways that this power can be used either for good or ill. In Chapter 3, I address some of the harms students might face in music learning spaces, as well as some ways that we as music teachers might mitigate them. But first, this chapter focuses on creating positive connections through music.

Recognizing Our Social Limits

According to the social brain hypothesis (SBH), the human brain is relatively large in comparison to other mammals and it handles a proportionally larger number of complex social relationships.[36] SBH scientists have calculated that humans can handle only a limited number of very intimate relationships (around your top five), but that we can handle a larger number (around 150) of casual friendships. On the other hand, we can handle being acquainted with, or knowing the names of, people in a larger group (approximately 1,500) because they take relatively less mental space, time, and energy.[37]

Although social media algorithms are set up literally with the SBH principle in mind,[38] our technological choices nevertheless have the potential to wreak havoc on the development and maintenance of trusting relationships, as we may find ourselves spending more time connecting virtually with people whom we wouldn't necessarily choose as our most intimate friends, or even friends in the "middle circle." As Vivek Murthy professes, "it's so easy to [. . .] spend more hours digitally chatting with people we barely know than connecting meaningfully with those we love the most."[39]

Of course, the number of manageable relationships varies from person to person—as does our tolerance for aloneness—because everyone has unique social needs and levels of introversion and extroversion.[40] Trauma histories and neurodiversity also play a role in the way one creates and maintains social connections. However, the SBH is instructive for music teachers in terms of the levels and kinds of care we can give others and the levels of social connection we can expect to experience in our lives (see Reflection Activity 2.6).

Knowing our limits can help us prioritize where we put our time and energy. First, it reminds us that we need a small but steady group of close friends and confidants with whom we can honestly share the full range of our ups and downs, our accomplishments and failures. Therefore, it is important to create a social support system beyond the classroom to be there for us—and us for them—as we care for students. Throughout this chapter I'll address some approaches to connecting with others even when it seems difficult to do so.

Second, the SBH reminds us that we can't be everything to everyone. (Feel free to reread that last sentence and let it sink in a bit, maybe taking a nice deep breath in and out, as I just did while writing it.) For music teachers, this is where the power of communal music-making comes in. Meaningful social bonding during group music-making can occur at the collective level, without it requiring all the cognitive load and energy of creating individual personal relationships. Group music-making experiences might occur in the "middle circle" of friendships, where we do not necessarily have intimate relationships but we still connect as friends. They might even occur the "outer circle," where we know others in the group but do not have a formal relationship with them. Of course, many of us have fostered some of the most intimate relationships of our lives through music-making—but it does not have to be the case for us to have powerful sociomusical connections with others when we make music together.

Thus far, I have addressed the need for connection in a social world where people have become increasingly lonely, and where the connections we do have are much more diverse and complex than in the past. It is important for music teachers to ensure that students have their physical and emotional needs met as they are creating relational and collective bonds. Doing so is the essence of care, through a process of reciprocity and responsiveness—as I explain next.

Reciprocal and Responsive Care

At this moment I am typing on a laptop, sitting in a recliner, while my spouse, Tawnya, is standing behind me but facing the other direction. She is completely consumed in a conversation with eight plants that are lined up in the windowsill, and she does not seem concerned in the least that I might hear her. She compliments one plant on its healthy green shoots and offers thanks to another for the way it radiates the space with its vibrant maroon leaves. She apologizes to another because it (apparently) needs a bigger pot with new soil. She notices the curve of the leaves in another plant that appears to have had too much sun exposure, and assures another plant that it will receive a bit less water next time. Each plant gets its individual turn of "Tawnya time," each receiving a unique amount of care and attention.

If I were the one caring for these plants, they would all get the same amount of water, exactly at 2:30 pm every Sunday. I wouldn't make much of the job beyond a systematic task on my to-do list. As a result, some plants would thrive while others would wilt, overgrow, or otherwise die a slow and painful death.

I do not have Tawnya's "green thumb," which I realize has nothing to do with the amount of moss on her hands, and everything to do with the sensitivity she has for the needs of the plants. She has developed this attunement to plants over many years by attending to their individual nuances. She tends to plants in a way that might offer a simple and workable illustration for care: She takes time and space to notice what each plant wants and needs to thrive, provides that individualized nurturing, and gives them space to do their own growing. She checks in from time to time in order to recalibrate the care, and delights in how they are each thriving in their own way as a result of that care. This is an example of reciprocal and responsive caring *for*.

Reciprocal and Responsive Caring *For*

Educational care theorist Nel Noddings explains how reciprocal and responsive caring *for* requires two parties—one who cares (the carer), and one who receives care (the cared-for).[41] In effective caring relationships, the one who receives care reciprocates by providing acknowledgment of, or feedback about, the care they receive. In turn, the one-caring responds with adaptations to their caring approach, continually making their best attempt to provide the kind of individualized care that the cared-for needs and wants. The carer benefits from this interaction through the sense of accomplishment and joy knowing that the care is received.

In music education, this kind of caring-for reciprocity and responsiveness might include the teacher providing space for the student to clarify their learning needs, or the student providing feedback about what is (or is not) helping, and so forth—to which the teacher can adjust their care.[42] To evaluate how effective their caring efforts might be, music teachers assess both formally, such as through evaluations of performance or musical creations, or informally, such as through students' smiles or looks of confusion or disappointment. They then demonstrate further care by adapting the ways in which they offer that care.

Caring for humans is never an exact science, as another person's needs and interests change continually. Furthermore, as I discuss later in the section on empathy, the process of attuning to another human almost always loses something in translation. But the point is that, theoretically, caring *for* another person is a reciprocal experience in which the one who cares sees a need, meets it as best they can, sees how the caring is received, and delights in that care. Caring *for* music students, beyond simply caring *about* music, shifts the assessment from "What went wrong?" to "What does this student need to get it right?"

Reciprocal and Responsive Caring *For* versus Caring *With*

It may be helpful to explain what I view as different between a reciprocal and responsive caring-*for*, versus a reciprocal and responsive caring-*with*, relationship. In caring *for*, the relationship is reciprocal but still asymmetrical. As Noddings explains:

> [W]e do not expect cared-fors, whether human or animal [or plant], to do for us what we do for them, nor do we expect payment of some sort. Instead, we look for signs that our caring has been received. What we do by way of caring satisfies a need in the cared-for, completes the caring relation, and enriches our lives as carers.[43]

In the case of caring for another, the benefit to the carer is that of satisfaction in having met a need (see Figure 2.1).

As I explained in the previous chapter, a caring-*with* relationship positions the teacher as a co-learner and is more equitable in terms of power. Of course the teacher will facilitate much of the learning and the direction it takes, based on dialogue between the teacher and student. They will also learn very different things due to their varied life experiences and musical skills. But in a caring-*with* relationship, both co-learners (teacher and student) remain open to dialogue and work toward shared goals, dare to try new things and take musical risks, and engage together to create authentic connections. Reciprocal and responsive caring *with* involves a kind of mutuality in which people attune to one another and respond as they learn alongside one another. There is still joy in the process, but it is more

Figure 2.1 Reciprocal and Responsive Caring *For*. (Design credit: Adam Symborski)

multidirectional. Caring *with* music students, beyond simply caring *for* them, shifts the assessment from "what does this student need to get it right?" to "what do we hope to learn together?" (see Figure 2.2).

Creating such reciprocal and responsive caring-*with* relationships requires daring acts from music teachers. Caring *with* requires courage to learn and try new things. It requires an openness to attune with students' needs, interests, desires, and learning pathways. It requires vulnerability to make mistakes in front of students. It requires flexibility and curiosity. It requires not only empathy but also humility and trust—which I address in the remainder of this chapter.

Empathy, and Its Relationship to Shame versus Connection

Earlier I explained how loneliness, distrust, and feelings of low self-worth can work together to exacerbate isolation and withdrawal—in part because these feelings may cause people to be less willing to be vulnerable and risk making social connections. Research has also associated such feelings with the experience of shame.[44] There are countless ways that music teachers might doubt themselves or feel a sense of shame, especially when they feel unprepared or at odds with others. For example, we might

Figure 2.2 Reciprocal and Responsive Caring *With.* (Design credit: Adam Symborski)

feel unprepared for new settings, content, or demographic populations; question our own musicianship; feel anxious about the unknowns and possible criticisms in public performance; experience any number of doubts and self-deprecation involved in competitive experiences or social comparisons; or doubt ourselves if we have differences in philosophies or methods compared to others.[45] Students will of course have similar experiences of self-doubt or shame when they face new things, don't feel like they fit in, or experience bullying or harassment.

In better news, according to vulnerability researcher Brené Brown, shame's antidote is empathy—and empathy is a twin sibling to connection.[46] Brown's research suggests that empathy works along with connection, power, and freedom to help people become resilient to shame.[47] Further, reaching out and empathizing with others may be even more effective in developing resilience to those demons in our own heads, than can our individual efforts to understand and empathize with ourselves. Stated differently, reaching out and connecting with others can help us break never-ending negative spirals inside of ourselves.

Empathy is defined as the ability to understand what other people are experiencing by thinking and/or feeling in attunement with them.[48] I devoted a full chapter of *Compassionate Music Teaching* to the study of empathy in its various forms. There, I explained how music teachers might exercise empathy to attempt to understand our students' needs, hopes, interests, and learning styles—and even to attune to how they might be receiving our care, or "getting" what we are attempting to teach.[49] I also proposed a kind of music teacher literacy in which we learn to "read" our students and adapt our lessons in response to what we sense they may better need in any moment.

Empathy is key to creating caring relationships. It is the "leading actor" in *Daring to Care* and will show up throughout the book taking on many different roles and wearing a variety of "outfits," including cognitive, affective, compassionate, mature, kinesthetic, and musical empathy; empathetic attunement; and empathic creativity. In this chapter I introduce the first four: cognitive, affective, compassionate, and mature empathy.

Cognitive empathy involves the way we think in our minds about what someone else might be experiencing. Meanwhile, *affective* empathy involves the way we feel in our bodies and emotions as we attune to the experiences of others. Our ability to appropriately empathize with others will typically mature over time: Children can very naturally experience affective empathy (think of the child who cries when another child cries, or a toddler dancing when they see someone dance on television). They can learn over time to consider, cognitively, how someone else's experiences might be similar or different from their own needs (think of asking a child, "do you think that Jasmine might want to play the piano for a while now?"). These forms of attunement can lead to *compassionate* empathy, where one not only feels or thinks with another but also feels compelled to act in that person's best interest—or at least what they think or feel is their best interest.

As I will address in later chapters, it's not always possible to know what people want or need, and it's not always our business to try to help others unless they want that help. Enter *mature* empathy, or "a sensitivity to subtle differences in the severity and quality of the consequences that different actions might have for different people."[50] As OHCME authors Guadalupe López Íñiguez and Heidi Westerlund explain, care requires an openness to the perspective of others, and mature empathy requires that we consider the wellbeing of others from *their* perspective, not ours. Such a willingness to act in someone else's best interest requires humility, as I address later in this chapter.[51]

According to Noddings, empathy might involve a kind of "engrossment" with students in which the teacher resists the urge to insert any sort of agenda into the act of "feeling with" students, and instead becomes fully receptive and attuned to *their* needs, feelings, and experiences. Engrossment reduces the propensity toward shallow "othering" that might happen with less mature forms of empathy.[52] Through engrossment we can attempt to discern feelings and needs of students to make informed choices about the most appropriate ways to act.[53] Therefore, mature empathy requires authentic listening, or the art of seeking to understand—yet it also requires an awareness that another person's values and goals may be different from ours. As I explain in *Compassionate Music Teaching*, truly listening will likely reveal disagreements with others, which—although often avoided or viewed as a sign of trouble—can, in fact, be positive catalysts for authentic connection when coupled with a genuine desire to appreciate another's perspective.[54]

Exercising Empathy: Handle with Care

Contrary to popular opinion, empathy is not innately positive. For example, one can feel or understand the needs of others without necessarily choosing to do anything about it. Second, some especially empathic people can lose their own sense of self when they attune to others' needs and feelings—thereby risking overwhelm, secondary traumatic stress (defined further in Chapter 8), or the inability to make or keep appropriate boundaries.[55] Furthermore, it is possible for people to use the information they gain about others' feelings to manipulate them in unhealthy ways, draw attention inappropriately to their own discomfort when hearing about the pain of others, or position themselves as rescuers to justify their own morality and superiority above others.[56] Mature empathy, however, involves practicing attunement with another's values and worldviews, and promoting action or support that is truly warranted or wanted.[57]

Anti-oppression scholar Juliet Hess and I have had many formal and informal conversations about the various faces and shades of empathy. Together we have written about the "pathways and pitfalls" of engaging empathically with other people.[58] We recognize empathy's potential for authentic connection but also how feigned or misguided empathy can do harm to others as well as ourselves. Using a hiking metaphor to consider the empathic journey a music teacher might take with a co-learner, we have offered several "cairns" to mark (but not dictate) safe paths for teachers to consider on such a journey (Box 2a). These cairns share a common theme of continual self-reflection and relational recalibration to ensure that neither person in a relationship is harmed by the other. Such self-reflection and courage to change requires humility, as described next.

Unselved or Ecological Humility for Caring *With*

Humility is the sibling of empathy and trust.[59] Many definitions and perspectives exist regarding humility, but here I narrow our focus to "unselved"[60] or ecological[61] humility involved in caring *with*. This kind of humility is not where we talk down about ourselves or talk up other people while we continue to compare ourselves to one another. In fact, it is not about how we view ourselves at all.[62] Rather, unselved or ecological humility involves maturing away from self-preoccupation, toward a sense of community and an awareness of how we fit within that community.[63] It is less about what we look like, and more about what we are open to learning and contributing.

Box 2a Cairns for Healthy Empathic Connections with Music Students

1. Center student voices. Allow students space to think for themselves and speak.
2. Center minoritized voices. Be aware of power dynamics and work to mitigate them.
3. Listen with openness to what students have to say. Even if you think they are wrong, show them you are on their side and engage in continual questioning to work toward understanding.
4. Recognize that it is virtually impossible to fully understand someone else's perspective.
5. Maintain a centered emotional state, where neither you nor the student expects or takes too much from the other.
6. Be aware of your own bias and privilege.
7. Let go of assumptions that you know what is right or best for another person.
8. Recognize the strengths and potentials that students have, rather than thinking of them in terms of their needs and deficits.
9. Be open to learning with and from students.
10. When others share their stories, consider how vulnerable they might be in sharing, and resist the urge to co-opt or use their story for your own purposes (even if you think it is helpful to a good cause).
11. Resist the hero narrative (as discussed in Chapter 1). Focus empathy-inspired action on making change to oppression, not on helping oppressed people.
12. Be open to how you might benefit from someone else's misfortune, and work to change systems that make it so.
13. Engage in continual self-reflection. Check in with yourself about your motives for listening to someone else.
14. Be willing to apologize and repair relationships where needed.*

*These cairns are paraphrased from Hendricks and Hess, "Troubling Empathy in Music Education." 17–22.

Unselved humility involves a willingness to be vulnerable, demonstrated by an "openness to new ideas, contradictory information, and advice for [...] relationships from sources other than self."[64] Ecological humility involves taking responsibility for mistakes and a willingness to learn from others, with a continued sense of curiosity and wonder.[65] As OHCME author Tawnya Smith explains, ecological humility involves a shift from an *ego*-centric awareness to an *eco*-centric awareness, in which we recognize how we fit and contribute to sustainable systems.[66] OHCME author C. Victor Fung also points to nonegoistic being within Taoism as an aspect of caring.[67] Unselved or ecological humility works alongside empathy and trust for musical improvisations[68] as well as the kind of improvisatory co-learning in caring-*with* relationships.

According to OHCME author June Boyce-Tillman, humility involves remaining authentic to our own selves and our own values while also listening openly to others' perspectives—recognizing that their truths might be just as valid as our own.[69] Humility is necessary for mature empathy, where we consider others' wellbeing from our best attempts at understanding what *their* values and perspectives are, rather than privileging ours. Unselved humility and curiosity are avenues for letting go of outdated, harmful beliefs and practices related to anyone or anything having to be "superior" to anyone or anything else. Instead, they allow us to consider what everyone's unique niche might be within a music-learning ecosystem.[70]

Unselved or ecological humility involves a willingness to learn from each and every interaction we have with another person—no matter who that person might be or what worldview they hold. OHCME author Amira Ehrlich uses a model for cultural humility, developed by health care scholar E-shien Chang and colleagues,[71] to consider how music teachers might practice authentic care to model self-questioning and opportunities for mutual learning with students from a variety of different cultural backgrounds.[72] E-shien Chang and coauthors use the acronym QIAN from the Chinese word 謙 (humbleness) to envision a curriculum whereby a healthcare professional might learn to explore, comprehend, and appreciate the cultural backgrounds and worldviews of their colleagues and patients.[73] The model is structured as follows:

Q: self-Questioning (reflecting on our own background and bias as it might affect our interactions with others);
I: bidirectional cultural Immersion (considering how cultural differences might play out to envision ways of treating another);
A: mutually Active listening (including paying attention to gestures, stories, feelings, and emotions); and
N: flexibility of Negotiation (a willingness to communicate and agree upon alternative approaches that are acceptable to both parties).[74]

The QIAN model works toward a "mindset of unknowing" in which the emphasis is not on learning goals and objectives, but on learning through relationships.[75] This model fits with the notion of caring *with*, as it causes us to consider how we can learn from every interaction with every person, no matter who they are (see Reflection Activity 2.7). It requires courage to take risks and be willing to deconstruct assumptions we have made about other people based on their background or culture, and instead to listen actively for the sake of learning about the other person.

Finally, unselved or ecological humility allows for open-mindedness to help us as music teachers recognize our own bias, for example when we might confuse a student's lack of growth in any given moment with lack of talent (as addressed further in Chapter 5). Exercising humility allows us to be open to patience and curiosity. It invites us to learn along with students as we figure out, together, new ways to approach technical passages, creative phrases, new music technologies, and various musical genres and styles, and to open up to the muse inside of us.

Unselved or Ecological Humility and Connection in Music Teaching

Mark Russell Smith is a sought-after honor orchestra conductor whose reciprocal and responsive approach to music directing I describe in Chapter 4. Mark practices unselved or ecological humility by keeping up his cello skills and playing in front of his students, including playing the things he asks students to play. In the quote below, he explains that he does this in part to ensure that he is asking something that is reasonable, but also to keep himself on the same level of humanness with his students:

> It's really important as a conductor, that you are capable of making sounds. I try to keep my cello up, but I'm not always successful. It's really important for humility and for understanding how difficult it is to really do what I'm asking. If I'm asking them to play a phrase, then I better be able to do it. So much is about expression, and so I always choose cello pieces that are expressive on purpose, where it's all the things I've been talking about with bow speed, connection, and with using silences.
>
> It's not that I want to show them that I can play. That's not it at all. It's "here's an example of what I've been talking about the past two days. Here's an example of [how] music can express things that words can't." It's my way of saying thank you. It's my way of saying "we're having a special experience together, and it means something to me."

As shown in this quote from Mark Russell Smith, humility is key for connecting with music students, as a way of attuning to what they might feel or need or want and ensuring that what he is asking is possible. Unselved or ecological humility allows for a kind of music education improvisation in which student and teacher can learn helpful and sustainable pathways together.[76] Creating these musical pathways requires trust.

Trust

I am puzzled at how seldom we talk about trust in the field of music education—or if we do, it is often by asking someone to trust someone or something, without explaining why or how (which is likely as ineffective as asking a horn student to perform a massive concerto without warming up). To me, trust is critical to conversations about care in music education because it is the backbone of what we do. There are countless things that we must trust as musicians:

- As performers, that the note will come out the same way it is in our head;
- As collaborators, that others in our group have done their share of practice, or that they will "nail it" in performance;
- As composers or songwriters, that those vulnerable parts of ourselves we stitched into the music will be understood by others, and that we can handle harsh criticism that may come from an unkind audience;
- As conductors, that a sound will emerge as our baton completes its first ictus;
- As teachers, that students will give our good intentions the benefit of the doubt and come along with our hard-earned ideas for a lesson;
- As people with trauma histories, that we can handle any unexpected triggers that might send us reeling into some other mental time and space;
- As students, that a music learning space is safe enough for us to take risks;
- . . . and so forth.

Trust is everywhere in music education, but is seldom noticed until it is missing. Trust can be lost in an instant, but it takes time to rebuild. Yet, trust *can* be rebuilt, and—no matter how brilliant two people may be in terms of socioemotional intelligence, they will likely need to rebuild and reinforce trust, over and over and over.

I wonder if one of the reasons that trust is understated in music education is that we live in an instant-gratification world, and trust does not work that way. But if any kind of teacher has the capacity to foster trust with and within their students, it would be music teachers—with all the time we spend with students, over a long period of time, coupled with the vulnerability involved in musical expression (see Reflection Activity 2.8). What a humbling responsibility. Throughout this book I offer strategies for helping students foster trust in their musical abilities and expressive musicianship. In this chapter, I focus specifically on fostering trust to create caring relationships with and between our students.

Relational Trust

Relational trust is defined by education scholar Megan Tschannen-Moran as the "willingness to be vulnerable to another based on the confidence that the other is benevolent, honest, open, reliable, and competent."[77] In an OHCME chapter on conflict transformation,[78] Boston University students and I define each of those facets of trust within music education as follows:

- Vulnerability: willingness to risk losing control of the decision but remaining responsible for the outcome.

- Confidence: expression of security and poise in face of risk.
- Benevolence: the understanding that the trusted individual will not exploit one's vulnerability and, instead, will protect one's wellbeing. As OHCME author C. Victor Fung further explains, benevolence is "a manifesto of sincerity and kindness *in action*."[79]
- Reliability: stability and regularity in expectations.
- Competence: successful demonstration of a skill. When a person is dependent on another, but some level of skill is involved in fulfilling an expectation, an individual who means well but who is not competent in that skill may not be trusted.
- Honesty: truthfulness, integrity.
- Openness: sincerity with personal vulnerability, willingness to share one's authentic self.[80]

Trust is multifaceted and dynamic, with each of these facets overlapping and interacting with one another.[81] Please take a look at Reflection Activity 2.9 and contemplate which of these facets might be most relevant to you and your work.

I provide more detail about each of these facets of trust in *Compassionate Music Teaching*. There, I conclude that music teachers can practice benevolence, reliability, honesty, and openness, while demonstrating competence, to help students build confidence—not only in other people, but in their own musical selves—so they can be open to the vulnerabilities involved in music learning and musical expression. And as you know, there are *many* vulnerabilities to face in a music classroom. Vulnerability is at the center of trust, as well as musical expression.

After researching trust for several years, I have come to believe that a willingness to be vulnerable is the principal ingredient in authentic musical connection. The strongest relationships are often those that have passed through multiple trials but have come out stronger with every mutual effort to rebuild and reinforce trust. Lack of conflict does not equate to trust; lack of conflict more likely equates to lack of communication or lack of authenticity.[82] Being human and interacting with other humans authentically will undoubtedly bring on conflict. It is in the ways that we handle conflict that trust is earned, kept, and built or rebuilt stronger.[83] That said, sometimes "talking it out" may not work—particularly when at least one party is affected by past or current traumas that impede their ability to remain calm or clear-headed in the present moment. I devote space in Chapter 3 to discuss how trauma-informed approaches might encourage students toward increasing levels of appropriate social and musical risk-taking.

Promoting Trust in Music Classrooms

Box 2b includes a list of some of the most effective ways for music teachers to foster trust in music learning spaces, based on a review of research.[84] Each

Box 2b Promoting Trust in Music Classrooms

1. Use consistent rules and routines to foster reliability and competence;
2. Create engaging, enjoyable lessons to encourage benevolence and openness;
3. Use specific, instructional praise to foster confidence, competence, honesty, and benevolence;
4. Promote collaboration rather than competition to encourage a sense of general safety and openness to risk-taking;
5. Encourage open communication and genuine listening to motivate benevolence, honesty, and openness;
6. Welcome student input and shared goals to emphasize openness and competence;
7. Model an openness to learning new things, including being willing to apologize where appropriate and continue improving oneself (balancing competence with vulnerability, honesty, and openness).*

*Hendricks, Dansereau, Bauman-Field, and Freeze, "Fostering Trust in Music Classrooms," 15.

strategy is shown alongside the facets of relational trust that apply. In general, the strategies highlight the importance of promoting consistency, collaboration, and competence-building as well as modeling our own openness, vulnerability, and willingness to learn.

Trust, Belonging, and Unconditional Love in the Teenage Years

In this larger discussion about trust, it seems fitting to highlight the teenage years, which can be especially volatile times for fostering trusting relationships. I have an absolute adoration for teaching teenagers, with all the challenges and possibilities for care (plus a whole lot of fun). Teaching teenagers provides ample opportunities to practice and model the facets of trust. For example, as young adolescent bodies are growing and changing, it can be difficult for a teenager to have a sense of reliability even within themselves, let alone anyone else. They are spreading their wings and testing their autonomy at the same time that they feel immensely vulnerable to judgments of adults and peers—and the social world of a teenager is not known to be benevolent (for example, see sections on bullying in Chapter 3 and microaggressions in Chapter 7).

As the teenage sense of self-worth plummets, so can their willingness to be open and honest with others—which can further feed the cycle of disconnection. Then there are growing bodies that make for an awkward-feeling physique, affecting students' sense of musical competence as bodies don't fit around instruments as they once did, and changing voices make all sorts of surprising sounds. Of course

Figure 2.3 Ducks in a Bucket. (Photo credit: Katie Le Sesne)

many teenagers wear orthodontic braces, which can completely obliterate a wind player's sense of competence or a singer's self-image.

The whole world seems to be spinning around teenagers as the ground shifts under their feet. It takes a very caring teacher indeed to maintain their own sense of groundedness while fostering trust among teenagers[85]—yet sometimes losing our own sure footing as teachers may be exactly what we need to care with, and learn alongside with, our students. In this section I offer ideas from three teachers of teenagers who are committed to creating spaces of trust, belonging, and unconditional love.

Ducks for Pedagogy and Connection

Indiana middle school music teacher Katie Le Sesne has taken on the young teenage teaching challenge with flying colors—*literally* with flying colors—as her classroom is home to over 200 multicolored rubber ducks, lined around the edges of the room for display, as well as in bins for student use (see Figures 2.3 and 2.4). The ducks have several purposes in the class, including as a prop or tool for teaching musical technique and as a safe, nonintrusive, and nonverbal way for Katie to check in with student emotions.

In Box 2c, Katie describes the various ways she uses ducks for pedagogy and connection. One thing that impresses me about the ducks in Katie's room is how very different they all are—much as the teenagers in the classroom are so uniquely different from one another (and even different themselves from day to day). The ducks symbolize to the students that they—and all of their emotions, quirks, ways

Figure 2.4 Ducks for Belonging. (Photo credit: Katie Le Sesne)

Box 2c Ducks for Technique, Ducks for Belonging

As a middle school teacher, my classroom is all about providing a safe space for students to learn not only course content, but also how to express themselves in a healthy way. The music room is home to an abundance of rubber ducks. We use them as teaching tools to help with posture, balance, and for preparatory technical exercises.

Every day, students choose a duck to use. The variety of emotions, themes, activities, and personalities portrayed by these rubber ducks allows students to communicate nonverbally about themselves. Some students will choose the same duck every time and others will choose a different one each class. Through seeing the students' choice of duck and observing how they treat it, I can check in informally with the students. This often leads to more meaningful conversations. The ducks help maintain morale in our community too. Kids can borrow ducks on a hard day to raise their spirits; similarly, when students move on to high school, they get to take a duck with them. On their last day of middle school, I present each student their own rubber duck to remind them of the community we have built in our class.*

*Personal communication, February 21, 2024. Used with permission.

of thinking and being—belong in that space too. As multipurpose tools for teaching technique, expressing emotion, and building community, those little ducks offer a power-packed way to foster relational trust, middle school style.

Belonging, No Strings Attached

Massachusetts instrumental music teacher Jessica Billings-White teaches classes at the elementary, middle, and high school levels. She uses an age-appropriate approach at each level to foster a sense of belonging and trust, drawing on customized approaches that students will resonate with depending on their age, interests, and backgrounds. As described further in Chapter 3, Jessica teaches elementary students to trust themselves and their peers to perform well by teaching specific skills to keep going no matter what happens in mock performances, whereas at the middle school level she has designated activities for making their growth visible.

At the high school level with older teenagers, Jessica is even more intentional with activities aimed toward social connection. Lexington High School, where Jessica teaches, has a decades-long tradition of very high performance both in academics and in music. Therefore, external stressors on students can be unremitting as the students are attempting to navigate their way through each day. Jessica wants to ensure that students in her classes have a place where they know they are welcome and accepted, not for their academic or musical performance but for who they are as people. In Box 2d, Jessica describes some of the social connection activities she has implemented to foster a sense of community in class and beyond.

As I explain in Chapter 7, music teachers can provide identity-responsive and identity-affirming pedagogies for students through fostering a sense of unconditional love within their music-learning communities. Jessica has been able to balance the high-stress performance expectations of her school district with a sense of

Box 2d Connection and Belonging, No Strings Attached

At the high school level, we do a lot of similar things as the middle school, but at a more in-depth level. I greet them all as they enter the room by name. I ask them how their classes are going. I ask the class as a whole if they are tired that day or if there are a ton of tests and quizzes or assignments given that week. High school students also help me organize movie nights where one night a month, I host a dinner and a movie night at school where students can just come, hang out and be surrounded by like-minded individuals and get to know each other better. I also bring my kids' Nintendo Switch and we have had Super Smash Brothers Tournaments or Mario Party games. Lots of fun. They look forward to this every month.*

*Personal communication, February 27, 2024. Used with permission.

belonging, where students know one another, help one another rather than compete with one another, and feel at home in her class:

> The biggest compliment that I get from my students are through random acts of kindness towards others or the anonymous notes I get left telling me that my class is the best way to start the day every day, or that my class they are incredibly relaxed and they just love coming because of how they feel there.[86]

Relationships First

A sense of unconditional love, trust, and belonging among teenagers is the catalyst for the music-teaching approach of Martin Urbach, who has taught over 10,000 students as a restorative justice practitioner, youth organizer, and teacher at a Title 1 public school in New York City. Martin describes the ways he aims to create "homeplaces,"[87] or brave spaces, where his students "can feel safe to rejoice and resist as they need, want or please"[88] and where he hopes and dreams along with his students toward the co-creation of a new world where trust flows easily. He argues that reaching out to students "with a sincere desire to understand"[89] is not enough to build trust. Instead, as he explains in Box 2e, we need to know them and love them.

Box 2e The Power of Education Is in the Symbiotic Relationship

I cannot possibly begin to understand most of the oppression(s) that the students I serve might be experiencing, thus I have to go beyond "a sincere desire to understand," and toward getting to truly know them, to break bread with them, to be in community with them as a catalyst to loving them. [We] cannot possibly love students whom we do not know. [. . .] The transformative power of education lies in the symbiotic relationship between teacher and learner, and those labels apply to all in the relationship. We are to learn how to love, and we are to teach how to love.*

*Martin Urbach, as quoted in G Smith, Waller-Pace, Urbach, and Powell, "Love, Care, Revolution, and Justice," 500.

As Martin describes, authentic connections can be forged as teachers and students teach and learn from one another—caring with one another, as co-learners. These connections cannot be forced but must be authentic, organic, and emergent, as co-learners move together "at the speed of trust."[90] By focusing first on relationships, we can learn from one another—and with one another—about how to trust, how to love, how to connect, and how to care. (See Reflection Activities 2.10–2.11.)

Chapter Summary and Conclusion

Human connection is necessary for our health and longevity, and loneliness is a bigger problem for more people than many of us realize. It is critical for music teachers to foster spaces where students feel safe enough to take appropriate social and musical risks so they can foster authentic connections with self, others, and the music. However, it is important to keep in mind that each of us has unique and individual ways and needs for connecting. Authentic care is reciprocal and responsive, meaning that the one caring attunes to the unique needs and ways of caring that the other needs.

Empathy (the "leading actor" in *Daring to Care*) helps us become resilient to shame, and it is key to connecting with others to create caring relationships. It is important, however, to practice empathy with appropriate boundaries. It is critical to let go of assumptions that we can ever fully understand another person, and to work toward removing power structures where harm might be perpetuated even in instances where we mean to care for others.

Practicing unselved or ecological humility is necessary for mature empathy and can help us self-reflect as we learn with and from our students. As Mark Russell Smith's quote suggests, sharing music with our students is a way of sharing our own humanness with students and letting them know how much we value our connections with them. Finally, teachers can create caring spaces by considering the facets of relational trust to promote consistent, collaborative, competence-building music spaces where students feel safe to take musical risks. In the next chapter I offer additional ideas for connection, with a focus on maintaining caring relationships.

Reflection Activities

2.1. How have you experienced isolation, versus loneliness, versus solitude as a music student? As a music teacher? Fill out Box 2f with each of your responses.

Box 2f Reflection on Isolation, Loneliness, and Solitude

How have you experienced isolation, versus loneliness, versus solitude as a student? As a teacher?

	Isolation	Loneliness	Solitude
As a music student			
As a music teacher			

Box 2g Navigating Isolation, Loneliness, and Solitude

How have you navigated each of these things and/or turned them into strengths?

	Isolation	Loneliness	Solitude
As a music student			
As a music teacher			

2.2. How have you navigated each of these things and/or turned them into strengths? Fill out Box 2g with each of your responses.
2.3. How have you noticed loneliness (vs. isolation or solitude) among your students?
2.4. What are ways that you encourage individual and collective bonding with your music students?
2.5. What are ways that you foster authentic connections with your students?
2.6. As you consider how different students have different needs for social connection versus solitude, how does this knowledge affect the way you might approach classroom management? How does it affect the ways you might care for, about, and with neurodiverse and trauma-affected students? (See later chapters for more information on these topics)
2.7. Think of the various interactions you have with people throughout your day. Consider the students who come ready and eager to learn, as well as those who appear to lack motivation or who continually struggle. Consider also the staff and other colleagues you work with. Thinking of the QIAN model, what might you learn from each of these people?
2.8. What are some of the vulnerabilities that students face in a music classroom? What are some of the vulnerabilities that teachers face in a music classroom?
2.9. Review the list of trust facets (vulnerability, confidence, benevolence, reliability, competence, honesty, and openness) and their definitions as provided in this chapter. Which of these facets comes easier for you? Which is more difficult? Why do you think so? What can you do to strengthen that part of yourself, as a person and as a music teacher?

2.10. What activities for connection and belonging do you practice in music learning spaces? What additional activities might you try?

2.11. What does it mean to "move at the speed of trust"[91] for you and your students?

Notes

1. Mark McCrindle and Ashley Fell, *Generation Alpha: Understanding Our Children and Helping Them Thrive* (Sydney, Australia: Hachette, 2022); Corey Seemiller and Meghan Grace, *Generation Z: A Century in the Making* (New York: Routledge, 2018).
2. Karin S. Hendricks, "Contexts and Conceptualizations of Care in Music Education," in *The Routledge Companion to Creativities in Music Education*, ed. Clint Randles and Pamela Burnard (New York: Routledge, 2022), 404–415.
3. Rachel Dirks, "Student and Teacher Mental Health: Nurturing Wellbeing within a Climate of Trust," in *The Oxford Handbook of Care in Music Education*, ed. Karin S. Hendricks (New York: Oxford University Press, 2023), 319–328; Karin S. Hendricks and Tawnya D. Smith, "Compassion, Care, Communication, and Connection in Instrumental Learning Spaces," in *Teaching Instrumental Music: Contemporary Perspectives and Pedagogies*, ed. Bryan Powell, Kristen Pellegrino, and Quincy Hilliard (New York: Oxford University Press, 2023), 95–102; Vivek H. Murthy, *Together: The Healing Power of Human Connection in a Sometimes Lonely World* (New York: HarperCollins, 2020).
4. American Psychological Association, "Stress in America: Generation Z. Stress in America™ Survey" (October 2018), https://www.apa.org/news/press/releases/stress/2018/stress-gen-z.pdf; Dirks, "Student and Teacher Mental Health."
5. Murthy, *Together*, xiii, 10.
6. Daniel A. Cox, "The State of American Friendship: Change, Challenges, and Loss," American Enterprise Institute for Public Policy Research (2021), https://www.aei.org/wpcontent/uploads/2021/07/The-State-of-American-Friendship.pdf.
7. Cox, "The State of American Friendship."
8. Murthy, *Together*, 10.
9. Murthy, *Together*, 54.
10. Murthy, *Together*, xiii.
11. Murthy, *Together*.
12. Julianne Holt-Lunstad, Timothy B. Smith, Mark Baker, Tyler Harris, and David Stephenson, "Loneliness and Social Isolation as Risk Factors for Mortality: A Meta-Analytic Review," *Perspectives on Psychological Science* 10, no. 2 (2015): 227–237, https://doi.org/10.1177/17456916145683.
13. Julianne Holt-Lunstad, "Loneliness and Social Isolation as Risk Factors: The Power of Social Connection in Prevention," *American Journal of Lifestyle Medicine* 15, no. 5 (2021): 567–573, https://doi.org/10.1177/1559827621100945.
14. Louise C. Hawkley and John T. Cacioppo, "Loneliness Matters: A Theoretical and Empirical Review of Consequences and Mechanisms," *Annals of Behavioral Medicine* 40, no. 2 (2010): 218–227, https://doi.org/10.1007/s12160-010-9210-8; Isabella Ingram, Peter J. Kelly, Frank P. Deane, Amanda L. Baker, Melvin C. W. Goh, Dayle K. Raftery, and Genevieve A. Dingle, "Loneliness among People with Substance Use Problems: A Narrative Systematic Review," *Drug and Alcohol Review* 39, no. 5 (2020): 447–483, https://doi.org/10.1111/dar.13064.
15. Murthy, *Together*, 9.
16. Edward G. Michaud and Karin S. Hendricks, "Teaching Self-Efficacy Beliefs and Commitment Among Rural Music Educators," *Journal of Music Teacher Education* (in press).
17. Murthy, *Together*, 9.
18. Murthy, *Together*, 9.
19. Lina Hejjawi, Charlene Ryan, Karin S. Hendricks, and Tawnya D. Smith, "The Role of Social Media Feedback in Performance Preparation, Self-Esteem, and Anxiety," manuscript under review.
20. Tawnya D. Smith, *Healing the Fragmentation of Psyche, Society, and Nature through Music Education: A Radical Ecopsychological Approach* (Routledge, under contract).
21. Brené Brown, "Shame Resilience Theory: A Grounded Theory Study on Women and Shame," *Families in Society* 87, no. 1 (2006): 43–52, https://doi.org/10.1606/1044-3894.34; Karin S. Hendricks, *Compassionate Music Teaching: A Framework for Motivation and Engagement in the 21st Century* (Lanham, MD: Rowman & Littlefield, 2018).
22. Stephanie Cacioppo, Munirah Bangee, Stephen Balogh, Carlos Cardenas-Iniguez, Pamela Qualter, and John T. Cacioppo, "Loneliness and Implicit Attention to Social Threat: A High-Performance Electrical Neuroimaging Study," *Cognitive Neuroscience* 7, nos. 1–4 (2016): 138–159, https://doi.org/10.1080/17588928.2015.1070136; Murthy, *Together*, 41.
23. Murthy, *Together*, 41–44.
24. Murthy, *Together*, 51.
25. Eiluned Pearce, Jaques Launay, and Robin I. M. Dunbar, "The Ice-Breaker Effect: Singing Mediates Fast Social Bonding," *Royal Society Open Science* 2 (2015), http://doi.org/http://dx.doi.org/10.1098/rsos.150221.

26. Eiluned Pearce, Jacques Launay, Pádraig MacCarron, and Robin I. M. Dunbar, "Tuning in to Others: Exploring Relational and Collective Bonding in Singing and Non-Singing Groups over Time," *Psychology of Music* 45, no. 4 (2017): 496–512, https://doi.org/10.1177/0305735616667.
27. See Karin S. Hendricks and June Boyce-Tillman, "Music, Connection, and Authenticity," in *Authentic Connection: Music, Spirituality, and Wellbeing*, ed. Karin S. Hendricks (Oxford, UK: Peter Lang, 2021), 5.
28. Elizabeth Cassidy Parker and Jennifer C. Hutton, "Singing and Caring," in *The Oxford Handbook of Care in Music Education*, ed. Karin S. Hendricks (New York: Oxford University Press, 2023), 267–268.
29. Parker and Hutton, "Singing and Caring," 268.
30. Tiri Schei, "The Vulnerability in Being Heard," in *The Oxford Handbook of Care in Music Education*, ed. Karin S. Hendricks (New York: Oxford University Press, 2023), 309.
31. Jorim Reid, "Marching Sound Machines: An Autoethnography of a Director of Bands at an Historically Black College and University" (PhD diss., Boston University, 2020), 19.
32. Cecil Adderley, Mary Kennedy, and William Berz, "'A Home Away from Home': The World of the High School Music Classroom," *Journal of Research in Music Education* 51, no. 3 (2003): 190–205, https://doi.org/10.2307/334537.
33. Kevin Shorner-Johnson, Martha Gonzalez, and Daniel J. Shevock, "*Convivencias* and a Web of Care," in *The Oxford Handbook of Care in Music Education*, ed. Karin S. Hendricks (New York: Oxford University Press, 2023), 69.
34. Karin S. Hendricks, Tawnya D. Smith, and Jennifer Stanuch, "Creating Safe Spaces for Music Learning," *Music Educators Journal* 101, no. 1 (2014): 35–40, https://doi.org/10.1177/0027432114540337.
35. Deborah Bradley, "Oh, That Magic Feeling! Multicultural Human Subjectivity, Community, and Fascism's Footprints," *Philosophy of Music Education Review* 17, no. 1 (2009): 56–74, https://www.jstor.org/stable/40327310.
36. Robin I. M. Dunbar, "The Social Brain: Psychological Underpinnings and Implications for the Structure of Organizations," *Current Directions in Psychological Science* 23, no. 2 (2014): 109–114, https://doi.org/10.1177/0963721413517118.
37. Dunbar, "The Social Brain"; see also Murthy, *Together*, 218.
38. Robin I. M. Dunbar, "Dunbar's Number: Why the Theory That Humans Can Only Maintain 150 Friendships Has Withstood 30 Years of Scrutiny," https://neurosciencenews.com/dunbars-number-social-brain-19210/.
39. Murthy, *Together*, 220.
40. Murthy, *Together*, 9.
41. Nel Noddings, *Caring: A Relational Approach to Ethics and Moral Education*, 2nd ed. (Berkeley: University of California Press, 2013).
42. David Baker, "Disability, Lifelong Musical Engagement, and Care," in *The Oxford Handbook of Care in Music Education*, ed. Karin S. Hendricks (New York: Oxford University Press, 2023), 98.
43. Noddings, *Caring*, xviii.
44. Brené Brown, "Shame Resilience Theory."
45. For a more extensive discussion of shame related to these experiences in music education, see Mara E. Culp and Sara K. Jones, "Shame in Music Education: Starting the Conversation and Developing Resistance," *Music Educators Journal* 106, no. 4 (2020): 37–38, https://doi-org/10.1177/0027432120906198.
46. Brené Brown, "Shame Resilience Theory."
47. Brené Brown, "Shame Resilience Theory," 46.
48. Hendricks, *Compassionate Music Teaching.*
49. Hendricks, *Compassionate Music Teaching.*
50. Martin L. Hoffman, "Empathy: Justice and Moral Judgment," in *Empathy and Its Development*, ed. Nancy Eisenberg and Janet Strayer (New York: Cambridge University Press, 1987), 65.
51. Guadalupe López Íñiguez and Heidi Westerlund, "The Politics of Care in the Education of Children Gifted for Music: A Systems View," in *The Oxford Handbook of Care in Music Education*, ed. Karin S. Hendricks (New York: Oxford University Press, 2023), 119.
52. Noddings, *Caring.*
53. Martin L. Hoffman, *Empathy and Moral Development: Implications for Caring and Justice* (Cambridge, UK: Cambridge University Press, 2001).
54. Hendricks, *Compassionate Music Teaching.*
55. Hendricks, *Compassionate Music Teaching*; Karin S. Hendricks and Juliet Hess, "Troubling Empathy in Music Education: Pathways and Pitfalls," *Bulletin of the Council for Research in Music Education* 239 (2024): 7–25, https://doi.org/10.5406/21627223.239.01; Tawnya D. Smith, "Teaching through Trauma: Compassion Fatigue, Burnout, or Secondary Traumatic Stress?," in *Trauma and Resilience in Music Education: Haunted Melodies*, ed. Deborah Bradley and Juliet Hess (New York: Routledge, 2022), 49–63.
56. Karin S. Hendricks, "Counternarratives: Troubling Majoritarian Certainty," *Action, Criticism, and Theory for Music Education* 20, no. 4 (2021), https://doi.org/10.22176/act20.4.5; Hendricks and Hess, "Troubling Empathy in Music Education"; Juliet Hess, "When Narrative Is Impossible: Difficult Knowledge, Storytelling, and Ethical Practice in Narrative Research and Pedagogy in Music Education," *Action, Criticism, and Theory for Music Education* 20, no. 4 (2021): 79–113, https://doi.org/10.22176/act20.4.79.
57. Hendricks, *Compassionate Music Teaching*; Hendricks and Hess, "Troubling Empathy in Music Education."

58. Hendricks and Hess, "Troubling Empathy in Music Education."
59. June Boyce-Tillman, "The Hospitality of Wonder and Its Relation to Care and Compassion in Music Education," in *The Oxford Handbook of Care in Music Education*, ed. Karin S. Hendricks (New York: Oxford University Press, 2023), 79–90.
60. John Marks Templeton, *Worldwide Laws of Life* (Philadelphia: Templeton Foundation Press, 1997), 412, as cited in Trampas J. Rowden, Steven M. Harris, and Katharine Wickel, "Understanding Humility and Its Role in Relational Therapy," *Contemporary Family Therapy* 36 (2014): 380–391.
61. Boyce-Tillman, "The Hospitality of Wonder," 79–91; Tawnya D. Smith, "Caring with the Earth, Community, and Co-Learners for the Health of Biological, Social, and Musical Ecosystems," in *The Oxford Handbook of Care in Music Education*, ed. Karin S. Hendricks (New York: Oxford University Press, 2023), 141–152.
62. Templeton, *Worldwide Laws of Life*, 382.
63. Tawnya D. Smith, "Caring with the Earth."
64. Trampas, Harris, and Wickel. "Understanding Humility and Its Role in Relational Therapy," 382.
65. Boyce-Tillman, "The Hospitality of Wonder"; Tawnya D. Smith, "Caring with the Earth."
66. Tawnya D. Smith, "Caring with the Earth."
67. C. Victor Fung, "Ways of Caring in Music Education through the Lens of Classic Confucianism and Classic Daoism," in *The Oxford Handbook of Care in Music Education*, ed. Karin S. Hendricks (New York: Oxford University Press, 2023), 130–140.
68. Bruce Ellis Benson, "Improvisation as Spiritual Exercise: The Improvisational Virtues of Empathy, Humility, and Trust," in *Authentic Connection: Music, Spirituality, and Wellbeing*, ed. Karin S. Hendricks and June Boyce-Tillman (New York: Peter Lang, 2021), 33–45.
69. Boyce-Tillman, "The Hospitality of Wonder."
70. Tawnya D. Smith, "Caring with the Earth."
71. E-shien Chang, Melissa Simon, and XinQi Dong, "Integrating Cultural Humility into Health Care Professional Education and Training," *Advances in Health Sciences Education* 17, no. 2 (2012): 269–278, https://doi.org/10.1007/s10459-010-9264-1.
72. Amira Ehrlich, "Cultural Humility and Ethics of Caring in Multicultural Settings of Music Teacher Education," in *The Oxford Handbook of Care in Music Education*, ed. Karin S. Hendricks (New York: Oxford University Press, 2023), 566–579.
73. Chang, Simon, and Dong, "Integrating Cultural Humility," 269.
74. Chang, Simon, and Dong, "Integrating Cultural Humility," 274–275, as cited in Ehrlich, "Cultural Humility," 567.
75. Ehrlich, "Cultural Humility," 570.
76. Tawnya D. Smith, "Caring with the Earth."
77. Megan Tschannen-Moran, *Trust Matters: Leadership for Successful Schools* (Hoboken, NJ: Jossey-Bass, 2014), 20.
78. Karin S. Hendricks, Delaney A. K. Finn, Cheryl M. Freeze, and Jessandra Kono, "Facilitating Trust and Connection through Musical Presencing: Case Study of a Conflict Transformation Facilitator," in *The Oxford Handbook of Care in Music Education*, ed. Karin S. Hendricks (New York: Oxford University Press, 2023), 217–230.
79. Fung, "Ways of Caring in Music Education," 134, emphasis in the original.
80. Hendricks, Finn, Freeze, and Kono, "Facilitating Trust and Connection," 217–218; See also: Wayne K. Hoy and Megan Tschannen-Moran, "Five Faces of Trust: An Empirical Confirmation in Urban Elementary Schools," *Journal of School Leadership* 9, no. 3 (1999): 184–208, https://doi.org/10.1177/105268469900900301; Megan Tschannen-Moran and Wayne Hoy, "Trust in Schools: A Conceptual and Empirical Analysis," *Journal of Educational Administration* 36, no. 4 (1998): 334–352, https://doi.org/10.1108/09578239810211518; Megan Tschannen-Moran and Wayne K. Hoy, "A Multidisciplinary Analysis of the Nature, Meaning, and Measurement of Trust," *Review of Educational Research*, 70, no. 4 (2000): 547–593, https://doi.org/10.3102/00346543070004547.
81. Hendricks, Finn, Freeze, and Kono, "Facilitating Trust and Connection," 221–222.
82. Hendricks, *Compassionate Music Teaching.*
83. Hendricks, *Compassionate Music Teaching.*
84. Karin S. Hendricks, Diana R. Dansereau, Betty Bauman-Field, and Cheryl M. Freeze, "Fostering Trust in Music Classrooms: A Review of the Literature," *Update: Applications for Research in Music Education* 43, no. 1 (2024): 10–18, https://doi.org/10.1177/87551233231183366.
85. See Bridget Sweet, *Growing Musicians* (New York: Oxford University Press, 2016), for a more detailed description of the middle school teenage experience.
86. Personal communication, February 27, 2024. Used with permission.
87. bell hooks, *Teaching to Transgress* (New York: Routledge, 2014).
88. Gareth Dylan Smith, Brandi Waller-Pace, Martin Urbach, and Bryan Powell, "Love, Care, Revolution, and Justice: Loving Oneself and Loving One's Students," in *The Oxford Handbook of Care in Music Education*, ed. Karin S. Hendricks (New York: Oxford University Press, 2023), 501.
89. Hendricks, *Compassionate Music Teaching*, 48.
90. Gareth Dylan Smith et al., "Love, Care, Revolution, and Justice," 500; see also Adrienne Maree Brown, *Emergent Strategy: Shaping Change, Changing Worlds* (Chico CA: AK Press, 2017).
91. Adrienne Maree Brown, *Emergent Strategy.*

3
Maintaining Caring Relationships

Chapter Overview

Just as there are countless ways that a student can learn, there are countless ways for a student to be harmed while attempting to learn music. The previous chapter addressed ways to create caring relationships, whereas this chapter focuses on strategies to sustain positive, life-giving, and enduring forms of care. The first half of the chapter offers several research-based suggestions for fostering community, maintaining relationships, and providing opportunities for validation when relationships may need to be repaired or maintained, or where trust has been broken. Topics include culturally responsive music education, practicing nonviolent communication, encouraging brave vocal expressions, daring to apologize, bully prevention, frameworks for inclusive caring, standing with students against gender stereotyping and harassment, addressing student mental health, and creating safe and brave spaces through peer mentoring. The second half of the chapter attends to trauma-informed approaches, including using trauma as a lens for student behavior and teacher response, seeing the student rather than their trauma, trauma-informed approaches to care in community music settings, and trust-focused strategies for all students no matter their trauma history. The chapter includes specific strategies for nonviolent communication, discussing mental health with students, and engaging in trauma-informed approaches.

Introduction

As discussed in the previous chapter, loneliness comes through isolation and is fueled by distrust. It is no coincidence that our current loneliness epidemic is accompanied by a societal decline in relational trust.[1] It makes sense, then, that our best chance of reversing a spiral of increasing distrust-disconnection is to muster up the courage to walk ourselves (and our students) through spirals of increasing trust and connection, taking risks to be vulnerable as we are honest and open with one another and work toward patterns of increasing benevolence, reliability, and competence.

This brave step may be easier said than done, however—especially when at least one party has a history of trauma. Further, just as there are countless ways

Daring to Care with Music Education. Karin S. Hendricks, Oxford University Press. © Oxford University Press 2025.
DOI: 10.1093/9780197777589.003.0003

that a student can learn, there are countless ways for a student to be harmed while attempting to learn music. In the groundbreaking text *Madness and Distress in Music Education*,[2] Juliet Hess offers several examples of how music education might cause students emotional and often physical distress, including:

- *a culture of perfectionism* that adheres to one standard of excellence and creates "a disdain for mistakes" rather than viewing them as opportunities for learning;
- *expectations that are unrealistic, impossible to attain, or not well guided*;
- *competitive events and philosophies* that cause music programs and teachers to work in a standardized way that is not necessarily beneficial to all students, and that privilege students with more resources;
- *harmful levels of pressure and stress* associated with a heavy workload and "grind" culture;
- *invalidations* of students' musical contributions, tastes, skill sets, and personhood—including music being prioritized over music-makers; and
- *abusive relationships* with teachers [and peers], in which students are bullied, harassed, or physically or verbally abused.[3]

In contrast, Hess suggests that music can also help students—particularly those with mental health concerns—through creating connections: fostering community, building relationships, having opportunities to feel seen and validated. (See Reflection Activity 3.1.)

Throughout this book I offer strategies for fostering positive experiences in music learning settings. In this chapter, I offer several research-based suggestions for fostering community, building relationships, and providing opportunities for validation when relationships may need to be repaired or maintained, or where trust has been broken. I continue the discussion of caring relationships from the previous chapter, focusing now on ways to sustain positive, life-giving, and enduring forms of care. In the first half of the chapter, I address ways to maintain and repair relationships and mitigate harm. The second half of the chapter addresses trauma-informed approaches.

Maintaining Positive Relationships, Mitigating Harm

In the previous chapter I discussed how collective music-making has been shown to be uniquely powerful for creating human connection. However, music learning spaces may not be enjoyable for students when care is absent, or when caring efforts are not received as such.[4] Even the best attempts at caring can be ineffective, or even destructive, when they are not reciprocal or responsive.

Maintaining positive relationships may require a variety of communicative strategies, whereas mitigating harm requires that we see students through the lens of their experiences, needs, and interests rather than their deficits. In this section I address ideas for maintaining relationships and mitigating harm, including envisioning music learning from the learner's perspective, practicing nonviolent communication, encouraging brave vocal expressions, daring to apologize, bully prevention, inclusive caring, standing with students against gender stereotyping and harassment, addressing mental health, and creating safe and brave spaces through peer mentoring.

Shaping Music Learning from the Learner's Perspective

One example of intended care gone awry is found in Box 3a, from *Oxford Handbook of Care in Music Education* (OHCME) authors Warren Churchill and Clare Hall in their chapter "Caring about Deaf Music in Culturally Responsive Music Education."[5] In this vignette, Churchill describes how accommodations were made for Amari, a second-grade student with a hearing impairment. However, when those accommodations were made, there appears to have been little input from Amari, nor any efforts to create music learning activities in class that were meaningful to Amari.

Churchill and Hall explain that the accommodations described in Box 3a appear to have stemmed from a medical model of thinking, in which deafness is considered a deficit that needs to be fixed or minimized. Missing from this scenario is a consideration of the student's own experience for determining effective accommodations and meaningful musical activities. Amari appears to have been cared *about*, as evidenced by the American Sign Language (ASL) activity, and the teachers took care *of* Amari by putting ASL in the performance. But reciprocity and responsiveness are not evident in this scenario, despite thoughtful efforts to consider Amari as a member of the class. (See Reflection Activity 3.2.)

To practice a more reciprocal and responsive caring-*with* approach with Deaf students, Churchill and Hall propose that the lesson planning mindset could be flipped upside down: Instead of thinking about what music will be learned and how to accommodate students, we might instead shape music learning from the learner's perspective—in other words, to consider whom we are teaching and what it is that *they* want and need. A more flexible and responsive approach involves responsiveness to Deaf culture:

> Rather than promote a list of how-to best practices that lead to notions of mastery over fixed skills, acknowledging the fluid cultural dimensions of communities to which Deaf[6] and hard of hearing students belong might inspire inclusive pedagogical practices that are more ethically aligned with [. . .] educational caring.[7]

According to Churchill and Hall, reciprocal and responsive approaches would resist actions that center in "pity" or "helping" members of the Deaf community and instead allow for dialogical engagement—caring *with*. This kind of dialogical

Box 3a Caring Efforts Gone Awry

It is the late 1980s and I (Warren) am a preservice teacher completing a teaching internship in upstate New York. At this public school I'm working with a quiet second grade student with a hearing impairment in a general music setting. Each week, Amari (a pseudonym) and their classmates excitedly scrambled to their assigned seats in the music room. Entering right behind, Amari's sign language interpreter greets my supervising teacher and gives her a microphone and FM transmitter set to wear during the lesson. Amari wears a corresponding pendant-like receiver that is connected to their hearing aids. The interpreter then sits in a chair directly facing Amari so they can see the interpreter signing clearly.

I understand that these accommodations are intended to facilitate Amari's access to spoken language, which are stipulated as part of their Individualized Education Program (IEP). I imagine that Amari's hearing aids give them some access to what is happening in our predominantly sound-based learning environment. However, my care for Amari's music education does not extend to informing myself to what extent musical sounds are made perceptual by the accommodations that allow access to spoken language. Therefore, I do not make any kind of music-specific accommodations for Amari. Nor was this modeled for me. Nonetheless, I suspect that my sponsor teacher has been grappling with these issues, albeit not so obviously. I suspect this because during the weeks leading up to the annual December concert, the entire second grade performed "I'd Like to Teach the World to Sing" using sign language while-singing.

Although I appreciate the inclusive efforts, what these students learned about the Deaf community was likely minimal given the limited rehearsal time and the rote approach to teaching the signed lyrics. Furthermore, I believe that this was a one-time collaboration to see whether a sign language enhanced choral performance could be successfully undertaken. Given these factors, I doubt whether students had the opportunity to meaningfully engage with sign language or to learn about the signing community in culturally responsive ways. As such, I wonder to what extent my supervising teacher and I had really enacted care for the Deaf community?*

*Churchill and Hall, "Caring about Deaf Music," 542–543.

engagement (whether verbal or otherwise) is critical for maintaining reciprocal and responsive caring-*for* and caring-*with* relationships with music students.

Practicing Nonviolent Communication

Nonviolent communication (NVC) practices developed by Marshall Rosenberg[8] can help us find a way to talk out concerns with another person in moments of conflict or stress. Tawnya Smith and I have written about using NVC in ensemble rehearsals to help students feel safe while also offering constructive suggestions.[9] NVC can help music teachers care *with* students, as we work "toward shared goals that are mutually determined, and connect with them as collaborators in the music-making and learning process."[10] The steps to NVC are as follows:

- I state what I observe that does not contribute to my well-being (observing without evaluation or judgment).
- I state how I feel in relation to what I observe.
- I state what I need or value that causes these feelings.
- I clearly request that which would enrich my life without making a demand.[11]

Box 3b includes examples of what each of these steps might be in a music ensemble rehearsal. I have left space for you to fill in your own ideas.

Encouraging Brave Vocal Expressions

There is an element of vulnerability in voicing what we need (as in the NVC examples above), but also when we use our voices to sing. Although singing may be part of a primal instinct for social connection (as described in Chapter 2), the personal nature of the voice-as-instrument also makes it vulnerable to all sorts of physical and emotional harms. OHCME author Tiri Schei describes the possibility for voice shame, especially in cases where students have been told or made to think that their singing—the instrument through which they learned to identify their social self—was not good enough. She explains how voice shame can be "a devastating self-punishment in the aftermath of exposure to an audience,"[12] and that negative feedback about one's singing voice can have an impact that lasts throughout their life:

> Unfortunately, experiences from early childhood can have a very negative impact. Many people are reluctant to speak or sing in groups because they "know" that they do not sing well. Such feelings may remain vivid throughout one's life. I have met teachers and elderly people who cling to this "truth" about their singing voice and have not dared to sing since their early schooldays.[13]

Recognizing that even music teachers with the best intentions will make mistakes, Schei advocates for a kind of care in which music teachers acknowledge the vulnerability inherent in music learning. She encourages us to remain vigilant and self-reflective about the ways that we might encourage students toward "bold vocal expression,"[14] where both students and teachers can become comfortable with uncertainty and exploration.

Box 3b Nonviolent Communication Practices in an Ensemble Rehearsal

1. I state what I observe that does not contribute to my/our well-being (observing without evaluation or judgment).

Examples:

a. "Did anyone notice intonation issues at Letter B? What might be happening?"
b. "Would you agree that we weren't quite together?"
c. [Add your own here]

2. I state how I feel in relation to what I observe.

Examples:

a. "I am disappointed because it sounds to me like people didn't practice this section. Is that true?"
b. "I feel like I'm counting out loud up here and it's not helping. Do you have thoughts about what we might do?"
c. [Add your own here]

3. I state what I need or value that causes these feelings.

Examples:

a. "It's important to me that we get this part in tune this week, so that we are ready to harmonize with the soloist when she comes to practice with us next week."
b. "From my experience, it's really important to get the rhythms together before we have a sense of how everything fits together. I want you to feel that magic."
c. [Add your own here]

4. I clearly request without making a demand.

Examples:

a. "How can I help support you with your home practice? Do you need more strategies for breaking it down? Would you like more ideas for how to fit in the time? What would help?"
b. "What strategies can you think of to help us get this part more together?"
c. [Add your own here]*

*Hendricks and Smith, "Compassion, Care, Communication, and Connection," 100.

OHCME author Kelly Bylica also envisions how music teachers might practice and model flexibility through the art of listening as a means of honoring another's experience, rather than listening merely to respond—both in terms of verbal communication, as well as in musical interactions.[15] We might aspire to go beyond listening for a "right" or "best" sound or answer and invite musical and verbal dialogue that represents the complexity and variety of student expression. Such practices may be especially important in helping students move beyond the possible types of shame and trauma within and beyond the music learning space, as students may need to learn how to practice flexibility, openness, and exploration. There are several activities for promoting musical risk-taking and expression in Chapter 4.

Daring to Apologize

Whether in music or in life more broadly, practices of flexibility, openness, and exploration may lead us in directions that we decide weren't really where we wanted to go after all. Openness to learning from mistakes is key, but in the case of maintaining relationships or mitigating harm, apologies may be necessary to rebuild and reinforce relational trust. While conducting and presenting research on this topic over the last decade, I have found that students seldom remember having had an apology from a teacher.[16] As I wrote in *Compassionate Music Teaching*:

> Teachers are often very good at demanding an apology *from* students—either to us directly or to another offended student. [However], we are not always as eager to apologize ourselves when circumstances warrant it. This reticence on our part may likely relate to a fear of losing our sense of authority, power, or control over students. However, considering the costs of distrust in a learning space (and particularly to one that involves the musical expression of emotions), a weak or incomplete apology might be much too great to risk.[17]

I have some possibly good news: In the last few years, as I have asked younger students if they remember receiving apologies from teachers, they are saying "yes" more than ever before. I do not have empirical data to support this observation, but I do hope it is an upward trend.

Do you find it hard to apologize? If so, do you know why you do? I feel that there have been times in my life where it has been easier or more difficult for me to apologize, but I never regret it when I do. I am in utter awe whenever my spouse or a friend or colleague comes to me with an apology, or even to clarify something they said previously (just in case it might have upset me), because I realize that they must value our relationship enough to be vulnerable in that moment. I can't think of a gift that means more to me. I am inspired, by their courage to be vulnerable, to open myself up more honestly as a result.

Most likely students will appreciate our apologies too. Not only is an apology an act of care that demonstrates our commitment to a relationship, but it is also a way to model learning from mistakes. Furthermore, several OHCME authors note the power of an honest apology to foster trust when working with traditionally marginalized or oppressed music learners, as they may have learned from past experiences not to trust people who hold power over them.[18]

Of course, we need to find the right balance here. For example, some teachers who are new or insecure may say they are sorry repeatedly when things don't go as they would like, focusing on their own inadequacies or skills-in-process rather than placing their attention on fixing the mistake and moving on. Over-apologizing and focusing on the mistakes might actually negate trust, as students sense a lack of competence in the teacher and begin to lose trust in their own progress. Instead, we might make an honest comment about what needs to be improved, sometimes even asking students for suggestions or ideas, to encourage mutual commitment to musical improvement. Whether building relationships or fixing musical errors, trust can be built most effectively when we communicate honestly what has not gone well, discuss steps for improvement, and then demonstrate an authentic commitment to that improvement plan.[19] (See Reflection Activity 3.3.)

Bully Prevention

Another way to maintain positive relationships and mitigate harm is through bully prevention. Bullying is also a concern for music students, and something for which teachers need to be particularly vigilant with their care. Bullying can cause serious trauma and can have adverse and lasting effects on victims.[20] The Centers for Disease Control and Protection reports that one in five high school students reported being bullied on school grounds, and one in three middle or high school students reporting cyberbullying.[21] These numbers are likely much higher for music students: One study found that male arts students were 69% more likely than male non-arts students to be bullied in school and 63% more likely to be victims of cyberbullying.[22] Compounded on these statistics are intersectional issues related to peer victimization based on race, gender, disability, sexual orientation, and so forth—all of which make bullying greater concern for music learners who identify in one or more minoritized groups.[23]

Students who have positive experiences in a music class may feel more empowered or more resilient to peer aggression.[24] On the positive side, students in music ensembles have been shown to demonstrate more prosocial behaviors and to stand up to bullies in comparison to their peers not enrolled in these ensembles.[25] However, music classes also present many unique opportunities for bullies to assert power over other students, which OHCME author Jared Rawlings suggests might make "a presumably safe space less so."[26] It is important for music teachers to note the ways in which musical risk-taking (such as performing a solo, playing or singing for a graded test in front of the class, or presenting a composition) might make students more vulnerable to bullying or other psychological harm.

We might also pay close attention to the ways that peer groups are formed within a music class, especially in ensembles where students are divided up by instrument type and may form social groups or cliques, where connections may be stronger among some students, but where other students may be marginalized. Students with disabilities are commonly separated from their peers in music classes in ways that can lead to peer victimization. For example, OHCME author David Baker offers an example of a partially sighted musician who was accompanied by a teaching assistant in music class and was bullied by other students in ways that led the student to opt out of music participation at school.[27]

Although music classrooms have unique ways for bullying to fester, they also have unique ways for students to learn about standing up collectively to stop it. Students can be provided with opportunities to explore such topics in their work as peer mentors (addressed later in this chapter) but also in their day-to-day musical experiences. It may be helpful to create curricular units, choose repertoire and concert themes, and design other activities related to social support and resilience in the face of bullying (see Reflection Activities 3.4–3.5).

Frameworks for Inclusive Caring

Bullying is of particular concern for students with disabilities. OHCME author Kimberly A. McCord draws on research to explain that students with disabilities are bullied more frequently than students without disabilities, and that students with learning disabilities, autism, and emotional disorders are bullied even more frequently than students with other disabilities.[28] Furthermore, many students with emotional or intellectual disabilities may be more likely to show bullying behaviors themselves.[29] Based on her work with a popular music course where students learned new rock band instruments, McCord offers six conditions of a safe music learning environment where students might thrive:

- Musicians feel valued by their peers.
- Musicians feel safe enough to receive feedback from their peers.
- Musicians feel supported as soloists by their peers.
- Musicians respond appropriately to others when confronted with differences.
- Musicians feel that they contribute musically in ways that make everyone sound good.
- Musicians feel a sense of community through making music with each other.[30]

As I describe in Chapter 4, McCord has found musical empathy an effective way for some students with autism to communicate freely with other students.

OHCME author Ryan Hourigan also points to the importance of safety for students with disabilities.[31] Full inclusion, according to Hourigan, "requires educators to embrace the idea that all students can be both victims and aggressors of behavior and other practices that contribute to either a safe or unsafe school environment."[32] Music educators have unique advantages for helping to create safe spaces. First, in many cases we have students over an extended period of time and we have the opportunity to create relatively deeper relationships with them—which may allow us a particular vantage point to notice changes in behavior. Further, if we foster trust over that longer duration of time, it might provide a space in which students will report safety concerns. Hourigan reminds us, however, to turn to trained counselors for those concerns that go beyond our expertise.

To encourage the creation of safe, caring, and inclusive music learning environments, Hourigan offers a framework for inclusive caring that involves five steps:

1. Coming to terms with our own biases,
2. Exploring and understanding family and support system perspectives,
3. Teaching empathy and emotion as part of the curriculum,
4. Celebrating identity through self-determination, and
5. Promoting safety.[33]

First, being self-reflective about the words and labels we use can help mitigate bias. Hourigan explains that cultural beliefs and practices can cause us to recognize certain behaviors from people in one group as strong or confident, but those same behaviors from people in another group can be labeled as disruptive or disrespectful. Recognizing cultural influences can help classroom management approaches to be fairer and more consistent. Second, understanding family and support systems can also help us create more equitable learning environments. Hourigan recommends a simple questionnaire asking about any constraints and needed accommodations (e.g., transportation, sibling conflicts) for which family and support systems might require extra assistance.

Third, Hourigan emphasizes the importance of all students having opportunities to foster empathy through music, as music has been found to "help us ignite, recognize, and predict our emotions."[34] In the process of understanding their own emotions through music, students may "learn to care about the emotions of their peers."[35]

Fourth, identity exploration is of particular concern for students with learning differences, as they may have different personality traits, interests, behaviors, and manners of communication. Students need ample opportunities to determine their own level and ways of participating in music learning activities, perhaps again through pre-class questionnaires or other protocols to signal choice and consent to participate. Finally, it is imperative for students to have systems in place where they can report concerns in confidence. Considering the earlier descriptions of relational trust, students may need demonstrations of a teacher's reliability and benevolence prior to disclosing these concerns.

Standing with Students against Gender Stereotyping, Objectification, and Harassment

Another common form of bullying stems from gender stereotyping, objectification, and harassment. For example, bullying and homophobic name-calling are commonly experienced by musicians who perform an instrument that is culturally associated with a different gender and by transgender or gender-expansive music students.[36] Although music classes offer a kind of emotional shelter for many gender-expansive students,[37] microaggressions (as described in Chapter 7) and gender-related bullying are still a serious concern for many music students.[38]

In a recent study of LGBTQ+ students and relational trust in music classrooms, one transgender jazz student named Rey explained that they were treated differently in professional jazz circles when they wore pants versus a dress—such as getting more gigs when wearing pants, yet experiencing marginalization and exclusion when wearing a dress. The opposite would also happen in other social circles in their school music classes, with marginalization and exclusion when they wore pants.[39] In other words, even within music spaces there was no place for Rey to experience a full sense of belonging due to different gender expectations in different music-making contexts.

Female-identifying musicians are routinely harassed, belittled, or hypersexualized when performing or learning music in areas commonly dominated by men (e.g., jazz, pop, rock)—but also in everyday situations in any kind of music genre. I can't count the amount of times I have heard stories from female musicians about the ways they were seen only for their looks, told to dress differently, told they needed to smile, made the brunt of sexual jokes, had their personal space invaded, excluded from networking opportunities, included in what they thought were networking opportunities that they found out were actually a date, not believed when they spoke their truth, or had their ideas taken and capitalized on by someone else, on top of not being recognized for their musical achievements.

In addition to having to fight off extra distractions and harassments, females must routinely work harder than their male peers to be taken seriously[40]—and then are regularly told they are "overly emotional" or "overexplaining" when they express frustration about this inequity. Compounded on these gender issues are intersectional characteristics related to race, class, disability, and so forth, which lead to a complex layered web of inequities and barriers to access and support—as I address further in Chapter 7.

OHCME author Emília Barna, who has studied female rock musicians in Hungary, explains how harassment or discrimination of females can come from music teachers as well. In the case of rock musicians, female students are often expected or required to take on a more masculine language or persona to fit with the dominant expectation for this art form. However, when they try to become something other than what they are, "they often fail in the eyes of their instructors, which leads to further derision and a self-fulfilling prophecy—that they never belonged here anyway."[41] This harassment and discrimination can be perpetuated by other women too; Barna describes an experience of a female teacher taking off her own high-heeled shoes and encouraging a female student to wear them, to attract the male gaze. According to the student:

> [Before my exam] we rehearsed my song one more time and suddenly [my singing teacher] came running up to the room, tearing her sandals from her own feet, saying, "Vera, put these shoes on immediately!" I asked her why. [She says] because the entire faculty [mentions names of male instructors] is talking about how pretty I am but I need high heels, because I was wearing a pair of boots. And I was just looking at her like this is a joke, I'm not going to put on those sandals, I'm really happy in my boots.[42]

Barna explains how the teacher likely believed she was caring *for* the student by helping to further her career in this way. However, as noted earlier in this chapter, authentic care is reciprocal and responsive—and in this case the student did not receive the gesture as caring. What the student appears to have wanted and needed was a caring-*with* gesture in which the teacher resisted such symbolic violence against her student and spoke up to the other faculty about this sexual objectification.

It is important for music teachers—no matter our gender—to resist falling prey to gender stereotypes and instead stand in solidarity with aspiring performers who may be in a position to break gender barriers with their art.[43] I know from personal experience that speaking up can lead to any number of reactions from those who hold power over others. However, as I address further in later chapters, even the smallest micro-interventions can make an impact.

Addressing Student Mental Health

As noted previously, mental health is on a downward trend just as loneliness is on the rise. OHCME author Rachel Dirks describes the many stressors on adolescent mental health.[44] Research conducted over a decade ago suggests that mental health has historically been worse under three conditions: (a) during times of dramatic societal changes and times of high threat; (b) times of decreased social connections; and (c) eras in history where "money, image, or fame were of greater societal value than community and connection."[45]

Folks, right now we are living all three of the stressors that Dirks describes. Adolescence is tricky on a good day, but a 3/3 social history score makes things especially challenging for youth. From my many conversations with music teachers it's clear that we're not always sure what to do about it or how we can help when student mental health is in crisis. Dirks honors that feeling of uncertainty—where we aren't sure if we are seeing what we think we are seeing, and if we are, we may not know what to do about it. She quotes Brené Brown to remind us to allow space to "just be" and sit with our concerns before jumping too quickly to respond:

> The space between the thing that grabs us and how we respond to it is, in my opinion, what differentiates leaders [and teachers]. [Teachers] blow air into that space. They make it bigger. They stay in the quiet. . . . They stay in the vulnerable and really think through the response.[46]

"Blowing air" into a situation (such as addressing a student's mental health) allows music teachers time to reflect and honor the student rather than jumping too quickly to "fixing" in ways that may not be helpful. Dirks offers three steps to supporting student mental health, using the acronym AIR (awareness, inquiry, response). I offer a brief overview here, but I highly recommend a full read of her entire OHCME chapter.

Awareness fits hand-in-glove with reciprocal and responsive care. It involves the same kind of attuning and attending to students, but with an increased dose of awareness where we might notice changes in student's behavior, physical appearance, socializing/withdrawing, and general disposition. When any of these things change dramatically or in concerning ways, we can observe and monitor to see if anything becomes more serious.

Inquiry relates to the Brown quote above, as we allow space to question, reflect, and further observe. Dirks recommends possibly having conversations with the student about particular stresses, or discussing concerns with school counselors, parents, or other teachers (where appropriate and respectful of the student's privacy). When conversing with a student, we might try open-ended questions such as "What's been the best part of your day so far?" or "I'd love your opinion on our rehearsal yesterday—how did you think the roll-out of that new piece went?"[47] to allow for more observation and awareness of a student's behavior and dispositions as they reply. It is also a way to demonstrate care and open a space for them to share as they are willing.

Response comes after sufficient awareness and inquiry have taken place and the teacher takes active steps to support the student. Dirks offers steps for this response, based on strategies provided by The National Alliance on Mental Illness.[48] These steps—and Dirks's practice of them with a hypothetical student named Shane—are shown in Box 3c.

Dirks reminds us that this is only one possible response. Depending on the situation, she could have also: (a) mentioned more about her observations, without mentioning self-harm; (b) gone directly to the school counselor to discuss her concerns; or (c) simply offered the student encouragement while continuing to monitor his situation. Dirks also recommends the AIR approach for teachers monitoring their own mental health. (See Reflection Activity 3.6, and the discussion of teacher stress and self-care in Chapter 8.)

Box 3c Strategies for Responding to Students with a Mental Health Concern, *Following Steps of Awareness and Inquiry*

Lean in. After class I asked Shane if he would visit with me for a few minutes.

Create a safe space. We held our conversation in my office, where Shane felt comfortable and knew that what we discussed would be private.

Get comfortable feeling uncomfortable. As I dug into the heart of the conversation, there were moments when I felt very uncomfortable and I could tell Shane felt the same. My drive to continue on this path, however, was fueled by my desire to support and care for Shane.

Start with, "I've noticed . . ." I shared some of the differences I had noticed in Shane's appearance and behavior and said that I was concerned about him.

Ask open-ended questions. Asking questions like "How have you been feeling lately?" were helpful questions to continue shaping the conversation.

Practice active listening. Throughout the conversation with Shane I would repeat what I had heard him say to make sure I was hearing him correctly and to affirm that I was actively listening to his concerns. I would often follow up some of his statements with prompts like "Tell me more."

If you are concerned for your student's safety, use direct language framed in empathy and compassion. After we had visited for a few minutes, it was clear that Shane was very low and my "red flag" was on alert. Even though I was scared of the answer, I asked Shane if he was considering hurting himself. When he said "yes," I knew I was out of my depth and needed to ask for help.

Know your resources. I was glad that I knew each member of the mental wellness team at our high school. As soon as I had decided to talk with Shane after class, I asked a student to tune the orchestra while I stepped into my office to call a school social worker whom I trusted. I informed her that I would be visiting with a student of concern after class and asked if she could be available in-case we needed further support. Once Shane had revealed how serious his situation was, I was able to extend the opportunity to visit with the social worker, a person I trusted, immediately. I offered to go with him until he felt comfortable for me to leave. That afternoon his parents were notified and he was able to receive the support he needed.*

*Dirks, "Student and Teacher Mental Health," 324.

Reconceptualizing Failure

As introduced in Chapter 2, instrumental music teacher Jessica Billings-White works in a school district where students have many external pressures to perform at consistently high levels, both academically and musically. Especially since the COVID-19 pandemic, however, Jessica has noticed that her students have become much more prone to simply give up when something doesn't work out for them the first time. She mentioned to me that if students cannot get a rhythm or musical passage right the first time, many of them just stop trying.

Currently, as I write this book, there is a lot of talk in our field about students not showing up to music lessons or fulfilling practice or work requirements at a far greater rate than in the past. Although some music teachers connect this trend to mental health concerns, other folks in music education have been quick to judge such actions as generational, or as a student's lack of care, or even pronouncing laziness on them. I address this concern more fully in Chapter 9, particularly how we as music teachers need to care differently than past generations of music teachers have done. I argue for a change in culture, suggesting that we do away with fear-based motivations that shut people down, and instead move toward a culture of love that welcomes people in. One of the first steps to change the culture may be to connect authentically with students and find out, together, the reasons behind their lack of engagement and work together to create new, more life-giving and engaging approaches.

Jessica is one music teacher who dares to care differently. She recognizes that the multifarious external stresses on her students may be spinning them toward a mental health crisis. One approach she takes is to teach them to reconceptualize failure, shifting their attention away from fear of mistakes, to instead viewing them as part of the path toward music-making. In Box 3d, Jessica explains the approach she takes to help elementary students learn how to keep going even when mistakes occur.

Recognizing Growth, Sharing Progress

Another approach that Jessica Billings-White uses with her middle school students is to make their growth visible and share their progress with peers in mutually supportive ways. As described in Box 3e, Jessica uses video technology to track student progress as a group, but also for individual practice: Students share video clips from their own practice sessions with one another in a private virtual space, offering tricks and tips with one another as they work through challenging passages at home. Research supports Jessica's approach, suggesting that mindful and healthful approaches to using social media for music performance feedback can help music students grow in their performance confidence.[49]

Creating Safe and Brave Spaces through Peer Mentoring

To avoid perpetuating instances of harm such as shame, bullying, harassment, and stereotyping, students need to feel physically safe and they need supports to feel emotionally and musically brave. *Safe spaces* can refer to protection from physical or emotional injury, but safety does not necessarily lead to growth or progress. *Brave spaces* are also those in which students and others can express their truth

Box 3d Reconceptualizing Failure

Student mental health has become a priority for me, more so than concerts or what used to be considered "success" based on a pre-pandemic rubric that I made up in my head or what I was brought up believing was the success/failure scale for everyone. Some things that I do with my elementary students to check in with them, is showing them what is possible through failure and not giving up. Let's say that we have a part of a song that we were memorizing for our Winter Orchestra Concert (vertical concert with elementary through high school) and we attempt to play through a song like Old MacDonald or The Trilogy of Baked Goods (Hot Cross Buns, Sad Soggy Buns, and Happy Jazzy Buns) without music.

This is a few weeks before our big concert and we have done some singing of note names and fingerings, but never really attempted to play through it. Kids are skeptical, but I tell them that I am with them the ENTIRE way and it's ok if they make a mistake! Just KEEP GOING! Move without sound if you have to until you get to a point where you can jump back in (and we give them a few spots where they can jump in easily because they repeat or they are an easy section that everyone remembers).

When we finally get to the end (and it probably was a train wreck in the middle, but we have practiced the beginning and the END so that no matter what, they get the first and the last note of the piece), I say something like "how many of you made a few mistakes like I did, but were still able to get to the first and last note with the entire group???" 99% of the entire class raises their hands every single time and I FEED off of that excitement and make it a HUGE deal! If they were able to do that, they will be able to make it through the concert no problem, especially if it were TODAY! And I am so proud of them! The key is big smiles and lots of energy. We then have a checkout ticket where they would have to tell me one thing they can't do YET and that is their goal for next week.*

*Jessica Billings-White, personal communication, February 25, 2024. Used with permission.

(whether speaking, dressing with a certain style, or making music) in a way that is personally meaningful and empowering.[50]

Safe versus brave spaces can be compared to the difference between inclusion and belonging. Whereas the notion of "inclusion" infers a kind of welcome into a preexisting space (with an assumption that a person will fit with already-established norms of the group), "belonging" affords people an opportunity to remain just as they are, with a feeling of welcome that does not require them to change. So, whereas inclusion might provide physical safety to people who embody difference in some way, a sense of belonging also encourages a sense of bravery—which enables an openness to vulnerability, trust, and meaningful progress, both socially and musically.

Box 3e Making Progress Visible

At the middle school level, we do a lot of "first time read through" recordings and then compare and contrast even something that happens later that week. Playing a musical instrument is HARD not only because there is so much body awareness and concentration that goes into every single movement and every single note, but also because we never create a physical product, so progress can sometimes be lost. That aural progress, even comparing weekly recordings is soooooo big and students are always amazed when at the end of the year, we listen to our "First Notes Together" recording and they laugh at how awful it was and how much they have improved over time.

I also do a practice assignment using Flipgrid* where students record a section of themselves practicing and teaching how to practice a certain section of their music. These videos are ONLY viewable by the students in their class and they can leave comments (and of course we have ground rules about these comments that are left). Students gain valuable insight from practicing for each other, even if it is an easy section. I tell them to pick either a section that is hard for them, or a section that they know they can succeed at and want to fine-tune. This helps students learn how to practice from their peers and not just from me "blah blah blah"ing at them all the time, lol.†

*"Personalized Learning Using the Power of Video," Flip, https://info.flip.com/en-us.html.
†Jessica Billings-White, personal communication, February 25, 2024. Used with permission.

I address several ways to foster brave spaces in future chapters. However, one way to help create *safe* spaces where students can protect one another from physical and psychological harm, while also supporting one another in *brave* spaces for music learning, is by implementing systems for peer mentoring.[51] Peer mentoring can be structured hierarchically, with a more advanced student supporting the learning and growth of another student. However, they can also be set up nonhierarchically, where students of similar abilities support one another in a reciprocal fashion.

No matter the kind of peer mentoring we may encourage in our classrooms, OHCME author Andrew Goodrich cautions us to use peer mentoring in ways that do not reinforce dominant power structures, as that may continue to cause harm to students who have been traditionally marginalized at school (due to their race, gender, sexual orientation, religion, disability, etc.).[52] Instead, Goodrich suggests that we make time and space to teach peer mentors various ways to care for, about, and with others in the classroom, and to be self-reflective about their own privilege and biases as they are working with other students. Additionally, in the spirit of reciprocal and relational care, it is important for the students to determine what "safe" means to them, rather than the teacher presuming to know. Peer mentoring offers one means whereby students might feel brave enough to articulate their needs and work together to co-construct a learning environment in which they feel safe, seen, and brave enough to take musical risks.

Goodrich recommends using the six facets of compassionate music teaching (trust, empathy, patience, inclusion, community, authentic connection) as a framework for teaching students the skills and dispositions they need to be effective and caring peer mentors. In *Compassionate Music Teaching* I offer an example of how one band director, Steve Massey, used peer mentoring as a principal strategy for ensuring a sense of community, ownership, technical proficiency, and expressive musicianship among band students. Steve devoted a seemingly exhausting amount of time every Friday morning before school to hold extra leadership training meetings—yet this investment of time reaped rewards far beyond the cost of Steve's time and energy, as the students formed communities of learning, leadership, and belonging that were self-motivating and self-sustaining. (See Reflection Activities 3.7–3.8.)

Trauma-Informed Approaches

There are times when even the most seasoned, caring, or well-loved music teacher just can't seem to "get through" to a student, or to connect authentically with a group of students. In such cases, the students may have trauma histories that impede their ability to connect with anyone. Many music educators are becoming increasingly aware of how trauma affects one's ability to function in music learning settings.[53] OHCME author Jared Rawlings, along with Shannan Hibbard and Erin Price, defines trauma as "an emotionally painful or shocking experience that might result in lasting impact."[54] The kinds of harm mentioned earlier in this chapter can be felt as traumatic events to some students. Additionally, students (and teachers) may carry a history of past trauma in their minds and/or bodies, which can affect their ability to function fully as they wish and thereby negatively impact their ability to learn and authentically express themselves.[55]

Traumatic events can cause many different reactions in different people but are typically manifest through dysregulation of stress hormones and a heightened sympathetic nervous system. The reactions that may occur in a trauma-affected person include:

- *Emotional*, such as anxiety, depression, or shame;
- *Physical*, such as sensory issues, sleep problems, or dysregulations of the heart, nerves, or skin;
- *Cognitive*, such as thinking or memory errors, excessive or unfounded guilt, idealization (rationalizing or justifying the event or remembering it as better or less problematic than it actually was), hallucinations, delusions, intrusive thoughts; or
- *Behavioral*, such as avoidance (missing school, not signing up for an audition), compulsivity (checking the door repeatedly, cleaning something that does not need to be cleaned, incessantly fixing something that isn't broken),

self-medication (using illicit drugs or alcohol to change one's physiological state), impulsivity (stealing, self-harm).[56]

Such reactions are often involuntary or unconscious, and they can occur at any time as a trauma-affected person experiences a "trauma trigger," or some event that stimulates a memory of past harm.[57] The often involuntary and inconsistent nature of trauma reactions makes them especially difficult to detect or manage in a classroom.[58]

Here, I offer a few ideas for working with trauma-affected students, and in Chapter 8 I address the impact of trauma on teachers. In truth, however, trauma can (and does) affect students and teachers simultaneously and reciprocally, as depicted in the vignettes offered below. I also highly recommend a full read of the Hibbard and Price chapter in the OHCME and other literature in the references for a deeper dive into compassionate approaches that may help stop cycles of trauma from reoccurring.

Trauma as a Lens for Student Behavior (and Teacher Response)

OHCME authors Shannan Hibbard and Erin Price explain that many students who are labeled as having a behavior disorder may actually be trauma victims who become further traumatized by the kinds of classroom discipline teachers use in their efforts to focus or calm the student.[59] For example, Box 3f contains a vignette written by Hibbard and Price, which describes how a well-meaning and very caring teacher is at a loss as to how to support a music student (Jamie) who seems unable to engage in music class without continually disrupting the lesson. The teacher's efforts to discipline the student appear unhelpful, and in fact are met with more outbursts and disruptions.

Meanwhile, Box 3g depicts the same situation through the student's eyes. As we consider this second vignette through a trauma lens, we can pick up on several clues about where Jamie might be triggered by something that causes him to react: teasing in the hallway, having no choice about being placed in a seat in the front of the class where he feels unsafe, hearing loud and unexpected crashes, laughing students, an angry adult voice followed by an angry adult glare. Despite Jamie's best attempts to stay calm, it becomes too much for him and he reacts, escaping to where he feels safe as quickly as he can—pushing anything in his path out of the way.

In Box 3h, the teacher reacts out of their own frustration and sense of a loss of control. Not only have they lost Jamie, but they may face feelings of embarrassment and shame that the vice principal has witnessed the scene. This loss of control, coupled with possible shame, can be similarly triggering to the teacher, especially if they have their own trauma history. The teacher attempts to reason with Jamie. However, as the teacher's own emotions escalate and they begin to yell, Jamie's triggers likely increase as well, and the situation does not improve.

Box 3f A Frustrated Teacher

I slump forward in my desk chair, my head in my hands. It's only lunchtime and I feel like a complete failure. Jamie, a student in whom I have been investing a lot of energy, had another blow-up in class this morning. Despite my efforts to put boundaries in place with a behavior chart, consequences, phone calls home, and an assigned seat in the front of the general music class, his explosive behavior always seems to come out of nowhere. And this time, he ran. Thankfully the assistant principal was in the hall to help diffuse the situation, but it only worsens my feelings of shame and incompetence.

I don't know how I can face Jamie again with a smile. As I go above and beyond to fix it, his outbursts and disruptive behavior only heighten. My frustration is at its peak, and even worse, I feel resentful and angry toward him—a child just seven years old. I sigh a breath of hopelessness. I just don't know what to do anymore.*

*Hibbard and Price, "Trauma," 385.

Box 3g The Student's Perspective

Jamie enters the general music room in line with his second-grade classmates. Teasing and conversations that began in the hallway get louder and more animated as students transition to their assigned seats in the front of the whiteboard. Jamie finds his spot right in front, just to the left of where his music teacher will eventually sit. He much preferred his old spot at the back and hates to sit here. He fidgets with his pant legs, crossing and uncrossing his legs. He nervously looks behind him and around the room.

As the music teacher tries to gain the attention of the students and quiet the room, a student playfully fiddles with a djembe in the corner, causing it to tip over. The drum falls into a shelf of hand percussion instruments, sending triangles and cymbals crashing. A half dozen cylindrical wood blocks roll in various directions across the floor. The intense sound of the mishap is met with the roar of giggles and shouts, several students rocking on their backs in response. The teacher raises her voice in exasperation, and several students scramble across the floor to help gather instruments. As Jamie's heart races in response to the chaos, the teacher's angry glare meets his eyes from above. In less than a second, he crawls up and toward the door, pushing students and kicking woodblocks from his path. He is gone from sight.*

*Hibbard and Price, "Trauma," 385–386.

Box 3h The Problem Escalates

I dart after Jamie, leaving the rest of the class unattended. He runs past the gym corridor, turning down a long hall that ends in an emergency exit. "Please, not the exit door today," I plead in my thoughts. Ten paces behind him, I round the corner to find the assistant principal standing in front of the exit door, one hand on the shoulder of a sweating, panicked Jamie. Relieved yet still furious and winded, I lay into Jamie, expressing anger and frustration with the choice he has made. Doesn't he understand that his choices affect his peers—who are now in the room alone? Why would he run like this, especially after we've discussed how unsafe this behavior is? What was he thinking? He looks at the floor in silence.*

*Hibbard and Price, "Trauma," 387.

Many of us have been both teacher and Jamie at different times of our lives. In this circumstance there is no right or wrong person; there are only stresses and frustrations and solutions to figure out. It appears from these vignettes that both Jamie and the teacher appear to be trying hard not to upset the other. However, as is often the case with trauma-affected individuals, their bodies and minds did not cooperate with their best intentions.

A Compassionate Lens: Seeing the Student, Not Their Trauma

There is room in this situation for the teacher to have self-compassion, and also to experience compassion for Jamie—especially as we define compassion not as giving up or "letting students walk all over us,"[60] but rather seeking to understand and connect with another, or to care *with* another).[61] Seeing students and ourselves through a lens of trauma can help us understand that our behaviors in any moment do not define us. Instead, we can strive to see students and ourselves as holistic and beautifully complex humans with unique needs and strengths to be discovered and communicated. As Hibbard and Price state, this view can help to "open awareness to the strengths, beauties, and joys of students and their cultures and communities."[62]

Whereas traditional classroom management perspectives cause one to consider what is *wrong* with students, Hibbard and Price explain that a trauma lens causes one to consider what *happened* to students. Considering the impact of trauma is an important first step. However, there are several problems with focusing directly on a student's trauma. First, teachers may not be privy to a student's trauma history to understand what might be triggering the student. Second, every person will react differently to different traumatic events, depending on several environmental factors as well as the length, severity, and recurrence of the event. Therefore, it is nearly impossible for someone to project assumptions about someone else's behavior based on trauma.

Third, focusing on a child's trauma draws the attention to the very thing that they are not (and that they do not want to be), rather than who they are and who they want to be. Focusing on a student's trauma rather than their potential might continue to perpetuate cycles of harm, as the emphasis stays on the problem and the attempt to control students (even if intended to improve their situation). For this reason, Hibbard and Price suggest that we shift the lens even further away from a deficit perspective of what *happened* to students, to consider what is *right* with students.

Changing What We Can

There is much that we cannot control in music teaching relationships, whether trauma-affected or not. However, what we can control is the ways in which we respond to student behavior. The first step may be to address our own trauma triggers so that we can remain focused and calm when engaging with disruptive behavior in the classroom. I invite you to consider Core Reflection activities in Chapter 5 as well as all of Chapter 8—and please consider working with a licensed therapist if needed.

The second step is to become more aware of the ways in which we have or hold power over students. In so doing, we can consider how that power differential might affect our perspective of them, and their potential fear of us. We might ask: Do we view students for their deficits and weaknesses rather than their strengths and unique needs and interests? Do they view us as a trusted individual, or do they possibly associate us with others who have harmed them or withheld good things from them?

The third step is to create a healing environment for students in which they receive validation and affirmation and gradually come to feel a sense of agency and trust.[63] Finally, we can communicate with students about what they want and need to be successful. In Box 3j, Jamie's teacher tries such an approach to relationship maintenance. Box 3k shows that relational work in action.

Trauma-Informed Circles of Care for Community Music Settings

In community music settings, lifelong learners may bring histories of trauma to group music-making experiences. Standard school curricula and pedagogical approaches may be less effective or out of place in these contexts, and trauma histories may impede a student's ability to focus or engage. Opportunities for connection, relationship maintenance, and healing are critical.

OHCME author Janelize Morelli offers a framework for using trauma-informed care in community music contexts that is based on principles of safety, connection,

Box 3j Relational Work

After sleeping on it, I recognize Jamie needs a new approach. His behavior seems out of both of our control, and his palpable shame isn't motivating him to change. I ask for a meeting with him at lunch, a time I usually observe him smiling and laughing with friends. It is a time when I am also at ease. Head and eyes to the floor, he enters the music room, taking quick, tentative glances up at me. I ask where he would like to sit. After a long silence, he points to the two cozy chairs in the corner. There our eyes can meet on a level plane, but Jamie eyes a puppet I use for Kindergarten classes. As I offer him the stuffed dog, I ask him if he has any pets. He perks up as he snuggles the puppet, sharing the details of his family cat, one his Mom began feeding as a stray. I feel surprised by his expressions of compassion.

Suddenly and with urgency, I interject an apology for what happened in the music room—the loud accident, my yelling, and the way I interrogated him. "I was angry and frustrated," I said, "but I shouldn't have acted like that. I bet you must have felt really awful." Jamie silently nodded at me, his countenance more curious, but still reluctant. I explain that I called him in so we could discuss strategies together that might help him have a better experience in music class. I express concern that he is missing out on music-making. Without blame, I also express concern for his safety. "I'm worried about you, Jamie—what can I do to help?" He returns the question with a shrug. "Would you like some suggestions?" I ask. After a long pause, he meets my eyes and nods. "Well, let's start with your seat—do you feel you can do your best work there?" He furrows his brow and shakes his head. "I want a new spot."

As we talk through several more strategies and changes to allow Jamie a better experience in music class, I feel him softening. He doesn't offer many solutions but provides clear opinions when I give him suggestions. He appears more relaxed than I've ever seen, and even though he is still very quiet, I feel good about the way I am able to speak with him. I am taking lessons from this peaceful moment that I hope will shape our class. I am hopeful.*

*Hibbard and Price, "Trauma," 389–390.

and managing emotions.[64] She has developed this framework based on her own experience facilitating community music workshops with learners of all ages in South Africa. The Musical Circle of Care framework has four steps: (a) welcoming one another, (b) extending hospitality, (c) becoming aware, (d) finding healing, and (e) taking leave.

In *welcoming one another*, community music facilitators can work to foster a sense of felt safety and creating connection. Morelli uses Dalcroze-inspired techniques in this phase, although any approaches can be used to help learners feel

Box 3k Relational Work in Action

Standing near the back of the line, Jamie enters the room with his classmates. With a quiet smile and elbow bump from his teacher, he goes to the sensory drawer and chooses a small fidget toy. As peaceful music plays in the room and students take their seats, they create body percussion patterns and read the agenda on the board—some silently, some sounding the words aloud. "Say hello! And how are you?"

The music teacher sings as she fades the soft music. Most students join her in singing, clapping in the rests. Jamie has chosen a chair from a stack in the corner and placed it behind the last row of students. He is content there, listening and popping his fidget in and out. He listens to the singing, rocking gently and swinging his legs back and forth. "Maybe today we will play that game where the eliminated players get to play the pattern on the xylophone?," he thinks to himself. He is hopeful.*

*Hibbard and Price, "Trauma," 391.

a sense of playfulness in a space where there is no discussion of performance nor space for failure. Learners find their way around the room, each with a unique path, while listening to music. They listen again, making eye contact this second time as they pass others (but without prolonged eye contact or touch). On a third listening they add acceptable touch by high-fiving others as they pass—gradually lifting the mood and fostering increased trust at the level that individual participants feel ready to engage.

Extending hospitality involves balancing an open welcome with the establishment of rules and routines. It is a moment to negotiate and define group member's responsibilities, where the facilitator can enlist the ideas and requests of group members to develop shared norms for group participation. Morelli recommends establishing relationships with group members prior to the workshop where possible, to establish stability and understood expectations from the outset before conflicts arise.

Becoming aware assists in the process of emotional regulation. It might involve activities to establish routine and rhythm, or to encourage self-regulation or mindfulness, or to help deescalate heightened emotions. Examples include having a visual card to check in with emotional states (green = all is fine, ready to engage; yellow = it's a bit much; red = feeling out of control; blue = lack of energy). Morelli offers a musical alternative in which music learners express their emotional state through free improvisations with their voice, an instrument, or movement.

Finding healing is a stage in the Circle of Care in which participants connect with one another by moving together or observing someone else's movements while they make music. Box 3m contains a vignette in which Morelli describes her experience

Box 3m Mirroring Movements for Kinesthetic Empathy

As the music started playing I held my hands up. This was our starting position. We held our hands close to each other without touching. I asked him to lead, knowing that this might be challenging. As I focused intently on mirroring his movements as closely as possible, I became more aware of the softness of his eyes. It was a strange feeling. As we moved along with the activity, I changed partners throughout until I could mirror every student in the group. On some level, I had gotten to know each of them better in those 15 minutes than I probably would throughout the rest of the semester.*

*Morelli, "The Musical Circle of Care," 164.

of mirroring the movements of various workshop participants while music played, and how this process connected them through kinesthetic empathy, or attunement to one another's movements.

Taking leave brings closure to the workshop. Because the emotional and musical state may take any unknown form at this point (from deep sadness to utter joy and musical effervescence), it is important for the facilitator to recognize what is needed and to offer activities that are befitting the mood. Morelli notes that workshops with older adults may need more space to honor life histories and grief. The process of taking leave may include a verbal or visual debrief, or a closing song. Although Morelli has considered it for use with community music groups where participants have lives or trauma or pain, its format is also applicable and malleable enough for use in a variety of settings.

Trust-Focused Strategies for All Students, No Matter Their Trauma History

Thus far, this section of the chapter has offered ideas for supporting students with trauma histories. However, I join many other trauma scholars to advocate for a trauma-informed, trust-promoting approach for *all* students, for several reasons. First, it is impossible to know or predict the severity or impact of any student's (or teacher's) trauma history. Second, labeling students according to their trauma focuses on deficits rather than strengths and possibilities. Third, the elements of trauma-informed care (safety, choice, collaboration, trustworthiness, and empowerment) are similarly advocated by educational psychologists as motivational approaches for all students. Using a lens of trauma when considering classroom management can help us to stop and consider particularly stressful behavioral issues through a lens of compassion and curiosity rather than viewing them as a student's or a teacher's personal failure.

In Chapter 2, I provided a list of specific ways to promote trust in music learning settings. which I aligned with the facets of relational trust. These strategies included: consistent rules and routines; engaging and enjoyable lessons; specific, instructional praise; promoting collaboration over competition; encouraging open communication and genuine listening; welcoming student input and shared goals; modeling an openness to learn new things. Recent research on trauma and music education suggests that these strategies are helpful to consider with trauma-affected music learners as well.[65]

Consistent rules and routines can help students repair their ability to regulate emotions, whereas enjoyable and engaging lessons can help students focus and thereby limit possibilities for distraction. Emphasizing collaboration can help students repair attachment patterns with adults and foster authentic connections with others. Instructive and specific praise can help students foster a sense of positive accomplishment and a growth mindset. Open communication, genuine listening, student input, and shared goals can help to create new patterns of safety in the classroom. Consent and choice are key to fostering such trust and felt safety—including taking students at their word, honoring their choices, and asking many clarification questions as needed to help them communicate if/how they need something different. Finally, modeling an openness to learning can help students learn healthy patterns of behavior for working through challenges. (See Reflection Activity 3.9.)

Conclusion

Music learning spaces can be rich with joy, but they can also be spaces of harm. This chapter has focused on ways to maintain reciprocal and responsive caring relationships with students, even when it is difficult. Communication is key—and this chapter has provided a variety of approaches to practicing communication, whether through an apology, asserting a need, or checking in with a student where instances of mental health or trauma may be impacting their ability to be present and focused. Maintaining reciprocal and responsive relationships requires that we adjust our lens of care away from student deficits, and instead focus on student needs, interests, and strengths. With an understanding of some ways to create and maintain caring relationships, the conversation turns in the next chapters to how we can immerse ourselves in the music-making process as it relates to caring for, about, and with our students and the music we make.

Reflection Activities

3.1. What are some ways that you have seen harm occur in music education spaces? What might you have done (or what did you do) to mitigate this harm?

3.2. Think of an instance when you, or another music teacher, made caring efforts that were not received in the way that was expected. What might have been a reason for this mismatch? What could have happened differently?
3.3. Think of a time when you received an apology that felt authentic. What made it seem so?
3.4. Was there ever a time when you were bullied in a music learning space? What did it feel like? What would have helped you?
3.5. Was there ever a time when you were a bully to someone else in a music learning space? What caused you to act the way you did? What would have helped you?
3.6. Considering the AIR approaches for mental health and the scenario in Box 3c, what are some other strategies that you have found effective?
3.7. What are some ways that you could implement hierarchical and nonhierarchical peer mentoring in your classroom? How can you do so without reinforcing dominance of some students over others?
3.8. Describe a safe versus a brave space in your own music learning history. What made the difference?
3.9. What did you find most surprising or most useful in the section on trauma-informed approaches?

Notes

1. See Pete Buttigieg, *Trust: America's Best Chance* (New York: W. W. Norton, 2020); Megan Tschannen-Moran, *Trust Matters: Leadership for Successful Schools* (Hoboken, NJ: Jossey-Bass, 2014).
2. Juliet Hess, *Madness and Distress in Music Education: Toward a Mad-Affirming Approach* (New York: Routledge, 2024).
3. Hess, *Madness and Distress in Music Education*, 147–166.
4. Nel Noddings, *Caring: A Relational Approach to Ethics and Moral Education*, 2nd ed. (Berkeley: University of California Press, 2013).
5. Warren Churchill and Clare Hall, "Caring about Deaf Music in Culturally Responsive Music Education," in *The Oxford Handbook of Care in Music Education*, ed. Karin S. Hendricks (New York: Oxford University Press, 2023), 542–553.
6. From Churchill and Hall, "Caring about Deaf Music," 546: "Big 'D' Deaf, [. . .] refers to people who use sign language as their primary language, as opposed to small 'd' deaf, which refers to the condition of being unable to hear, or those who have lost their hearing but are not affiliated with the signing community."
7. Churchill and Hall, "Caring about Deaf Music," 547.
8. Marshall B. Rosenberg, *Nonviolent Communication: A Language of Life* (San Diego, CA: PuddleDancer Press, 2003).
9. Karin S. Hendricks and Tawnya D. Smith, "Compassion, Care, Communication, and Connection in Instrumental Learning Spaces," in *Teaching Instrumental Music: Perspectives and Pedagogies for the 21st Century*, ed. Bryan Powell, Kristen Pellegrino, and Quincy Hilliard (New York: Oxford University Press, 2023), 95–102.
10. Hendricks and Smith, "Compassion, Care, Communication, and Connection," 99.
11. Rosenberg, *Nonviolent Communication*, 6–7.
12. Tiri Schei, "The Vulnerability in Being Heard," in *The Oxford Handbook of Care in Music Education*, ed. Karin S. Hendricks (New York: Oxford University Press, 2023), 312.
13. Schei, "The Vulnerability in Being Heard," 309.
14. Schei, "The Vulnerability in Being Heard," 315.
15. Kelly Bylica, "Critical Listening and Authorial Agency as Radical Practices of Care," in *The Oxford Handbook of Care in Music Education*, ed. Karin S. Hendricks (New York: Oxford University Press, 2023), 482–493.
16. Hendricks, *Compassionate Music Teaching*.
17. Hendricks, *Compassionate Music Teaching*, 47, emphasis added.

18. Justin McManus and Bruce Carter, "Accompanying LGBTQIA+ Students in the Music Classroom," in *The Oxford Handbook of Care in Music Education*, ed. Karin S. Hendricks (New York: Oxford University Press, 2023), 179–192; Rebecca D. Swanson and Mary L. Cohen, "Music-Making in Prisons and Schools: Dismantling Carceral Logics," in *The Oxford Handbook of Care in Music Education*, ed. Karin S. Hendricks (New York: Oxford University Press, 2023), 517–530.
19. Hendricks, *Compassionate Music Teaching*, 46.
20. Jared Rawlings, "Using the Lens of Psychological Safety to Understand the Effects of Bullying within the School-Based Music Ensemble Classroom," in *The Oxford Handbook of Care in Music Education*, ed. Karin S. Hendricks (New York: Oxford University Press, 2023), 292–293.
21. Centers for Disease Control and Prevention, "#StopBullying," last modified Oct 3, 2019, https://www.cdc.gov/injury/features/stop-bullying/index.html.
22. Ken Elpus and Bruce Carter, "Bullying Victimization among Music Ensemble and Theatre Students in the United States," *Journal of Research in Music Education* 64, no. 3 (2016): 322–343, https://doi.org/10.1177/0022429416658642.
23. Jared R. Rawlings, "Middle School Students' Perceptions of Bullying," *Bulletin of the Council for Research in Music Education*, no. 209 (2016): 7–26, https://doi.org/10.5406/bulcouresmus edu.209.0007; see also Tawnya D. Smith and Karin S. Hendricks, "Diversity, Inclusion, and Access," in *Oxford Handbook of Musical Performance*, ed. Gary E. McPherson (New York: Oxford University Press), 528–549; Emilia Barna, "Popular Music Education, Aesthetic Judgment, and Gender Relations in Hungary," in *The Oxford Handbook of Care in Music Education*, ed. Karin S. Hendricks (New York: Oxford University Press, 2023): 530–542; Karin S. Hendricks, "Compassionate Pedagogies for LGBTQ+ Student Visibility, Radical Welcome, and Authentic Expressions of Music and Personhood," in *The Oxford Handbook of Gender and Queer Studies in Music Education*, ed. Nick McBride and Colleen Sears (New York, Oxford University Press, in press).
24. Rawlings, "Using the Lens of Psychological Safety," 292.
25. Jared Rawlings and Jacob Young, "High School Band and Orchestra Musician's Willingness to Intervene in School-Based Relational Victimization Experiences," *Contributions to Music Education* 46 (2021): 207–223.
26. Rawlings, "Using the Lens of Psychological Safety," 295.
27. David Baker, "Disability, Lifelong Musical Engagement, and Care," in *The Oxford Handbook of Care in Music Education*, ed. Karin S. Hendricks (New York: Oxford University Press, 2023), 99.
28. Kimberly A. McCord, "'This Guitar Hurts!': Empathy and Caring in Inclusive Ensembles," in *The Oxford Handbook of Care in Music Education*, ed. Karin S. Hendricks (New York: Oxford University Press, 2023), 248.
29. McCord, "This Guitar Hurts!," 248.
30. McCord, "This Guitar Hurts!," 249, adapted for a broader music education audience.
31. Ryan M. Hourigan, "Music as a Vehicle for Caring for Students with Learning Differences," in *The Oxford Handbook of Care in Music Education*, ed. Karin S. Hendricks (New York: Oxford University Press, 2023), 381–383.
32. Hourigan, "Music as a Vehicle," 377–378.
33. Hourigan, "Music as a Vehicle," 382.
34. Hourigan, "Music as a Vehicle," 382.
35. Hourigan, "Music as a Vehicle," 382.
36. McManus and Carter, "Accompanying LGBTQIA+ Students"; Rawlings, "Using the Lens of Psychological Safety," 295.
37. Erin M. Hansen, "Roles of Music Making in the Lives of Sexual and Gender Minority Youth," (PhD diss, University of Michigan, 2016), http://hdl.handle.net/2027.42/120873; Karin S. Hendricks, Cheryl M. Freeze, and Tammy S. Yi, "Spaces and Facets of Trust for Secondary School LGBTQ+ Music Students," in *The Oxford Handbook of Gender and Queer Studies in Music Education*, ed. Nick McBride and Colleen Sears (New York, Oxford University Press, in press).
38. Matthew L. Garrett, and Joshua Palkki, *Honoring Trans and Gender-Expansive Students in Music Education* (New York: Oxford University Press, 2021).
39. Hendricks, Freeze, and Yi, "Spaces and Facets of Trust."
40. Barna, "Popular Music Education."
41. Barna, "Popular Music Education," 538.
42. Barna, "Popular Music Education," 536.
43. Barna, "Popular Music Education."
44. Rachel Dirks, "Student and Teacher Mental Health: Nurturing Wellbeing within a Climate of Trust," in *The Oxford Handbook of Care in Music Education*, ed. Karin S. Hendricks (New York: Oxford University Press, 2023), 319–328.
45. Dirks, "Student and Teacher Mental Health," 319.
46. Brené Brown, "Brené with Dr. Susan David on the Dangers of Toxic Positivity, Part 2 of 2," March 8, 2021, in *Dare to Lead*, produced by Brené Brown, podcast, Spotify, 52:36, https://brenebrown.com/transcript/brene-with-dr-susan-david-on-the-dangers-of-toxic-positivity-part-2-of-2/.
47. Dirks, "Student and Teacher Mental Health," 323.

48. Sally Spencer-Thomas, "How to Ask Someone about Suicide," *National Alliance on Mental Illness*, September 6, 2019, https://nami.org/Blogs/NAMI-Blog/September-2019/How-to-Ask-Someone-About-Suicide.
49. Lina Hejjawi, Charlene Ryan, Karin S. Hendricks, and Tawnya D. Smith, "The Role of Social Media Feedback in Performance Preparation, Self-Esteem, and Anxiety," manuscript under review.
50. Brian Arao, and Kristi Clemens, "From Safe Spaces to Brave Spaces," in *The Art of Effective Facilitation: Reflections from Social Justice Educators*, ed. Lisa Landreman (Sterling, VA: Stylus Publishing, 2013), 135–150; Hendricks, Freeze, and Yi, "Spaces and Facets of Trust."
51. Andrew Goodrich, "Developing Trust and Empathy through Peer Mentoring in the Music Classroom," in *The Oxford Handbook of Care in Music Education*, ed. Karin S. Hendricks (New York: Oxford University Press, 2023), 280–291.
52. Andrew Goodrich, "Valuing Racialized Student Voices: Transforming Learning through Peer Mentoring," *Action, Criticism, and Theory for Music Education* 21, no. 1 (2021): 142–171.
53. Tawnya D. Smith, "Teaching through Trauma: Compassion Fatigue, Burnout, or Secondary Traumatic Stress?," in *Trauma and Resilience in Music Education: Haunted Melodies*, ed. Deborah Bradley and Juliet Hess (New York: Routledge, 2022), 49–63.
54. Rawlings, "Using the Lens of Psychological Safety," 297.
55. Patricia A. Jennings, *The Trauma-Sensitive Classroom: Building Resilience with Compassionate Teaching* (New York: WW Norton, 2019); Smith, "Teaching through Trauma."
56. These examples are adapted from a list provided by Rawlings, "Using the Lens of Psychological Safety," 297. See also Bessel van der Kolk, *The Body Keeps the Score: Brain, Mind, and Body in the Healing of Trauma* (New York: Penguin Books, 2015).
57. Van der Kolk, *The Body Keeps the Score.*
58. Shannan Hibbard and Erin Price, "Trauma: A Compassionate Lens for Music Teaching," in *The Oxford Handbook of Care in Music Education*, ed. Karin S. Hendricks (New York: Oxford University Press, 2023), 384.
59. Hibbard and Price, "Trauma," 384; see also Juliet Hess, "Rethinking 'Bad Behavior': A Compassionate Response to 'Acting Out' in Music Education," in *Trauma and Resilience in Music Education: Haunted Melodies*, ed. Deborah Bradley and Juliet Hess (New York: Routledge, 2022).
60. Hendricks, *Compassionate Music Teaching*, 6.
61. Hendricks, *Compassionate Music Teaching*, 5–8.
62. Hibbard and Price, "Trauma," 389.
63. Karin S. Hendricks, Diana R. Dansereau, Betty Bauman-Field, and Cheryl M. Freeze, "Fostering Trust in Music Classrooms: A Review of the Literature," *Update: Applications for Research in Music Education* 43, no. 1 (2024): 10–18, https://doi.org/10.1177/87551233231183366.
64. Janelize Morelli, "The Musical Circle of Care: A Framework for Relationship Building and Healing through Musicing," in *The Oxford Handbook of Care in Music Education*, ed. Karin S. Hendricks (New York: Oxford University Press, 2023), 158; see also Howard Bath, "The Three Pillars of Trauma-Informed Care," *Reclaiming Children and Youth* 17, no. 3 (2008): 17–21.
65. Betty Bauman-Field, "Trauma-Informed Classroom Management in Music Education: A Literature Review," *Update: Applications of Research in Music Education*, (2023), https://doi.org/10.1177/87551233231173149; Erin E. Price, "Behavioral Strategies for Trauma-Informed Elementary General Music Education for Students with Emotional/Behavioral Disorders: A Review of the Literature," *Update: Applications of Research in Music Education, 41* no. 2, (2023): 38–47, https://doi.org/10.1177/87551233221120235.

4

Caring with Musical Expressions

Chapter Overview

This chapter explores various ways that music teachers and their co-learners connect authentically with self, others, and the music they make. Topics include: musically meaningful goals; caring about and for the music we make; musical authenticity and integrity; sharing an ethic of responsibility with co-learners; caring with and *through* the music; promoting "enthusiastic commitment" through cycles of connection; encouraging musical expression through singing-caring relations; caring connections through the lifespan; and the various roles of empathy in musical expression (fostering empathic expressions, musical empathy, empathic creativity, promoting empathy through jazz and jazz-inspired activities, and cultural attunement and co-learning). Several specific strategies and approaches are offered for creating brave spaces for musical risk-taking.

Introduction

I've found that one of the most challenging things about writing a book is deciding what order to present the material. I have you, the reader, continually in my mind—wondering if everything will make sense to you in the way I write it. As is the case with preparing lesson plans, things rarely turn out as anticipated. Just like when making music, the process of writing is far more holistic and spontaneous than our pen-and-paper approach allows. In both writing and music teaching, many of the best ideas can get lost in translation, and many books or music lessons take an unforeseen direction as things unfold. Slowly and gradually I'm beginning to accept that this process of creativity and improvisation is what life, writing, music, and teaching are all about.

The original plan was to place this chapter later in the book, after the one on musical development. I thought to myself, "of course, develop the skills first . . . ." However, the chapter on expression seemed like such an easy continuation of the previous one—so much so, that I started experiencing writer's block as I tried to work against what felt natural. I had been privileging thinking over feeling and, as a result, was getting nowhere. Then, once I decided to put the chapter on expression before the chapter on musical development, everything felt so much easier.

Daring to Care with Music Education. Karin S. Hendricks, Oxford University Press. © Oxford University Press 2025.
DOI: 10.1093/9780197777589.003.0004

In that moment I recalled an experience that happened to me over a decade ago, one that forever changed my perspective on music teaching and learning. I was born to the daughter of an army colonel, and thus I was raised to be a Type-A personality who loves a good system, a sequenced checklist, and a "perfect" plan. If plans are to be changed, then that change needs to be written into the plan—you know the type. This kind of systematic lifestyle works very well when there are rules to follow and one singular standard to uphold, but it also falls flat when real life happens—including in music classes with real music and real music learners who each have their own ideas, identities, and expressions.

(As an aside: Over many years in the field of music teacher education I've seen some of the best lesson plan writers struggle in the classroom when they fail to extend themselves beyond the plan, to engage with the students before and beside them. Here is where connection, trust, empathy, and humility play a role for teachers: balancing what we *think* is the best approach to reach an objective, with what our students need and want and contribute to their own learning.)

So, imagine me as a Type-A teacher in my early years of teaching, attempting to soak up everything I could from seasoned, successful teachers around me like a sponge. Then, taking that information, I devised systems for learning musical technique and expression—which I would then uphold in the classroom like a golden standard. Some of these systems seemed to work well for me and the students I taught, especially in later years when I relaxed a bit and learned to treat them as a template rather than a rule.

One of these systems was "Hen's Pecking Order," my version of the traditional "order of operations" for musical elements used in many music classes, where teachers suggest that students should focus first posture and rhythm, and so forth, and then add on more elements as they are ready. "Hen's Pecking Order" poked fun at the nickname my students had given me while also providing them with a prescribed order for prioritizing various elements of string instrument performance. It also gave us a rubric for self-assessment. Figure 4.1 is a picture of a "pecking order" poster created by Jordanne Burgess, a former orchestra student who is now an orchestra teacher herself. This poster resides in the classroom where I once taught, and where Jordanne now teaches.

Back to the story: Enter Becky Roesler, my good friend and colleague, with whom I have presented several sessions at music education conferences across the United States. Once, while preparing slides for a presentation we were preparing to give on expressive performance, I proposed that the "pecking order" might be a helpful way to introduce students to elements of musical expression. I suggested to Becky that it might prevent overwhelming students with too much to think about at any one time.

Becky looked up at the screen, with her eyes squinting, appearing deep in thought as she studied this system. After a pause and a "hmmm," she said with kindness, "I wonder . . . if it's really so linear." I watched as she used her hands to

Figure 4.1 "Hen's Pecking Order." (Photo credit: Jordanne Burgess)

flip the sequence upside down, placing the expressive elements on the top like an umbrella with all the technical pieces underneath them. She explained that, in her mind, expression is the overarching goal—and music teachers would do well consider all the other elements less as an order of operations, per se, and more as they work toward an expressive goal. Otherwise, musical targets are isolated from their connective expressive purpose, and very often teachers and learners will end up putting expression at the end of the order—where it gets the least attention, if any.

Rather than seeing the performance elements as isolated steps (where one was unable to move on until each step was perfected), Becky helped me to see music teaching and learning as a holistic process where the goal of musical expression was always in the forefront. Figure 4.2 illustrates what Becky envisioned through the analogy of an umbrella, with various elements of music working together toward musical expression. String pedagogues Kristen Pellegrino and Joel Schut offer further insight into how technique can be taught through expressive goals, as students learn to blend various amounts of bow placement, angle, weight, and speed to create a broad palette of musical sounds.[1]

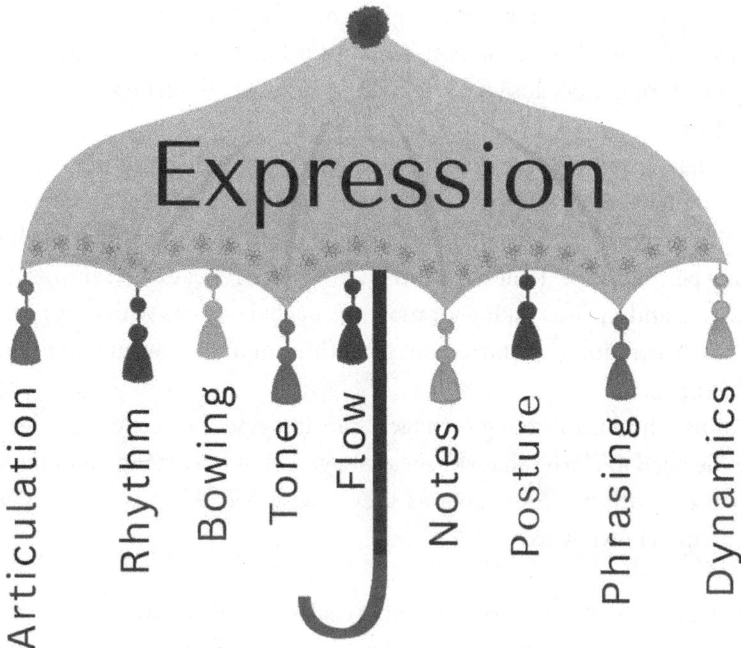

Figure 4.2 "Roesler's Expressive Umbrella." (Design credit: Adam Symborski)

Musically Meaningful Goals

Around the same time we gave the presentation described above, Becky Roesler published a *Music Educators Journal* article on the importance of starting with such expressive goals in mind.[2] Comparing music learning to reading, Roesler draws on research[3] suggesting that students can have better reading retention when they read with the intent to seek solutions to problems, rather than reading merely to gain whatever information is put in front of them. In other words, students may be able to make the most sense out of content when they have choice and control to select, organize, and integrate it toward tangible goals. Reflection Activity 1.6 in Chapter 1 might be an example of this strategy. Similarly, in music, all the technical elements that go into a performance can make more sense to students when they can envision them through an expressive goal.

Authentic goals such as those related to musical expression focus on meaningful outcomes. They run opposite to *avoidance* goals, where we might focus on doing something in order to avoid failure or embarrassment.[4] As I explained in Chapter 2, feelings of shame, failure, or embarrassment can lead to social withdrawal, whereas care-filled music-making provides powerful opportunities for authentic connection. Roesler agrees, stating that "there are few things quite as satisfying as connecting with another human being through music."[5] Interpersonal goals (such as sharing music with listeners, evoking a reaction from listeners, creating a feeling in listeners, conveying a message to listeners) help us focus on learning in "musically meaningful" ways, not only for the giver but also the receiver.[6] As Figure 4.2 illustrates, technique is still fundamental, but it may have a better chance to permeate the experience because it comes with meaning and purpose. (See Reflection Activity 4.1.)

Roesler tells a story of how she experienced the joy of purposeful learning when she was simultaneously a teacher and a listener to the music her students made—as her middle school students took on a challenge to move her emotionally in the upcoming performance. It all began when they were rehearsing a slow and tender composition, and she was asking for more connected phrases with only partial success. In her frustration she blurted out something akin to "I want you to make me cry at the concert!"

Any of us who know young teenagers can imagine the scene that ensued, including the need to clarify that she meant "a *good* kind of crying," and the various individual chatterings of students as they envisioned the possibility. The story continues, in her own words:

> I had no idea how effective this impromptu challenge would prove to be. It changed the tenor of our rehearsals. Thinking about what would need to happen in music in order to affect another human being transformed their learning. Instead of trying to do the things I was telling them to do just because they were told, the students were now motivated by a deeply human, interpersonal, intrinsic goal: to create an emotional reaction in their teacher. In each rehearsal we practiced what would increase their chances of accomplishing their newfound objective. They learned to save their bows to have room to grow the phrase. They learn to balance each other, according to where the moving melody was. They learned to create different colors of sound by varying their bow contact point. While pursuing this communicative goal, they were receptive to acquiring and refining the skills that would increase their musical maturity and expressiveness.[7]

The simple, off-the-cuff comment about wanting her students to make her cry—and the collective challenge taken up by these curious youth—led to a transformation in both learning and teaching. There was no longer a need for external motivation to learn or practice. There was no need for talk about an adjudicator rating, or even what others in the audience might think. The students worked together for a holistic, expressive goal, working technical elements with focus yet flexibility. Although I wasn't there, I can imagine how the lesson plan waxed, waned, and wove as students likely asked more questions than usual, stayed more focused, and encouraged one another to do so as well.

We can't leave this story without knowing the ending: Did it work? Did the students make her cry in the performance? Roesler goes on:

> During the performance, they played beautifully. It was sensitive and poignant, with moments of mature stretching and phrasing. Truly, I was deeply moved, as

> were several parents in the audience. And, I must say, I have never seen a group of [middle school] students so concerned about the emotional state of their teacher following a performance. More important, they truly experienced expressive performance as they sought to communicate with their audience—with me.[8]

Although music does offer the possibility to communicate and connect, Roesler's article ends with a reminder that this is not always the case. As I discuss elsewhere, music learning spaces can also be places of disconnection and even harm. Additionally, many if not most students enter music learning spaces already inhibited from being fully expressive in one way or another.

With these various tensions in mind, I offer a variety of vantage points for encouraging and facilitating authentic musical connections through expressive goals. In the pages that follow, I explore how we might care for and about the music itself—including through fostering musical integrity and sharing an ethic of responsibility with co-learners. I then explore what it might look like to care with and through the music as we connect with others throughout our lives, including through enthusiastic commitment, singing-caring relations, and empathic attunement.

Caring for and about the Music

Oxford Handbook of Care in Music Education (OHCME) author Estelle Jorgensen shares similar sentiments about driving our work with musical goals. She reminds us that, as music teachers, we possess skills and multiple knowledges for using music as a tool for expression—a tool that we can share with learners of all ages so that they, too, can express themselves authentically.[9] Part of this work involves music teachers maintaining and continually expanding our own sense of musicianship. As the world around us changes rapidly and we gain increasing technologies for musical distribution and production, Jorgensen reminds us to focus on those aspects of music-making that give voice to our individual and collective expressions of our unique and shared life experiences. Caring for and about the music in this way involves practicing musical integrity, caring to connect, and sharing an ethic of responsibility with students.

Musical Integrity

I once had a very accomplished flute player explain to me that every note they played was like its own kind of sanctuary to them—and they wanted to honor every single note with their best breath, their best focus, their best expression. The flute player's perspective was not rooted in a kind of competitive aim where their "best" would be compared to anyone else's "best." Rather, it was about giving the utmost care to each and every note they played, out of respect for the process of music and the sounds that would go out into the world. To them, caring for and about the music was all about invoking authenticity and integrity into every note.

This same kind of reverence for the process and product of music is evidenced in the teaching style of Steve Massey, a secondary school jazz and concert band teacher whom I featured in *Compassionate Music Teaching.* Steve's friend and jazz legend Wynton Marsalis described how integrity was at the core of the work Steve did:

> Integrity is a word we hear all the time, but we see it very seldom, because integrity costs. [Steve Massey] possesses tremendous integrity. . . . When he walks into a room, all of our music is brought into the room with him because of the level of his integrity and the depth of it. . . . He loves his kids. That's why they play the way that they play. He loves the music. He's willing to sacrifice for it, and he knows about it. Love manifests itself in knowledge, and he has been dedicated for such a long time. . . . Soul means when you walk into a room, people feel better when you leave than they felt before you came in. This is what he has.[10]

In the quote above, Wynton Marsalis points to several aspects of integrity, as he noticed them in Massey's teaching style. First, integrity costs something—in other words, it doesn't just show up innately in the music or in our teaching, but it requires that we take particular care to produce music that has such integrity—integrity in sound, in shape, in flow, and so forth. Second, a person who shows such a high level of authentic care about music education embodies it. In other words, students and others may sense the level of authenticity and integrity through their interactions with that person. Third, authentic care for the integrity of the music relates to an authentic love for it. Fourth, and relatedly, authentic care for students relates to an authentic love for them. Fifth, this kind of love is demonstrated by the ways that one cares to learn about something (music) and about and with someone (students). Finally, such authenticity and integrity have a tangible impact.

I also view authenticity and integrity as inseparable. The concept of authentic connection, as I have defined it, should not be conflated with just any "electric" experience that might occur as we make music with co-learners. Instead, authentic connection requires a deep level of integrity—of care, consistency, and honesty. As I have written elsewhere, authenticity is "connection with our true selves, as well as the integrity we display in our interactions with others." For *Courage to Teach* author Parker J. Palmer, "good teaching comes from the [. . .] integrity of the teacher."[11] And as Wynton Marsalis mentioned in the quote above, such integrity is rare because it costs. But it can be powerfully impactful—and worth far more than the cost.

Caring to Connect Is Worth More Than the Cost

The "cost" of time and effort involved in create authentic connections with music students is something that Sundas Mohi-Truong, an award-winning high school orchestra teacher in Texas, considers critical for long-term success. I asked Sundas to share some reflections about caring for, about, and with students as she prepared for her recent performance at the Midwest Band and Orchestra Clinic (a highly-celebrated honor for K-12 music teachers in the United States).[12] Specifically, I asked Sundas to think about the high levels of care required for each and every note expected at a Midwest Clinic performance—juxtaposed with the kind of care for individual humans that is so needed in this world, perhaps especially with teenagers whose mental and physical health should be at the forefront of teachers' minds.

I asked Sundas to share with *Daring to Care* readers what she thought are keys to such care-filled performances and practices where students learn to care for, about, and with each other—while also caring for and about the music. In her response, Sundas describes the importance of honesty and openness for building authentic connections, as well as setting up expectations for practice that would benefit everyone in the group:

> The product is always better when there is a genuine relationship between individuals who are working together. I find this to be especially true with teenagers, who are navigating a tough time in their lives where they are trying to discover who they are. I believe that relationship building is a skill that any teacher can learn, just like any other pedagogical skill we train.[13]

As explained in Chapter 2, an element of fostering trust with students involves honesty and openness. Sundas explains the specific ways in which she cares for the intricacies of the music, while also caring for and with students, by setting clear expectations for the learning environment and communicating openly with students about how their actions impacted others in the group:

> A key aspect to care-filled performances is kind and firm transparency. I shared with my students how important it was to me that [the Midwest Clinic] performance be their absolute best, and how much I wanted this moment to be one that they remember for the rest of their lives. There were points of frustration along the way and I was open with them about how it made me feel. I did not raise my voice or "yell." I did say that it felt disrespectful and hurtful that, when I and others put in so much time, some of their actions made it seem like they don't care as much. I described those actions (not marking their music, not practicing during our advisory time, not contributing in class); AND explained what I would like to see clearly (if you make a mistake, mark it; if you can't play something in class, practice it in advisory). I had many one-on-one conversations to explain to students what

I was seeing and how it came off, and allowed them to share their perspectives. This was time consuming, but important.[14]

The time and care that Sundas put into creating a community of responsibility is also mirrored by the work of Mark Russell Smith (described in Chapter 2 and later in this chapter), in the work he does to establish relationships and expectations over the course of a weekend performance event.

Finally, Sundas also shared with me the importance of fostering student ownership over any musical performance. As she explains, "If we want students to care about every note, we must give them as many opportunities to own their music and experiences as we possibly can." Performing at the Midwest Clinic was not *her* goal for them; it was *their* goal, something they decided on together and actively pursued together:

> My students chose the repertoire, helped me reserve it on the Midwest portal, contributed bowings and fingerings (some had to be corrected, but I gave them the opportunity). They picked our merchandise, wrote program notes, picked the graphic art for the programs and posters, created music binders, designed our shirts, helped pick where what sights we were going to see . . . the list goes on and on.[15]

Sundas made a point to ask herself, at every step along the way, "Is there any possible way I can involve students in this, even if it seems like a rudimentary task?" And then she involved them in those ways—thereby fostering trust, demonstrating belief in their competence, and creating a community of expectation and responsibility.

Sharing an Ethic of Responsibility with Co-Learners

Caring *for* music, just like caring *for* others, requires an acceptance of the responsibility involved in such caring. Such acceptance leads to action as we are attentive and attempt to understand the unique and nuanced ways that care is appropriate in a particular context.[16] Accepting responsibility in this way causes us to consider how we might, at the very least, do no harm to ourselves and others.

As I think on Jorgensen's call to care for the music (cited earlier), I wonder about the impact of various new technologies, including artificial intelligence, on our music-making. I think about all the ways it can enhance and support our creativity—all the ways we might get excited about what it can do for us. I have a colleague who is into all the latest gadgets, and he is absolutely thrilled by how such technologies can level the equity playing field for many would-be musicians, by providing musical access to those who might not otherwise have such opportunities. I had not considered this important perspective before interacting with him.

On the other hand, other teachers express concern about how an overstep of AI might leave music feeling contrived or inauthentic, or perhaps even cause harm to the careers of musical artists. I wonder: What do these technologies do for you and your students? What do they mean to you and your students? What are your anticipations? What are your concerns? (See Reflection Activity 4.2.)

OHCME authors Brent C. Talbot and Cara Faith Bernard consider some of the ethical tensions associated with music technology in their chapter titled "An Ethic of Expectation Surrounding the Virtual Performance."[17] Virtual ensembles went viral during the COVID-19 pandemic, and many parents and administrators have since come to expect high-quality productions like this from their own schools—but without stopping to consider all the costs, time commitment, skills, and technological access required to do so. Talbot and Bernard note how such a focus on "product" might take away from other social, individual, and educational value that comes from focusing first on musically meaningful goals.

Some of the positive outcomes of virtual ensemble performances include (a) attaining musical, social, and individual goals; (b) expanded opportunities for music-making; (c) an ability for self-study and self-improvement; and (d) expanded musical skills. On the other hand, there are potential hazards or tensions that music teachers, families and support systems, and administrators need to keep in mind, including: (a) cost and access required for certain technologies, (b) extra student or teacher labor required for editing and production, (c) ethical concerns related to manipulating student performances, and (d) the absence of an in-person experience.[18] Talbot and Bernard suggest that music teachers might consider virtual ensembles through a lens of care and compassion to promote authentic connections and student engagement.

Box 4a contains a vignette written by Talbot and Bernard, in which they illustrate a hypothetical (but very likely) scenario in which Mx. Stevenson, an accomplished choral director, wrestles with the ethics of altering performers' tone, pitch, volume, or other expressive elements in their digital audio workstation (DAW). On one hand, Mx. Stevenson recognizes the limitations of working with prerecorded student clips in that they cannot offer in-the-moment cues to students to help students with their diction and breath support. There is also no opportunity to move students around to help one another, as they would typically do in an in-person rehearsal or performance. Mx. Stevenson is torn between their desire to maintain the school music program's strong reputation, and the ethics of stitching students' voices together. Mx. Stevenson wonders: Is manipulating student voices akin to silencing their musical expression?

Mx. Stevenson continues to contemplate this conundrum in Box 4b. An issue of trust and self-efficacy arises: If Mx. Stevenson "over-functions" for students by doing all the mixing and mastering for them, the students may lose an opportunity to learn these skills and may also come to assume that Mx. Stevenson does not trust their musical insights. As shown in the vignette, Mx. Stevenson decides to bring the

Box 4a Mx. Stevenson's Conundrum with Virtual Ensembles

Acclaimed choral director Mx. Stevenson is working on blending all the voices in the DAW and observes in the recordings that a few students are not matching pitch well; a few other singers have poor breath support; and two students are holding the "s" too long while another singer places the "s" too early. Mx. Stevenson reflects that, in a live setting, upon hearing these sounds: "I would put these students next to other singers who have a stronger sense of pitch and who model good breath support in order to blend and balance the group." Additionally, Mx. Stevenson acknowledges the importance of visual cues, recognizing they would typically use conducting gestures or some movement to show better breath support or to indicate exactly where the "s" is to be placed. They elaborate, "I want students' hard work to be represented well." Mx. Stevenson struggles with continuing their legacy of lauded performances: "How am I to accomplish this without overly altering, silencing, or muting the students' voices?" In this virtual performance setting, Mx. Stevenson struggles with how to utilize and represent all singers' voices without having to manipulate their recordings.

Worried about maintaining their program's excellent reputation, Mx. Stevenson debates how to accomplish creating a performance that truly represents all the singers, while also maintaining the high level of quality for which the choir is known. As Mx. Stevenson considers this dilemma, they realize that the technology is an impediment rather than an enhancer to the goals and processes to which they have become accustomed. In a live rehearsal or performance Mx. Stevenson would never ask a student to mouth the words or to not sing. However, stitching students' voices together in a DAW makes Mx. Stevenson question the ethics of this endeavor, leaving them with an uneasy feeling about how to address the disparities of acoustic spaces and errors in the recorded submissions.*

*Talbot and Bernard, "An Ethic of Expectation," 49–52.

students into the production process. Students are invited to consider not only the mechanics involved in production, but also the ethics of voice manipulation.

When the students brainstorm along with Mx. Stevenson, they come up with suggestions for improving on the sound but without manipulating voices—including adding accompaniment and rerecording their parts with the support of a practice track. Students learn new skills and gain additional motivation to improve their own performance. Further, Mx. Stevenson can produce a recording they can feel proud to share with the music program community.

When I first read the ending of Talbot and Bernard's vignette, I let out a sigh—not only from relief at a problem solved, but also an "ahhh yes, I've been there" moment. For example, I think about all the times that I had no idea what to do to solve

Box 4b Problem-Solving with Students

Conscious that their decisions might lead to over-functioning for the students, Mx. Stevenson decides to play the aligned yet unaltered tracks for the students in the homophonic sections and center them in the decision making. Collaboratively, students name and negotiate the "ifs and whys and hows" of how they, as a group, want to proceed with the project. They consider how the changing conditions of a recording warrant a different set of expectations and actions, including how a live performance more easily welcomes errors in a one-off listening session versus a recorded effort where audience members expect the highest of quality and can return to the source for multiple listenings. Mx. Stevenson poses the ethical dilemma of muting, silencing, or autotuning voices to the students and they discuss the ramifications, deciding that acting upon these choices would not represent the group's personality. Mx. Stevenson also offers the option for the group to not share the piece as a public product.

The students describe that the ensemble typically performs unaccompanied works; however, one student with amateur recording skills suggests that within the recorded environment, adding accompaniment might facilitate better blend of disparate acoustic spaces and cover up some of the non-aligned breaths and sustained singing. As a group, they decide to add a piano and strings accompaniment that will help cover up some of the issues discussed, as well as improve the blend of the acoustic space.

Students also suggest that anyone is welcome to re-record their part. One of the students volunteers to create a new practice track with two full measures of them count-singing the meter and providing a starting pitch, establishing a strong tonal and rhythmic center for recording. Students could then submit a portion of the piece each week for feedback. Mx. Stevenson would listen to each voice individually and consider ways to scaffold the recording process to better address pitch issues, vowel unification, tone production, phrase shaping.*

*Talbot and Bernard, "An Ethic of Expectation," 52–53.

a musical concern—but when I was brave enough to bring the concern to students and invite them to problem-solve with me, I was regularly and routinely amazed at how effective their creative ideas were. What's more, in such cases I didn't have to worry about how to sell the idea to them because they already owned it.

As an aside: Early in my orchestra conducting career I would require pencils at the ready, conduct routine pencil checks for prizes, and say silly phrases such as "the shortest pencil is greater than the longest memory" to encourage students to write down and remember what I had asked them to do. But then, when I stopped asking students to do what I wanted and started asking them instead what they thought was possible, pencil checks were unnecessary because the pencils were already out and the minds were already engaged. And I was amazed daily at the kind of musical expressions that they envisioned, designed, constructed, and *remembered.*

Caring *through* the Music

Thus far in this book, I have focused on three kinds of caring: caring *for*, caring *about*, and caring *with* students and the music they make. A fourth kind of caring—caring *through* music, is important in a discussion of musical expression. OHCME author Marissa Silverman explains that having a goal to care through music and music education means that the goal extends beyond the music to achieve some other aim.[19] Caring through music can be evidenced when we use music to raise awareness or act for a greater good. One iconic example is when, in 1985, many of the era's music superstars produced the single "We Are the World" to raise money for famine relief. Countless examples also exist at local levels (see Chapter 9 for some of these).

Beyond using music as a vehicle for caring for something outside of the musical process, Silverman offers a vision of caring *for* another person, *through* music that we make together. Such an act might be considered "musical empathy," such as when we connect cognitively and affectively with other people through music in a music ensemble. Musical empathy also occurs when we sing and dance along with a singer/songwriter in a concert and honor their story by reciprocating with our own musical expressions. We may even come to identify with their music as if it were our own experience by expressing something like "that's my song!"[20]

In Chapter 2, I explained how making music with others while moving together affords a collective synchronized experience that connects people with others in ways that are unique to music. As Silverman describes, caring through music "instantiates that music teaching and learning is the vehicle for which caring can, and often does, occur. It also allows for the possibility that when [making music together], we can be our caring bests."[21]

On the other hand, the power of such musical synchrony has the potential to be especially harmful when in uncaring spaces—or even spaces intended to be caring where there is trauma or some other form of misunderstanding (see Chapter 3). With this caveat acknowledged, I turn now to a discussion of how caring *for*, *about*, and *with* students *through* music might lead to musical connections—and what those musical connections might look like.

Encouraging "Enthusiastic Commitment" through Cycles of Musical Connection

As I described in Chapter 2, music provides a unique avenue for creating connections with others, even within a short amount of time.[22] For this reason, it is probable to assume that co-learners can forge reciprocal and responsive relationships even during a short-term event such as a conductor-led large ensemble festival. OHCME author Al Legutki and colleagues describe how they observed orchestra conductor Mark Russell Smith establish "enthusiastic commitment"[23] with high school honor orchestra students through three cycles of increasing musical connection: (a) establishing his trust and authority as a conductor, (b) relaxing into roles and expectations, and (c) balancing authority and collective ownership.[24]

Mark began the first rehearsal by *establishing trust and authority* as a conductor, in ways that honor orchestra students would likely expect based on their prior learning experiences within the Western classical tradition. At this early stage, the teaching was clearly teacher-directed and focused on caring *about* the music, which he had selected in advance and prepped his score to convey the composer's intent through his own conducting. Yet Mark also demonstrated care *for* the students by considering pacing for the weekend in his initial plan (such as factoring in string-heavy rehearsals after loud, brass-heavy rehearsing to give brass players a break). As Mark explained, festival rehearsals can be "punishing"[25] so he took care to ensure that his plan was sustainable for student focus, stamina, and physical wellbeing.

Second, while trust was still developing, Mark made space for the players (and himself) to *relax into roles and expectations* for performance, orchestral etiquette, and support of one another. He made a point to clarify these roles and expectations to the students, not only through explanations of general rehearsal etiquette (for example, "players on the inside of the music stand are responsible for turning the pages" or "warm up in your seat before the rehearsal time begins") but also by building community, such as inviting them to listen to one another and shuffle their feet in celebration for another student's or section's success and inserting humor into the rehearsal at opportune moments. At this stage, Mark emphasized the importance of listening and responding to students rather than conducting a preplanned routine. He also explained his interest in teaching the students to listen and respond: "I try not to overconduct—even kids—because I conduct the kids just like I do a professional orchestra. . . . When you stop conducting, they start listening."[26]

Third, as Mark established even more trust over time, he was better able to *balance the role of conductor with student-shared musical ownership*. He did so by inviting the students to bring their own musicianship and expression to the group both verbally and through their musical expressions. This caring-*with* environment was established as Mark (a) opened up moments of dialogue and discussion about musical interpretation; (b) guided student listening and response by asking students to provide feedback and ideas to one another; (c) attended to student ideas and expressions through responsive gestures in his own conducting; and (d) shared some of his own vulnerabilities and joys as a musician, including by playing his cello for the students as a final "parting gift" prior to their own performance.[27]

Even in this traditional conductor-led ensemble event, Mark Russell Smith was able to work gradually from a caring-*about* environment to one of caring-*for*, and eventually to a caring-*with* experience where he could share musical ownership with students. Establishing trust first was key, however. In some cases (especially within the Western classical tradition) where students are not used to having such ownership over their learning, it can be jarring, scary, or even be misconstrued erroneously as incompetence when a teacher is not forthright about establishing goals. In these instances the students may need a bit of transition time (including an opportunity to develop trust and gain a sense of competence with the director, themselves, and their peers) before they may be ready to share such collective ownership. Therefore, in some cases where students are more accustomed to a teacher-led experience, it may be important to start with more structure and invite them gradually into the process through many of the approaches listed above.

Encouraging Musical Expression through Singing-Caring Relations

As noted throughout this book, singing is a powerful way to connect people to their felt emotions and to one another. We can care for others through singing in countless ways, such as through a lullaby to a child, singing at a memorial for people grieving a lost loved one, and so forth. We can even care for ourselves through singing when we are completely alone, as we tap into our own felt sensations and respond with vocal expressions. I'm one of those people who sings in response to just about everything—whether singing along with my favorite artist in the car or continually making parodies when someone says something (anything, really) that reminds me of song lyrics. There is a constant Broadway musical going on in my head, and I often have no choice but to sing out loud to release the musical pressure valve!

One particularly compelling avenue for reciprocal and responsive caring is through choral ensembles. OHCME authors Elizabeth Cassidy Parker and Jennifer C. Hutton draw on their experience as choral directors to offer a model for singing-caring relations, which involves three aspects: inclusion, balance, and connection.[28] *Inclusion*, or a commitment to giving everyone a space to belong, is put into practice by affirming everyone's vocal timbre—which has been found to connect with racial and cultural identity. Their suggestions for inclusive singing practices are found in Box 4c.

Next is the importance of *balance* for creating singing-caring relations. In Chapter 2, I discuss how group bonding can occur in choirs even without members needing to create individual relationships with one another. Parker and Hutton caution us, however, that the collective expressive goal of group singing should not override caring for individual musical expressions. Noting the tensions between group unity and individual expression, they offer some practical ideas for balancing the two (see Box 4d).

The third aspect of singing-caring relations comes through *connection*. Humans develop their ability to vocalize from birth, simultaneously as they develop relationships with others. "Thus," Parker and Hutton exclaim, "the voice reflects the self-identity and the amalgam of one's experiences."[29] Similarly, music teachers can encourage students to connect with themselves, others, and the world around them by attuning to their body and the sounds they make while singing. Suggestions for practicing connection while singing are offered in Box 4e.

Box 4c Singing for Inclusion

Because vocal quality and timbre are central elements of vocal development and expression, honoring and making space for exploration of varied vocal timbres can create an inclusive space that supports singer development. In teaching high school choral singers, I (Jenny) aim to explore vocal technique by incorporating singers' musical preferences into instruction and by affirming diverse vocal timbres. Using Estill Voice Training® techniques based on Jo Estill's philosophy that "everyone has a beautiful voice" . . . , singers in choir classes first engage in physical exploration of sounds, then match that exploration to characteristics they hear in their favorite vocal recordings. After gaining further understanding of vocal anatomy, they apply that understanding to their own physical experience of singing and experiment with physical adjustments that create different timbres in the choral repertoire. Singers have expressed a musical passage's mystery and intimacy using breathy, aspirate onsets; they have used high-larynx, twang timbre for musical theatre and for Mongolian folk music; and they have sung in speech-like qualities to enhance text and phrasing in pop, R&B, and jazz. This process has provided space where singers expressed feeling valued, cared for, and respected for the flexible, diverse voices they bring to the group and to the music they enjoy.

In working with younger singers in community choral programs, I (Elizabeth) have learned to embrace their expansive ranges. When I meet a child for the first time, I encourage them to sing a comfortable pitch and we work from their choice rather than from mine. Connected to this idea, I have noticed that bringing the lighter mechanism (commonly known as head voice) into the heavier mechanism (chest voice) through warm ups can exclude singers. To revise this practice, I have begun applying speech as a transition to singing, and using familiar songs or hymns reflecting singers' experiences rather than vocal exercises that may be unfamiliar. I have incorporated individual voice checks a few times each year where I have the opportunity to affirm each singer's voice, to talk with them about their role models, and discuss aims for their singing. I use one-on-one interactions to plan repertoire and structure activities that empower singer capabilities. In rehearsals, I ask singers to model how phrases should be sung for one another, which helps to build additional singing-caring relations.*

*Parker and Hutton, "Singing and Caring," 272.

Caring and Compassionate Connections throughout the Lifespan

Social bonding motivates many of us and our students to continue making music throughout life. The human need to belong is satisfied by intimate relationships that endure over an extended period of time,[30] and shared musical experiences can provide older adults ways to continue lives of joy and connection with others.[31]

Box 4d Singing for Balance

Within the school choral ensembles I (Jenny) work with, singers mostly experience full-ensemble singing as predictable and secure. Conversely, small group activities require greater flexibility and attention as the open-endedness of musical tasks and interpersonal interactions make processes less predictable. Work in small groups can provide new opportunities to appreciate singers' unique contributions. For example, after groups of five or six singers arrange short, known songs and perform them for the larger class, listeners customarily offer praise for their peers' musical choices, singing styles, and performance personalities. Small group activities focused on musical interpretation can lead to similar recognition. To help singers explore expression in a musical passage, I sometimes group singers by voice part, offer each group time to explore and come to consensus, and invite them to perform their interpretation for the larger group. By working within their smaller group and hearing each section's distinct interpretation, singers learn how to reconcile differing ideas to balance individual with group needs. Full-group activities that invite individual singers to share can also help singers feel seen and recognized. Simple classroom practices make space for singers to show gratitude for peer contributions to the choir or school, to discover and discuss their personal strengths, and to share everyday experience, entertaining stories, or wisdom gained from recent events. These experiences provide multiple levels of singing-caring relations while helping to balance the notions of individual and group.

The COVID-19 pandemic highlighted the interconnections between group and individual, and injected feelings of chaos and uncertainty in our community choral program. Like many, we held synchronous meetings on Zoom each week. For the first time, I (Elizabeth) attended to each singer's face and facial expressions because of their closeness on the screen. As a group, we prioritized learning about one another because the choral rehearsal could not operate in the same way as it did in person. Though some singers had difficulty with synchronous rehearsal platforms and kept their cameras off, all seemed to rally when they relied on one another to improvise a pattern or pass a musical idea to another singer. Those who described feeling disappointed with the loss of in-person singing still submitted audio recordings when I asked to hear their progress. Through those audio interactions I came to know their voices and strove to meet singers individually where they were.

As we emerged later in the pandemic to begin socially distant, outdoor singing, we worked to become an in-person collective. Because of those individual interactions, the close proximity of faces on Zoom and time we shared, we found ways to weave ourselves together as a group. I had never experienced such interconnectedness between the individual and group in a choral setting. Going forward as an organization, we will seek greater balance of individual and group activities to build singing-caring relations between each singer. The chaos and uncertainty will be viewed as an opportunity to remain present and care for each individual.*

*Parker and Hutton, "Singing and Caring," 273–274.

Box 4e Singing for Connection

I (Jenny) have noted singing activities that invite focus, quiet attention to sound and silence, and space for musical experiences to "breathe" can help high school singers experience connection through co-creation of beauty. Wordless beginnings within rehearsal act as "an invocation, designed to move us into reverence" for the sound of unified voices,[*] and starting warm ups or group improvisations with soft, collective hums brings voices into connection with one another. Activities involving listening to others' voices, such as building on singer-generated vocal or rhythmic loops, encourage musical experiences to unfold organically while highlighting the group's ability to create meaningful and beautiful music. At the end of a musical experience, purposefully leaving silence and omitting instructional commentary provides space for singers to sense the power of their collective voices.

For some singers, dimming the lights or standing in a circle facilitates a sense of connection, reverence, and attunement, and singers request such adjustments when they sense the group's musical experience is particularly powerful. Singers also build connection by identifying repertoire's emotional essence or its purpose for the community. In one activity, singers in a circle take turns describing the essence of a piece of music with one word. The group gains multiple perspectives on the music's meaning, and singer perspectives often coalesce into deeper understanding of musical expression and awe for the collective musical experience.

As educators who aim to model vulnerability as a strength, we (Elizabeth and Jenny) strive to open ourselves to emotional experiences that occur within and outside of music-making. Singers sense when we feel moved by a song. Synchrony of breath, sound, and text makes space for experience-sharing, or compassion and support derived from shared understanding.[†] By joining in group improvisations, singing alongside group members, or stepping away from a conductor role, we can facilitate possibilities of greater connection and unity. Sharing our vulnerability as persons fosters a sense of collective trust as students come to know their teachers as people and builds interdependence.[§]

*Tobin Hart, "Beauty and Learning," in *International Handbook of Holistic Education*, ed. John P. Miller, Kelli Nigh, Marni J. Binder, Bruce Novak, and Sam Crowell (New York: Routledge, 2019), 25.

†Hendricks, *Compassionate Music Teaching*.

§Parker and Hutton, "Singing and Caring," 275–276.

OHCME authors Lisa J. Lehmberg and C. Victor Fung list a wealth of benefits related to caring connections in music that older adults may experience, including cognitive function; community engagement; connection with others; enjoyment; heightened sense of wellbeing; increased self-confidence and musical self-efficacy; lessening of isolation and loneliness; having an opportunity to "give back" to their community by sharing music; overcoming limitations caused by aging; positive effect on moods; a sense of accomplishment, belonging, identity, purpose, and/or resilience; and spiritual fulfillment.[32] Human connection is one of the principal aspects of shared music-making that makes it meaningful.[33]

As OHCME author Fiona Evison points out, people at all stages of life benefit from music participation, as they can experience "a sense of connection to others, mutual respect, belonging, and physical and emotional wellbeing."[34] Although older adults tend to become more selective in their social interactions, music groups have been found to be a place they stay, due to the opportunities it provides for self-expression, rich and meaningful social connections, and opportunities to reach out and make an impact in the world.[35] Teachers of younger students may have more responsibility to care for their students, but community groups and teachers of adult students provide spaces where co-learners can care for one another. Evison discovered this to be the case in her research of community choirs, especially during times of crisis (such as the COVID-19 pandemic), when music leaders had extra stresses and were able to rely on adult choir members to offer support. When group music leaders are open enough to allow for this kind of reciprocal and responsive caring with adult learners it can further create a sense of connection.

Private piano studio teacher Kaitlyn Leahy takes a caring-*with* approach with her adult students to create caring connections. As a part of her efforts to make music learning meaningful for adults, she has studied the ways that a focus on the qualities of compassionate music teaching (trust, empathy, patience, inclusion, community, authentic connection)[36] can help her attune to their musical goals.[37] In Box 4f, Kaitlyn describes the ways that she tries to attune to beginning adult students' goals and interests by providing them a range of possible options and then affording them the space to gravitate toward certain topics, genres, and even learning approaches.

Empathy, Listening, Attuning, and Moving beyond "Fixing"

Perhaps the most tangible avenue for musical expression and connection comes through music's relationship to empathy. Throughout the OHCME, authors describe a variety of ways in which music-making activities help us to attune to one another emotionally, cognitively, physically, and spiritually. Earlier in this book, I cited research showing a link between synchronized music-making and increased social connection. Even more specific, however, is the correlation between music-making and the development of empathy, which researchers in and beyond music have been studying for decades.[38] As one empathy expert outside our field wrote, "music is famous for its ability to bring people together and to increase their feelings of care and warmth."[39]

It is critical to promote empathy development early in life because, as humans grow older, we face experiences where our empathy may be either boosted or stunted.[40] Music education seems an ideal place to foster empathy, given its potential for social connection[41] as well as the way it taps into our emotions and sensitivities.[42] Furthermore, group music-making invites humans—whether professional musicians,[43] adolescents,[44] children,[45] or infants[46]—to connect with the expressions of other music participants and respond in positive ways.

Box 4f Affording Adult Beginners Space to Create Their Own Musical Goals

Most of the adults I work with are beginners. Many have not taken any sort of music lessons before, and I often find myself supporting them in identifying their musical goals. So in these lessons we're often doing a little bit of everything, trying lots of different things on for size. We might build music literacy skills, try a little bit of rote learning, playing by ear, or improvising. And we might explore a variety of musical styles. What I find really fun, is that (1) they tend to really know what they like, and (2) there are no hard rules.

Although I personally am a big rule-follower and lover of structure, if an adult is spending their valuable time and money to engage in music-making at the piano, who am I to tell them that they simply MUST learn a particular style in a certain way? There is a lot of freedom in being able to follow a new music student's lead, especially if they aren't necessarily aware of, or if they don't ascribe to the beliefs, biases, and rules set by tradition. So, I am thrilled when a student is able to tell me how they prefer to learn, what genres they'd like they explore, or what kinds of musical experiences they would like to have. Who else do we need to answer to?*

*From Kaitlyn Leahy, used with permission.

But before we celebrate music and empathy too naively, however, it is important to proceed with caution (and care). It would be irresponsible to jump on the music education advocacy bandwagon too aggressively and start advocating for any and all kinds of music education because of what it *might* do in *some* contexts. Not all music learning situations are equally conducive to the promotion of prosocial skills and traits such as empathy—in fact, some can cause harm and shut people down (as discussed in Chapters 3 and 9). Research suggests that empathy is fostered most effectively when it is intentionally cultivated.[47]

Additionally, what we sense or feel in relation to another is very unlikely to be exactly what they are feeling or experiencing because our perception still comes from within us, not from them. We enter dangerous terrain when we begin to make assumptions about other people's feelings or needs, especially if we attempt to inappropriately "fix" something about someone else (see Box 2a in Chapter 2).[48] Music education should never be used to control or dominate over other people's feelings, experiences, or identities,[49] especially not when making music for self- and group-expression. With these cautions in mind, I offer a few ideas below for fostering positive empathic expressions.

Fostering Empathic Expressions

Research suggests that it is helpful to cultivate empathic connections through specific and intentional empathy-building activities rather than simply hoping that what we already do will innately foster empathy. For example, in one comparative study, participants in an experimental group were asked to engage in composition and improvisation activities specifically designed to boost empathy-related skills (identification with others, understanding different perspectives, compassion, and behavioral response).[50] Specifically, the students who engaged in empathy-boosting activities had been asked to:

- provide musical responses to given musical phrases;
- create music sequences to describe visual art;
- articulate, through music, another participant's point of view or emotion;
- create musical sequences in response to famous literary phrases;
- play musical expressions that matched the mood of a classmate;
- improvise body movements in response to the musical improvisations of other students.[51]

Students who participated in these activities scored significantly higher on empathy and cooperation skills afterward, and compared to students in a control group who were treated to a more traditional, noncooperative music education program. As I look at the list above, I am struck by how these activities are general enough to be adapted to nearly any music class, with any set of instruments, voices, or technological tools. (See Reflection Activity 4.3.)

Musical Empathy

Musical empathy relates to the ways in which the content of the music—phrases, structure, pitches, rhythm, and so forth—expresses a particular emotion or mood, which one person can express and then another person can receive and reciprocate.[52] It is the substance of reciprocal and responsive relationships *through* music. Musical empathy is defined and contextualized by OHCME authors Kimberly A. McCord, in her chapter on inclusive rock ensembles, and Troy Davis, in his chapter on jazz improvisation. Both authors describe how music can be a means for communicating something to another person without words.

Musical empathy is different from cognitive or affective forms of empathy because it relies entirely on musical elements for expression.[53] Therefore, McCord celebrates the possibilities for people with social challenges to relate with others through music.[54] For example, in her own music teaching and research, she has observed students on the autism spectrum respond musically to other musicians in ways that surpass their social communication, as they match others' mood through elements such as tempo, harmony, rhythm, and expressive phrasing. McCord quotes musicians with autism expressing how music-making with others offers "a welcome refuge" from some of the otherwise judgmental interpersonal interactions they often face when engaged in nonmusical social interactions.

Reciprocal and responsive musical relations are nearly ubiquitous in jazz music. In his research, Troy Davis found musical empathy to be critical for professional jazz musicians. The jazz performers explained to Davis how improvisation was like "a deep, caring [. . .] conversation" that they created together through musical content. Davis distinguishes between different types of empathic perspective taking: third-person (where someone imagines someone else's thoughts or feelings), versus first-person (where someone imagines how it might feel to be someone else).

It would be notable to imagine how different musical activities might encourage first- versus third-person perspective taking (see Reflection Activity 4.4). Also, keeping the empathy cairns in mind (see Chapter 2, Box 2a), it might be worth imagining how such musical perspective taking could afford students an opportunity to "be with" another person and respond to their expressions without dominating the exchange through their own interpretations or reactions.[55] (See Reflection Activity 4.5.)

Promoting Empathy through Jazz and Jazz-Inspired Activities

Given the connections between reciprocity and jazz described above, it makes sense that jazz may be an especially generative avenue for promoting musical and other forms of empathy.[56] Jazz performance requires *empathetic attunement*, or refined sensitivity to others in the group, whereas improvisation affords a space for such attunement to be expressed through musical response. Box 4g contains several suggestions from Davis's OHCME chapter for fostering empathy among jazz students. These suggestions are general enough to be adapted to other non-jazz settings. (See Reflection Activity 4.6.)

Box 4g Promoting Empathy in Jazz Pedagogy

- Engage students in group composition, in which students actively create musical content together;
- Give all students opportunities to improvise, even in small chunks, so they can learn to listen and respond to one another;
- Provide regular opportunities for "call and response," not only from teacher to student but also from student to student;
- Switch up standard "call and response" mimicry by asking for a response that extends on the call in some way;
- Encourage musical cues and facial expressions to facilitate musical attunement;
- Encourage peer mentoring that allows for artistic flexibility, including by having students take turns leading the class through small sections of music;

- Ask students to work in pairs to transcribe one another's improvisations;
- Engage in open-ended dialogue by asking questions (for example, about phrasing or shaping) without a pre-determined answer;
- Facilitate deep listening between students by encouraging verbal, embodied, and/or musical responses;
- Ask students to share thoughts and feelings about lyrics to a jazz standard;
- Ask students to share their experiences from home practice and development process with other students;
- Invite students to engage in free improvisation on a secondary instrument;
- Engage place-based pedagogy by associating repertoire with the places in which it was written, or where it was inspired, including through field trips;
- Offer care through confirmation, such as words of affirmation or specific, constructive praise to encourage progress;
- Invite students to extend confirmation to one another. These confirmations might come through verbal means, but could also be offered through musical improvisations.*

*Strategies compiled from Troy Davis, "Empathy and Deep Listening in Jazz Improvisation," 205–216.

Empathic Creativity

A similar concept to musical empathy is that of empathic creativity, which involves the processes of attunement and response that people might experience as they engage in creative music-making together. Unlike musical empathy, however, cognitive and affective empathy are also at play in empathic creativity, as musicians connect with one another through thoughts and feelings as well as their musical expressions. There are up to six elements of empathic creativity that can occur as people create music together:

1. *Imitation*, or musical mimicry;
2. *Entrainment*, or connecting rhythmically and/or emotionally to another;
3. *Disinterested pleasure*, or shared joy in the musical process but without a set musical agenda;
4. *Flexibility*, or an openness to change while attuning and responding to another;
5. *Ambiguity*, or allowance for musicians to create their own musical interpretations without a need to align with those of others; and
6. *Shared intentionality*, in which musicians experience disinterested pleasure, flexibility, and ambiguity in such a way that each musician can express themselves fully while also attuning to, and honoring, the full expressions of others.[57]

Some music-making approaches and genres lend themselves better to each of these steps than others. However, it is worth reviewing this list to consider how we might alter or adapt what we do to make more room for elements of empathic creativity in different music learning settings.

An Example of Creative Attunement

As one example of creative attunement, let's take one of the most top-down music traditions: the director-led orchestra. Even though orchestral musicians tend to work from a score, there are ways to expand beyond the written page to encourage creative engagement. I'll never forget watching my mentor Louis Bergonzi conduct a middle school honor orchestra where he and the orchestra members decided together in rehearsal that they would add a minute of freestyle individual playing prior to performing an arrangement of a grade 2 piece. Hypothetically, this activity could have been a one-time experience in a rehearsal to help students attune to one another. However, Louie generously shared this creative process with the audience in the concert, as follows:

One student played the song's main melody as a solo. Next, the rest of the students entered, at whatever moment they wished, and played whatever they felt inspired to play as it related to the melody. The musicians settled gradually into the mood of the song, as they felt ready to do so. Then, with a very slight gesture from Louie, the orchestral piece began. The improvisatory sound was cacophonic yet exhilarating as the students attuned to the soloist's melody, then to their own inner expression, and then to one another (while also embodying their own sense of expression) prior to beginning the piece—which then began with tremendous cognitive, affective, and musical focus.

Cultural Attunement: Respectful and Honest Attempts at Co-Learning

I reached out to Louie while writing this chapter, and he reminded me of some very important details about the project I described above. The piece through which he facilitated an instance of empathic creativity was an arrangement of the Korean folk song "Arirang."[58] Louie engaged in this activity with the students as a way of breaking down the traditional structures of European classical music, to resist colonizing the music of another culture within European music performance traditions while also attempting to learn more about a culture that was not his own.

Louie explained how he aimed to learn about the song along with the orchestra members, which included several Korean students. He asked the students to extend an invitation to their families to share their individual and unique experiences with the song. Mrs. Kim, a Korean mother, accepted the invitation and offered many insights. In rehearsals, the students studied several culturally authentic versions of the song together, learned about the folk song's origins, and thought together about the various interpretations that it might take.[59] They observed the shaping and contour, who was performing where, and they conjectured as to why—learning that there is no one "right way" to perform it. Next, Louie and the students considered together how they could adapt the arrangement to eliminate some of the most basic European aspects that distanced the song from its cultural origins (such as fast tempo, lots of vibrato), instead changing bowings and other aspects to reflect how the song might sound if sung.

The process of empathic attunement I witnessed on stage reflected the way Louie and the students decided in rehearsal to present the piece to their audience, and how Louie taught the students the piece—aurally, but not in a structured call-and-response approach. Rather, he taught it in the way Mrs. Kim described that the folk song would be learned; picked up over repeated hearings. As such, Louie merely played it on his own while sitting in a chair at the podium, inviting students to also play it on their own or with partners as they felt inspired to do so.

Louie had learned along with his students how pervasive the folk song is to this day in Korean culture. Therefore, they decided together that a conductor-led ensemble did not reflect the personal and private nature of the song. As he described it, they decided together that they would perform without a conductor, using their own arrangement, "not as a showcase—or worse, as a stunt—but as our way of reflecting the song's place in its culture."[60]

Louie took a caring-*with* approach to learn, along with his students, about engaging in music from a culture that was different from his own background, but similar to the backgrounds of some of the students in the ensemble. He chose to learn through care-filled questions, exploration, and deep respect rather than avoiding the song altogether or "[failing to] connect this folk song to its folk for fear of offending someone by making a cultural faux pas."[61] He engaged in dialogue with students and culture-bearers about creative adaptations of the song to make it more culturally authentic yet without naming or labeling certain features in stereotypical ways. Finally, he facilitated creative attunement in the learning and performing of the song, allowing space for each student to engage in a personal and private way with the song before performing it together. This process of shared learning afforded meaningful connections that would otherwise not have happened. He explained:

> By including *Arirang* on the program I came to know [the students] in a way that was very different from that gained via my other experiences as a guest conductor. Yes, we learned our pieces and put on a concert that sounded very good. But we didn't leave our cultural backgrounds at the door. We saw and celebrated them as part of the music and as part of our common and diverse experiences.[62]

As a member of the audience, I can attest to the authentic connection that this experience afforded to both musicians and audience, as Louie dared to care *with* his students. (See Reflection Activity 4.7.)

Conclusion: Creating Brave Spaces for Musical Risk-Taking

This chapter has covered a variety of ways for supporting students in their musical expressions, focusing on several different approaches for caring *about*, *for*, *with*, and *through*. I first addressed the importance of having musically meaningful goals, and how the different elements of music work together to attain those goals. I then addressed the importance of authenticity and integrity and our ethic of responsibility when caring for and about the music we make, including a discussion of music technology as both friend and foe to our expressive goals. I next addressed ways to care for, about, and with others *through* the music, including creating cycles of musical connection, creating singing-caring relations, caring throughout the lifespan, and various forms of empathy (empathic expressions, musical empathy, empathic creativity, and empathy in jazz pedagogy).

The strategies and approaches offered throughout this chapter can be combined or adapted to function in any number of ways, or in a variety of music learning settings, with co-learners of all ages. One thing these strategies share in common is their potential to help create brave spaces for musical risk-taking. As noted in Chapter 3, "brave spaces" go beyond "safe spaces" in the way that they afford students space to express their whole selves in ways that are personally meaningful and empowering.[63] Safety offers opportunities for inclusion and community, but not necessarily full expression or risk-taking. Brave spaces, on the other hand, offer a space for musical risk-taking as well as a sense of belonging in which one feels open to vulnerability, trust, and meaningful expression of their full self. In the chapters that follow, I lean more into the ways that caring-*with* approaches can foster brave spaces for full expression of identity, first through an understanding of the many pathways to musical development, and then through identity-responsive and identity-affirming pedagogies.

Reflection Activities

4.1. Think of an instance in which music learning was especially meaningful to you. What made it so?

4.2. What is your philosophy and approach regarding artificial intelligence and other technologies that can alter or produce musical performance? What are your hopes? What are your concerns?

4.3. Consider the six dot-point suggestions under the "Fostering Positive Empathic Connections" section in this chapter. How might you adapt these activities to your own teaching context?

4.4. Design a lesson in which students improvise in ways that promote first-person perspective taking, and third-person perspective taking. How would the activities differ?

4.5. As you consider empathy-promoting musical activities, how can you ensure that students have an opportunity to "be with" one another, without one student dominating the musical conversation or misinterpreting the expressions of another student?

4.6. Consider the suggestions in Box 4g, "Promoting Empathy through Jazz and Jazz-Inspired Activities." What additional ideas can you think of to further foster empathy among co-learners? How might these suggestions be applied to other settings?

4.7. As a supplemental resource, read Louis Bergonzi's "World Music in Orchestra and String Education: Understanding Reggae-Sprinkled 'Twinkle'"[64] and consider different ways that you might be respectful of other musical cultures while attempting to learn about them with your students.

Notes

1. Kristen Pellegrino and Joel Schut, "Pedagogies for Teaching the Right Hand to String Players," in *Teaching Instrumental Music: Perspectives and Pedagogies for the 21st Century*, ed. Bryan Powell, Kristen Pellegrino, and Quincy Hilliard (New York: Oxford University Press, 2023), 259–270.
2. Rebecca A. Roesler, "Musically Meaningful: The Interpersonal Goals of Performance," *Music Educators Journal* 100, no. 3 (2014): 39–43, https://doi.org/10.1177/00274321135177.
3. Richard E. Mayer, "Learning Strategies for Making Sense Out of Expository Text: The SOI Model for Guiding Three Cognitive Processes in Knowledge Construction," *Educational Psychology Review* 8 (1996): 357–371, https://doi.org/10.1007/BF01463939.
4. Roesler, "Musically Meaningful," 40; Brené Brown, "Shame Resilience Theory: A Grounded Theory Study on Women and Shame," *Families in Society* 87, no. 1 (2006): 43–52, https://doi.org/10.1606/1044-3894.34.
5. Roesler, "Musically Meaningful," 41.
6. Roesler, "Musically Meaningful," 40–41.
7. Roesler, "Musically Meaningful," 41–42.
8. Roesler, "Musically Meaningful," 43.
9. Estelle Jorgensen, "On Caring for Music Education in Troubled Times," in *The Oxford Handbook of Care in Music Education*, ed. Karin S. Hendricks (New York: Oxford University Press, 2023), 22–30.
10. As quoted in Karin S. Hendricks, *Compassionate Music Teaching: A Framework for Motivation and Engagement in the 21st Century* (Lanham, MD: Rowman & Littlefield, 2018), 23.
11. Parker J. Palmer, *The Courage to Teach* (San Francisco, CA: John Wiley and Sons, 2007), 10.
12. "About the Midwest Clinic," The Midwest Clinic, https://www.midwestclinic.org/.
13. Personal communication, February 13, 2024.
14. Personal communication, February 13, 2024.
15. Personal communication, February 13, 2024.
16. Tula Brannelly, "Mental Health Service Use and the Ethics of Care: In Pursuit of Justice," in *Ethics of Care: Critical Advances in International Perspectives*, ed. Marian Barnes, Tula Brannelly, Lizzie Ward, and Nicki Ward (New York: Polity Press, 2015), 219–232; Marissa Silverman, "Caring about Caring for Music Education," in *The Oxford Handbook of Care in Music Education*, ed. Karin S. Hendricks (New York: Oxford University Press, 2023), 31–45.
17. Brent C. Talbot and Cara Faith Bernard, "An Ethic of Expectation surrounding the Virtual Performance," in *The Oxford Handbook of Care in Music Education*, ed. Karin S. Hendricks (New York: Oxford University Press, 2023), 44–56.
18. Talbot and Bernard, "An Ethic of Expectation," 46.
19. Silverman, "Caring about Caring," 34.
20. Silverman, "Caring about Caring," 40.
21. Silverman, "Caring about Caring," 34.
22. Eiluned Pearce, Jaques Launay, and Robin I. M. Dunbar, "The Ice-Breaker Effect: Singing Mediates Fast Social Bonding," *Royal Society Open Science*, 2 (2015): 150221, https://doi.org/10.1098/rsos.150221.
23. Allen R. Legutki, Karin S. Hendricks, Tawnya D. Smith, and Kristi N. King, "Fostering Reciprocal and Responsive Musical Relationships in a Youth Instrumental Ensemble: One Guest Conductor's 'Caring With' Approach," in *The Oxford Handbook of Care in Music Education*, ed. Karin S. Hendricks (New York: Oxford University Press, 2023), 257; see also Mark Russel Smith, "Mark Russell Smith," Smartcat, 2020, http://markrussellsmith.net/.
24. These stages align with leadership research by Yaakov Atik, "The Conductor and the Orchestra: Interactive Aspects of the Leadership Process," *Leadership and Organization Development Journal* 15 no. 1 (1994): 22–28, https://doi.org/10.1108/ 01437739410050123.
25. Legutki et al., "Fostering Reciprocal and Responsive Musical Relationships," 259.
26. Legutki et al., "Fostering Reciprocal and Responsive Musical Relationships," 260.
27. Legutki et al., "Fostering Reciprocal and Responsive Musical Relationships," 263.
28. Elizabeth Cassidy Parker and Jennifer C. Hutton, "Singing and Caring," in *The Oxford Handbook of Care in Music Education*, ed. Karin S. Hendricks (New York: Oxford University Press, 2023): 267–268.
29. Parker and Hutton, "Singing and Caring," 275.

30. Roy F. Baumeister and Mark R. Leary, "The Need to Belong," *Psychological Bulletin* 117 no. 3 (1995): 497–529, https://doi.org/10.1037/0033-2909.117.3.497; see also Hendricks, *Compassionate Music Teaching.*
31. Felicity A. Baker and Julie Ballantyne, "'You've Got to Accentuate the Positive': Group Songwriting to Promote a Life of Enjoyment, Engagement, and Meaning in Aging Australians," *Nordic Journal of Music Therapy* 22, no. 1 (2012): 7–24, https://doi.org/10.1080/08098131.2012.678372; Lisa J. Lehmberg and Victor C. Fung, "Caring Connection, Music Participation, and Quality of Life of Older Adults," in *The Oxford Handbook of Care in Music Education*, ed. Karin S. Hendricks (New York: Oxford University Press, 2023), 395–409.
32. Lehmberg and Fung, "Caring Connection," 400.
33. Lehmberg and Fung, "Caring Connection," 401.
34. Fiona Evison, "'Sometimes I Just Crawl under the Covers and Hide': Caring by, for, and with Community Music Leaders during Crises," in *The Oxford Handbook of Care in Music Education*, ed. Karin S. Hendricks (New York: Oxford University Press, 2023), 231–243.
35. Lehmberg and Fung, "Caring Connection."
36. Hendricks, *Compassionate Music Teaching*
37. Kaitlyn Sarah Leahy, "Compassionate Music Teaching with Adults Learning Recreationally in Lessons: A Narrative Inquiry" (PhD diss., Boston University Theses and Dissertations, 2024).
38. See Hendricks, *Compassionate Music Teaching*, 61–64, and other references below.
39. David Howe, *Empathy: What It Is and Why It Matters* (London: Palgrave Macmillan, 2013), 170.
40. Laura Cuervo and Emilia Campayo, "The Potential of Group Music Education for Developing Empathy: An Empirical Study," *Psychology of Music* online first (2024): https://doi.org/10.1177/03057356231183873; Tal-Chen Rabinowitch, Ian Cross, and Pamela Burnard, "Long-Term Musical Group Interaction Has a Positive Influence of Empathy in Children," *Psychology of Music* 41 (2012): 484–498.
41. Pearce, Launay, and Dunbar, "The Ice-Breaker Effect."
42. Eun Cho, "The Relationship between Small Music Ensemble Experience and Empathy Skill: A Survey Study," *Psychology of Music* 49, no. 3 (2021): 600–614.
43. Troy Davis, "Empathy and Deep Listening in Jazz Improvisation," in *The Oxford Handbook of Care in Music Education*, ed. Karin S. Hendricks (New York: Oxford University Press, 2023), 205–217.
44. Cho, "The Relationship between Small Music Ensemble Experience"; Kimberly A. McCord, "'This Guitar Hurts!': Empathy and Caring in Inclusive Ensembles," in *The Oxford Handbook of Care in Music Education*, ed. Karin S. Hendricks (New York: Oxford University Press, 2023), 245–255.
45. S. Kirschner and M. Tomasello, "Joint Music Making Promotes Prosocial Behavior in 4-Year-Old Children," *Evolution and Human Behavior* 31, (2010): 354–364; Rabinowitch, Cross, and Burnard, "Long-Term Musical Group Interaction"; Glenn E. Schellenberg, Kathleen A. Corrigall, Sebastian P. Dys, Tina Malti, and Joel Snyder, "Group Music Training and Children's Prosocial Skills," *PLoS ONE* 10, no. 10 (2015): 1–14, https://doi.org/10.1371/journal.pone.0141449.
46. David Gerry, Andrea Unrau, and Laurel J. Trainor, "Active Music Classes in Infancy Enhance Musical, Communicative and Social Development," *Developmental Science* 15 (2012): 398–407.
47. Cuervo and Campayo, "The Potential of Group Music Education."
48. Karin S. Hendricks and Juliet Hess, "Troubling Empathy in Music Education: Pathways and Pitfalls," *Bulletin of the Council for Research in Music Education* 239 (2024): 7–25, https://doi.org/10.5406/21627223.239.01.
49. Tawnya D. Smith, *Healing the Fragmentation of Psyche, Society, and Nature within Music Education: A Radical Ecopsychological Approach* (Routledge, under contract).
50. Cuervo and Campayo, "The Potential of Group Music Education."
51. Cuervo and Campayo, "The Potential of Group Music Education," 6.
52. Davis, "Empathy and Deep Listening in Jazz Improvisation," 211; Adam Ockelford, "Towards a Developmental Model of Musical Empathy Using Insights from Children Who Are on the Autism Spectrum or Who Have Learning Difficulties," in *Music and Empathy*, ed. Caroline Waddington and Elaine King (Abingdon: Routledge, 2017), 39–88.
53. McCord, "This Guitar Hurts!"
54. McCord, "This Guitar Hurts!," 246.
55. Kelly Bylica, "Critical Listening and Authorial Agency as Radical Practices of Care," in *The Oxford Handbook of Care in Music Education*, ed. Karin S. Hendricks (New York: Oxford University Press, 2023), 482–493.
56. Davis, "Empathy and Deep Listening in Jazz Improvisation."
57. Ian Cross, Tal-Chen Rabinowitch, and Felicity Laurence, "Empathy and Creativity in Group Musical Practices: Towards a Concept of Empathic Creativity," in *The Oxford Handbook of Music Education*, Vol. 2, ed. Gary E. McPherson and Graham F. Welch (Oxford: Oxford University Press, 2012), 337–353; Karin S. Hendricks, "Contexts and Conceptualizations of Care in Music Education," in *The Routledge Companion to Creativities in Music Education*, ed. Clint Randles and Pamela Burnard (Abingdon: Routledge, 2022), 404–415; Karin S. Hendricks and Adam Symborski, "Empathic Creativity in Child-Adult Musical Play," *International Journal of Music in Early Childhood* 18, no. 2 (2024): 125–143.

58. The piece that Louie used for this performance was *Arirang: Korean Folk Song* arranged by Michael Story (Belwin Mills, 2005).
59. Louis Bergonzi, "World Music in Orchestra and String Education: Understanding Reggae-Sprinkled 'Twinkle,'" in *Teaching Music through Performance in Orchestra*, Vol. 3, ed. David Littrell (Chicago: GIA publications, 2001), 9–33.
60. Bergonzi, "World Music in Orchestra and String Education," 24.
61. Bergonzi, "World Music in Orchestra and String Education," 25.
62. Bergonzi, "World Music in Orchestra and String Education," 26.
63. Brian Arao and Kristi Clemens, "From Safe Spaces to Brave Spaces," in *The Art of Effective Facilitation: Reflections from Social Justice Educators*, ed. Lisa Landreman (New York: Routledge, 2013), 135–150; Andrew Goodrich, "Developing Trust and Empathy through Peer Mentoring in the Music Classroom," in *The Oxford Handbook of Care in Music Education*, ed. Karin S. Hendricks (New York: Oxford University Press, 2023), 280–291; Karin S. Hendricks, "Compassionate Pedagogies for LGBTQ+ Student Visibility, Radical Welcome, and Authentic Expressions of Music and Personhood," in *The Oxford Handbook of Gender and Queer Studies in Music Education*, ed. Nick McBride and Colleen Sears (New York: Oxford University Press, in press); Karin S. Hendricks, Cheryl M. Freeze, and T. S. Yi, "Spaces and Facets of Trust for Secondary School LGBTQ+ Music Students: A Multiple Case Study," in *Oxford Handbook of Gender and Queer Studies in Music Education*, ed. Nick McBride and Colleen Sears (New York: Oxford University Press, in press); Justin McManus and Bruce Carter, "Accompanying LGBTQIA+ Students in the Music Classroom," in *The Oxford Handbook of Care in Music Education*, ed. Karin S. Hendricks (New York: Oxford University Press, 2023), 179–192.
64. Bergonzi, "World Music in Orchestra and String Education."

5

Caring for Musical Development

Chapter Overview

This chapter addresses the countless possible pathways for musical development, inviting readers to challenge their own previously conceived notions of giftedness and talent by self-reflecting on prior assumptions and biases. It offers strategies for meeting various learners wherever they are, including ideas for collaborating with students to address their own interests, needs, and goals. Topics include understanding the complexity of musical development; recognizing our biases; supporting students' unique pathways for learning; promoting competence, autonomy, and relatedness; using empathy as a means of attuning to student needs and interests; caring with adult learners; and using core reflection to support our own development as teachers as we practice self-and-other caring.

Introduction

One of the things that thrills me most about music teaching is the element of surprise. Some people liken teaching to daily performances on the classroom "stage," but for me teaching is like a lifetime of constant video games where you never know where the next bit of action is going to come from. No matter how well a teacher plans in advance—and no matter how important that plan may be—the lesson will undoubtedly turn out differently than expected: A child becomes fixated on something you didn't even notice and steers everyone's attention away from what you had planned, it starts snowing outside, a reed breaks, a peer mentor cracks the code on a technical issue with another student that you've been trying to fix for weeks, the lead soloist loses her voice, the shy teenager who hasn't said a word all year improvises with an outpouring of emotion, the student who routinely disrupts lessons writes a song about how much they admire their mother, and so forth. And that's just Monday.

One delightfully unpredictable area of music teaching has to do with a student's musical development—the countless changes and surprises that occur along the musical journey for students at all ages and stages. Sometimes the student whom we expect to be the next musical Wunderkind surprises us by leaving formal music education altogether, to take up painting or car mechanics or some other passion. Sometimes the student who struggles mightily with rhythm has something click

Daring to Care with Music Education. Karin S. Hendricks, Oxford University Press. © Oxford University Press 2025.
DOI: 10.1093/9780197777589.003.0005

inside (or outside) and turns into a leader and mentor for others. Movies are made from these kinds of stories, and as music teachers we get to watch them unfold in real life, every day.

Just like the movies, however, it can be tempting to try to predict the ending prematurely, without watching the action unfold on its own. And as it turns out, our perceptions and expectations of what might happen for certain students can impact what does happen, for better or worse. Said differently, our own biases and our often-restricted vision may have the potential to reinforce positive musical development for some students while limiting opportunities for others. In this chapter I join you, the reader, to reflect on some of the ways in which music teachers and learners might create an expanded repertoire for supporting students in their beautifully unique aims toward deepening their musical connections.

Understanding the Complexity of Musical Development

In the *Oxford Handbook of Care in Music Education* (OHCME) chapter that I co-wrote with Gary McPherson, we describe some of the complex and unpredictable paths that music students might take toward attaining musical competencies.[1] Figure 5.1 contains a simplified version of the Differentiated Model of Giftedness and Talent (DMGT),[2] which is further detailed with specific examples in our OHCME chapter. In this model, "gifts" refer to abilities a student might naturally possess (and then further develop), whereas "talents" refer to specific musical competencies that are developed over time. It is important to note that the natural abilities on the left are not considered "God-given" or "innate" as some people believe. Rather, they represent the potential for musical development, but only if conditions happen to support that musical growth. The DMGT illustrates the various pathways toward musical talent, relating to:

- *Natural gifts or abilities*, including intellectual capacities, creativity and imagination, social skills, perceptual skills, muscle strength, motor control, and so forth. Although we are born with certain traits, natural abilities are still developed or strengthened (or, conversely, inhibited) over the course of our lives.
- *Environmental catalysts*, including the structural, cultural, and social supports we receive; the care we receive from families, teachers, and other community members; the kinds of provisional support we get through certain educational approaches, and so forth.
- *Intrapersonal catalysts* such as physical appearance, health, personality, temperament, self- and other-awareness, values and interests, individual perseverance, and so forth.

As shown in Figure 5.1, all these unique and varied talent "ingredients" are blended through, and impacted by, the developmental processes that occur throughout our

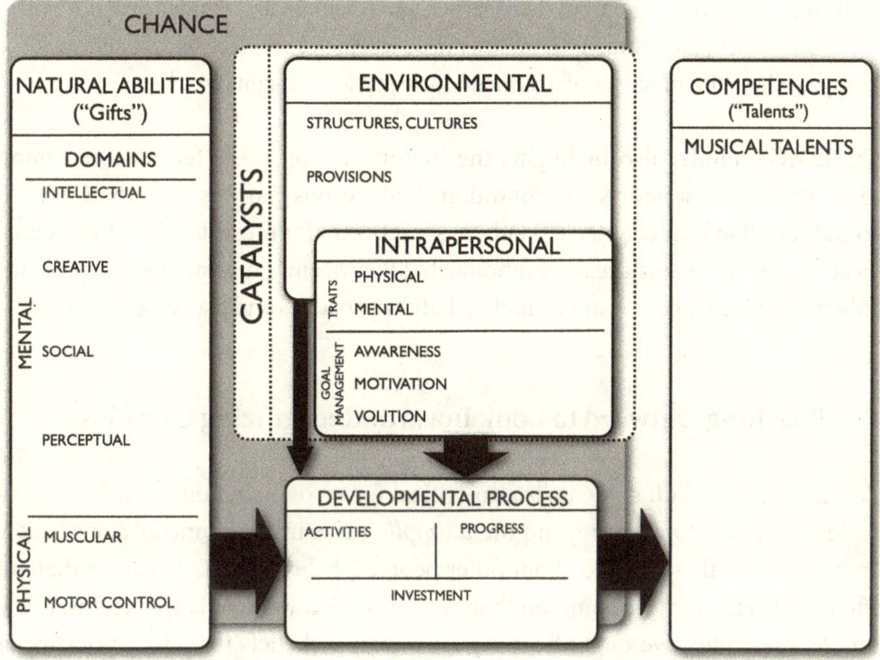

Figure 5.1 Simplified Version of the Differentiated Model of Giftedness and Talent (DMGT). Adapted from Françoys Gagné, "Building Gifts into Talents: Detailed Overview of the DMGT 2.0," in *Leading Change in Gifted Education: The Festschrift of Dr. Joyce VanTassel-Baska*, ed. Bronwyn MacFarlane (Austin TX: Prufrock Press, 2009), 61–80.

lives. Such developmental processes might be influenced by access to certain activities or content; notable events or turning points in progress; and investments of time, money, and energy. These developments lead to certain musical competencies or talents—but the opposite is true if we lack access, resources, support, and so forth. Finally, as shown at the top of the model, many of these characteristics, events, and pathways are affected by chance, as we happen to be at the right/wrong place at the right/wrong time to receive or experience (or not) what we need to thrive. (See Reflection Activities 5.1–5.3.)

When considering these various pathways toward musical development, it becomes clear that music learning is not a "one size fits all" endeavor. Therefore, McPherson and I argue that it is potentially harmful for music teachers to presume that some students are more gifted than others simply because of the way they might respond to certain teaching styles:

> [A]dherence to a philosophy of "one right path" to expert musicianship can lead to false and hurtful assumptions that some students just "don't care," or that they simply lack the motivation to put forth the necessary effort. Instead, a consideration of the various pathways and destinations for musical development honors

the uniqueness and agency of each learner, and opens up an abundance of options for supporting each student. It invites music teachers to replace "carrot and stick" approaches with practices of openness, curiosity, and imagination.[3]

The DMGT model also highlights the importance of music teachers becoming advocates for the supports and conditions that various learners need to thrive[4]—a point I revisit in later chapters. Finally, it is important for music teachers to communicate openly with music learners about what *they* deem important and helpful, not only in big-picture goals but in smaller, daily approaches and learning pathways.[5]

Reaching Outward to Look Inward: Recognizing Our Biases

Communication with students is also critical for recognizing our own biases and for learning how to work beyond them. *Implicit* bias involves unconscious beliefs or associations that we hold about other people—beliefs and associations that are often not true. It is more common than we realize that we hold biases against other people, even when we might have *explicit* values or beliefs that are supportive of these same people.[6] Biases can develop in a similar way to the development of musical talent: over time, as a product of environmental and interpersonal catalysts, and encouraged by the world around us.

Biases also come from stereotypes and socially learned beliefs about people, which of course can be hurtful to a music student who is judged unfairly—not only by teachers or other students, but also when the student also begins to believe the stereotypes and does not perform to their own capability or desire.[7] For example, OHCME author David Baker describes folklore associated with disabled people such that they are particularly gifted with certain other capacities because of their disability (e.g., believing that blind people are innately exceptional with aural skills).[8] Relying on such socially contrived assumptions rather than considering the individual strengths, needs, and interests of each individual student can be detrimental to both their musicianship and their sense of identity.

One example Baker gives is how thinking of blind students as being able only to learn by ear can limit their opportunities to engage with genres and ensembles where written music is used. Instead, he advocates for making adaptations to meet the considerations of the student, in the ways that are most useful to them. Baker emphasizes the importance of involving disabled learners in the decision-making process for their musical development, as many accommodations continue to privilege a nondisabled perspective (for example, recall Box 3a from Chapter 3 and see Reflection Activity 5.4).

Biases come from our own life experiences and the things we are exposed to (or not).[9] Therefore, we all have biases, no matter who we are, or how long we have been caring for, about, and with co-learners. Just knowing this about ourselves and leaning into this awareness can be a first step toward expanding our caring-with sensitivities and our accompanying pedagogical repertoire.[10] In Box 5a, Gary McPherson I share some strategies for working against bias in music education spaces.

Box 5a Strategies for Recognizing and Mitigating Bias in Music Education

- *View action as imperative for both individuals and communities.* Simply put, it takes all of us—individually and collectively—to make change.
- *Recognize the multifaceted nature of stereotypes and biases.* Rather than pointing fingers at someone else—or, conversely, taking on the burden of responsibility alone—we might consider the complex array of habits of mind, body, and sociality that are at play. Then we can begin, step by step, to change what we have the power to change.
- *Adopt epistemic humility.* Music education has a history of viewing the teacher as the "maestro" or "master," a perspective that unfairly disallows a teacher from being able to admit mistakes, let alone make them. Moving from a "deficit" to a "strengths" perspective, and engaging with what students bring rather than judging how they fit (or not) within a particular pedagogy, requires teachers to remain open to vulnerability, and to learning along with their students.[*]
- *Encourage perspective taking through humility, toward action.* Music teachers can practice empathy for, and with, their students to overcome biases and foster more inclusive classrooms where students can thrive in different ways. Learning to see the perspective of another can lead to "questioning, wondering, dialogue, authentic allyship, and collaborative action toward social change"[†]—so long as the process involves humility. Mature or authentic empathy "requires letting go of superiority or 'hero' narratives and exercising compassion not as a badge of morality, but as a way of recognizing common humanity."[§]
- *Exercise an experimental mindset.* An experimental mindset moves beyond "fixed" beliefs" or even the belief in "growth," to a mindset of openness and curiosity to what is currently unknown.[**] Earlier in this chapter I challenged the notion of "innate talent" (which presumes a mindset that talent is fixed) to suggest that ability development involved a complex system of processes whereby student ability could grow in any number of ways.‡ Applying an experimental mindset to music education might mean that music teachers better serve a variety of student needs and dispositions by practicing curiosity and imagination, with a willingness to try new things and a disposition to let go of what does not work.

- *Practice diversified experimentalism.*[§§] In the stock market, diversification involves having an array of investments so that one does not go bankrupt from putting too much money into any one bad investment. Anti-bias scholar Alex Madva suggests that we might apply the concept of diversification to anti-bias work, to "explore a bunch of different individual and social experiments and interventions to see which ones stick and which ones stink."[***] Applied to music education, teachers and students might try many different approaches for inclusive pedagogy—recognizing that not everything will be successful, but that different approaches will work better in certain contexts or at different times.[†††]

*Hendricks, *Compassionate Music Teaching.*

†Hendricks, "Counternarratives," 59.

§Hendricks, "Counternarratives," 76; Tawnya Smith, "Caring with the Earth, Community, and Co-Learners for the Health of Biological, Social, and Musical Ecosystems," in *The Oxford Handbook of Care in Music Education*, ed. Karin S. Hendricks (New York: Oxford University Press, 2023), 141–152.

**Alex Madva, "Integration, Community, and the Medical Model of Social Injustice," *Journal of Applied Philosophy* 37, no. 2 (2020): 211–232, https://doi.org/10.1111/japp.12356.

‡See also C. S. Dweck, *Mindset: The New Psychology of Success* (Random House, 2008).

§§Madva, "Integration."

***Madva, "Individual and Structural Interventions," 241.

†††These strategies are adapted from suggestions by Alex Madva, "Individual and Structural Interventions," in *An Introduction to Implicit Bias: Knowledge, Justice, and the Social Mind*, ed. Erin Beeghly and Alex Madva (New York: Routledge, 2020), 233–270.

A Personal Story about Bias

What biases might you bring to music education spaces? How might bias limit your vision of students' musical potential or how to support them? I'll start, by offering an example from my own experience.

Early in my career, I had just moved to a school district where I had the opportunity to co-teach with several well-seasoned music teachers, and where parents were heavily involved in our music program. The area was overwhelmingly white with a small Latine population and an even smaller percentage of Asian students. There was a relatively large economic disparity across the district, with some students very well off and others very much less so. The Latine students tended to live in an area of town that was on the lower end of the socioeconomic spectrum.

One day, one of my music teacher colleagues suggested that the eighth-grade orchestra should perform a song to feature a young cellist in the class who was also, according to the teacher, an "up-and-coming" concert pianist. This student (whom I will call Paris) had very wealthy parents who paid a lot of money for her to take extensive private lessons with a well-respected piano teacher. Paris came to class every day dressed impeccably, often with silk bows in her hair and toting a very valuable cello. It was obvious that she was well cared for in terms of any material needs she might have, and she was already doing quite well in terms of checking the boxes on the musical development graphic described above. My colleague's suggestion that she might solo with the orchestra would, of course, add another opportunity to further her musical career.

Delighted for a fun new musical adventure, I picked out a piece for piano and orchestra that I thought the class could perform well. I spoke with Paris about it, and she agreed with delight. I immediately made plans to rehearse the piece. On the day that the student librarians handed out the music to the class, I announced that Paris would be performing the solo.

After class, a young Latino boy (whom I will call David) came up to talk to me. Because I was new to the school district, I didn't know David well. However, he appeared to have much less money than Paris did, at least by the look of his worn-out jeans and because he played on a budget-level violin. He and I hadn't spoken much up to this point, if at all; he was rather quiet and seemed content to sit in the middle of the second violin section playing upbeats without a fuss.

David got right to the point: He asked me if he might audition to perform the piano solo I had just publicly assigned to Paris. I hadn't even thought about holding an audition because it was simply recommended to me that I feature the young woman. But out of respect for David's request, I went ahead and opened up auditions to anyone who might want to play that solo.

I admit, I had zero expectations that David would come close to playing at the level of Paris. I anticipated that it would be a kind gesture for a young man with some very high dreams, and that we would then simply go back to the original plan after the auditions took place. As the auditions commenced, however, I quickly discovered that David's technique, focus, and artistry were every bit as strong as those of Paris. I had known nothing about David's musical background beyond what I saw from the second violin section each day. I had no idea that he played the piano, let alone that well. I was flabbergasted. Because these were the only two students who signed up for the auditions, and because they both played so exceptionally well, I made space for both to perform part of the piece on the concert.

A few years later, Paris dropped out of orchestra when her other, non-cellistic musical dreams took precedent and she began to make her way toward a very successful music career in a different genre. However, David stayed in the orchestra program until he graduated from high school. Over the five years I spent with David I got to know more about his musical background as well as his deeply caring and sensitive personality and musical touch.

I was curious as to how David developed such brilliant musical prowess on the piano when his family did not have money for private lessons. One day he explained to me that, when he was a little boy, he would often make visits to visit a "lonely old man" who lived down the street. David made these regular visits to connect with his neighbor, simply to reach out to someone who, he believed, could use a friend. It turns out that this "old man" happened to be a piano virtuoso and retired music professor, who reciprocated David's kindness by sitting at the piano with him day after day, year after year. David's benevolence and care for a lonely neighbor came back to him in the form of exceptional piano technique and lifelong musicianship.

When David approached me that day about an opportunity to audition for a solo, I had falsely assumed that he would not be able to play the piano as well as he did, simply because I supposed he could not afford lessons. I didn't look deep enough. I didn't look beyond financial resources to envision how a student might develop expertise in a musical area that was not part of our school curriculum. I didn't envision the kinds of musical landscapes that children might have outside my class.[11] Yet David, who dared to reach out to an older man in his neighborhood for the sake of human connection, also reached out to me and gave me grace. In so doing, he gave me not just the gift of broader vision, but a gift of his music.

For years after this experience, David stayed after school to play the grand piano in the orchestra room while I entered grades and responded to emails. From my office next door, I had the opportunity to witness his caring touch on the piano keys as he practiced. To this day, decades later, I cannot hear Debussy's "Clair de lune" without remembering his exquisite rendition.

Neither Paris nor David needed my help to be successful musicians; they were both already well under way when I met them. However, I would have been remiss not to have recognized and celebrated each of their full musical selves. I am so grateful David dared to ask me to look beyond my limited vision about musical development—yet I am left to wonder about any other students who, for whatever reason, did not feel like they could similarly advocate for what they needed in my classroom to reach their dreams. I am committed to try, to ask questions, and to earn students' trust, no matter how many times I might make mistakes in the process.

Supporting Students' Unique Pathways for Learning

Supporting students in their individual pathways toward musical development requires that we envision and trust in students' potential to learn. According to OHCME author Elizabeth Mitchell, it is critical to practice unconditional positive regard, which includes "a genuine belief in every human being's capacity for development."[12] Paradoxically, Mitchell reminds us that, "in order to change, people need to be first accepted as they are."[13] I provide ways to offer holistic acceptance in the discussion of identity-responsive and identity-affirming pedagogies in Chapter 7.

Supporting students' individual pathways also requires that we communicate with them about our vision and trust in their potential. Sundas Mohi-Truong, the high school orchestra director whom I introduced in Chapter 4, explains that students "must feel that you are proud of their growth, and [must know] that you believe that they can perform at a high level." As Sundas sees it, our care for each student is the avenue for encouraging them to care for their musical development: "Students can only perform their best and focus on caring about every note when they know that you believe they can do it, too."[14]

Despite the large numbers in her ensemble, Sundas considers it time well invested to acknowledge students' unique pathways to success on an individual level:

> Before every "competitive" performance opportunity, I hand write notes of encouragement to each student in the ensemble, outlining ways I noticed that they have grown personally and musically. These notes are distributed the day before the performance, to remind them that the most important thing is that they grew through the music, and that I believe they will perform their best.[15]

Such trust in a student's possible future(s) can be viewed in terms of what educational care theorist Nel Noddings calls *confirmation*, which occurs "when we attribute the best possible motive consonant with reality" to that student.[16] Confirmation involves visualizing and continually affirming those characteristics of another that help to bring out their ideal self—what I have elsewhere explained as the "Michelangelo phenomenon."[17]

Attuning to students' versions of their own ideal self requires understanding students' lives beyond the immediate music learning context, to get the full picture of who they are and what they feel they want to be. Sundas also considers these aspects of her students as she encourages their individual development. As she explains on her music program website, "we celebrate the visible and invisible qualities that make each person unique."[18] With care, music teachers can come to understand these various parts of students through practices of mature empathy, using the empathy cairns described in Chapter 2. The following sections address several ways we can support students' musical development, including by promoting competence, autonomy, and connection; using empathy as a means of attuning to student needs and interests; and caring with adult learners.

Promoting Competence, Autonomy, and Relatedness

Earlier in this chapter I advocated for us to replace old-school, extrinsic, "carrot and stick" motivation approaches with practices of openness, curiosity, and imagination. Self-determination theory, a framework for intrinsic motivation developed by psychologists Edward Deci and Richard Ryan,[19] offers some helpful insights that apply to caring *with* music students while also encouraging their musical growth. This framework focuses on the importance of fostering student wellbeing, ownership, and agency—in essence, encouraging teachers to trust students and provide tools whereby they can be agents of their own musical development—with win-win results!

Self-determination theory focuses on three basic psychological needs that humans have:

- *Competence*, or tangible demonstrations of achievement;

- *Autonomy*, or a student's sense of independence and self-regulation; and
- *Relatedness*, or the connections one makes through engagement in an activity or in life.[20]

As mentioned in Chapter 2, *competence* is one of the critical components for students to foster a sense of trust in themselves and in others. Students feel a sense of competence through their own sense of achievement and their belief in their ability to accomplish specific tasks (also known as self-efficacy belief), as well as their sense of a group's capability (also known as collective efficacy). Music teachers can help students gain a sense of competence by (a) communicating and negotiating manageable goals, and then supporting them through the accomplishment of those goals over time; (b) providing positive and encouraging models for them so they can visualize what their success can look like, while resisting unhealthy social comparisons; (c) providing students with timely, task-based, constructive, and supportive feedback; and (d) helping them learn to prioritize their physical, mental, and emotional wellbeing.[21]

Autonomy in a music classroom involves balancing structure and agency so that students feel supported but also trusted and valued for their own ideas, insights, and musicianship. Communicating with students about musical goals is key to promoting a sense of autonomy. Autonomy-supportive approaches include communicating with students about their expressive intent and trusting them to be their own muse, while also providing them with the supports that *they* deem they need and want to develop musical independence[22]—which can encourage lifelong music-making long after they leave our classrooms or studios.[23]

Relatedness involves feelings of belonging and authentic connection, and it is fundamental to fostering and maintaining caring relationships (as introduced in Chapters 2 and 3). When considering relatedness with musical development, however, it is important to note that musicians' specific needs for relatedness will change over time. Research suggests that students may desire warm and fun interactions early in their musical career that allow students to connect with a love of music; however, as their musical skills develop they may desire student–teacher relationships that prioritize time spent on skill development and task-based proficiency.[24] Of course, the point of *Daring to Care* is that we can (and should) maintain warmth and care at all levels of musical development. Yet in terms of student needs and interests, the pace and focus of content will vary. (See Reflection Activity 5.5.)

Differentiating the Ratios

As noted previously, students will have different needs and desires regarding competence, autonomy, and relatedness depending on their goals and levels of musical development. For example, younger or less-experienced musicians may need more emphasis in relatedness while they develop competence and begin to sort out their own goals. Adolescents may desire more autonomy, whereas more advanced players may already have goals in mind and desire to focus their attention on detailed, fast-paced, competence-boosting activities. Finally, adult amateur musicians may have very different reasons for continuing music participation, so it is important to communicate with them about their goals and aims for music study.[25]

Of course these are just general ideas; every student will have different needs and desires at different times. Box 5b includes a vignette from Ryan Hourigan, envisioning how we might foster competence, autonomy, and relatedness with students who have a variety of different disabilities and learning needs. In cases where students may not be able to advocate for themselves (such as those with communication challenges or learning differences), it is important for teachers to check in regularly to ensure that a student's unique needs for competence, autonomy, and relatedness are being met.[26]

Box 5b Teacher Story Centered around Self-Determination and Children with Disabilities

I introduce the ukulele in my 5th grade general music classes. Two students with visual impairment that included no functional vision attended one of my 5th grade classes this past school year. During the day, these students received paraprofessional support, but not during specials (music, visual art, and physical education). Knowing that these students were about to begin the ukulele without assistance, I purchased two adaptive tools for the ukuleles in the event that these students struggled with finger position. These tools attached to the ukulele at the nut of the fretboard and had single buttons for the students to press to form a chord. As we began, I guided these students on where to place their finger(s) for each chord and how to strum with the other hand using hand over hand guidance. Once my 5th graders were playing more than one chord, I could tell that my students with visual impairment were determined to play the ukulele without additional support. As soon as ukuleles were passed out to the students during each music class, they immediately began to familiarize themselves with the layout of the instrument (distance between frets, location of the four strings, and which part of the instrument to strum) by moving their hands and fingers over the instrument. They would lean close to the fretboard to better hear their sounds, and they would adjust their fingers if the sound wasn't correct. Chord changes became easier, and they seemed to enjoy making music on their ukuleles. If we had any down time in which the class as a whole was not playing their ukuleles, these students would immediately practice on their ukuleles so they could better hear their chords and practice chord changes. While I had the adaptive tools to make playing the ukulele chords easier, I didn't want to get in the way of what these students were capable of doing on their own.

—*Elementary* General Music Specialist in the Southeast United States*

*Hourigan, "Music as a Vehicle," 378.

I have found the need for differentiated ratios of competence, autonomy, and relatedness in my own teaching, especially as I begin forging relationships with new students or in situations where I might not be familiar with the traditions and levels of the musicians. Sometimes I have entered a space too "friendly" and with a pace too slow, whereas other times I have come in too task-focused for the vibe of the group and have led them toward musical disenchantment before they even got going. By exercising cognitive and affective empathy, and by "checking the temperature" of the room, I have been able to make quick adjustments to get into a working rhythm that better supports the students' needs for competence, autonomy, and relatedness.

As an example, my first teaching job was in a beginning strings program in a rural area where the students had had little (if any) exposure to Western classical music. I had just completed a performance degree at the Oberlin Conservatory, and I brought that same high-level expectation and system of demands into the elementary classroom with me. I asked fourth graders to become perfectionists on isolated notes in pursuit of a greater whole that they couldn't even visualize yet. My focus was 100% on competence development without any measure of autonomy or relatedness—and as you can imagine, that didn't go over well! I quickly learned to slow the pace, connect technical parts with the whole, bond with the students first as humans, and encourage each musician to love what they were doing so that they could develop competence over time.

In contrast, two decades later I sat down with my cello in an instrumental lab class at Boston University, where music education students were practicing grade 2 literature on secondary instruments. The students did not yet know me so I took this as an opportunity to foster relatedness with them as we played together. Because the repertoire was at a typical middle school level, I demonstrated a typical "middle school" energy, smiling and cracking a few jokes moving at a pace much too slow for these university students.

I sensed immediately (due to the lack of eye contact and other subtle cues) that students were not amused, so I switched gears. Maintaining the smile but picking up the pace, I started focusing on refining my intonation, lining up entrances exactly with the first violinist, and ensuring that my bow matched the placement of the viola in our shared melodies. The vibe in the room changed immediately and I appeared to earn their trust as I demonstrated competence at the task. At this point they immediately started to reciprocate eye contact and smiles as my goals matched theirs. Then, the jokes and lessons about how to engage with delightfully goofy middle schoolers would follow later, after I had earned the students' trust. (See Reflection Activity 5.6.)

Looking at Competition through the Lens of Competence, Autonomy, and Relatedness

Because self-determination theory focuses on intrinsic motivation, it is important for music teachers to evaluate how extrinsic motivations such as competitive events and audition-based rankings might influence students' sense of competence, autonomy, and relatedness. How, if at all, is a sense of competence gained and experienced in a hierarchical system where the emphasis is more on comparison to others than on task-specific achievements? How, if at all, is autonomy experienced when goals are determined by set requirements and standardized metrics? How, if at all, is relatedness achieved among students who are competing against one another?

There are ways to work within competitive structures to support student growth and intrinsic motivation, especially when competition is not the goal in and of itself.[27] First, competitive events can be used to inform competence development (through adjudicator comments or peer review), rather than as a "fear-of-failure" motivational approach meant to control how much time students spend practicing, working on a composition, and so forth. Second, competence, autonomy, and relatedness can be encouraged by focusing on expressive goals rather than on beating out or winning over others—the latter of which may give a temporary buzz of excitement but may leave students feeling disconnected from others and perpetually dissatisfied.[28] Third, focusing on competitive experiences as a means of learning from other students can be helpful, as long as students are encouraged to envision how they, too, can build the skills to accomplish such musical expressions.[29]

After several decades serving as an adjudicator for competitive festivals, I can't express strongly enough how important it is for music teachers to start first by checking in with our own motivations for engaging students in such events. Our philosophies, fears, hopes, and interests transfer to our students; they are astute and attuned, and they will sense our true intentions. If we enter the events with musically meaningful goals, a desire for musical growth, and authentic trust in our students, it is more likely that students will too.[30] (See Reflection Activity 5.7, and a discussion of the detriments of competitive climates in Chapter 9.)

Using Empathy as a Means of Attuning to Student Needs and Interests

Because students' needs for musical development are so individual and unique, nothing can replace consistent communication to help us know how to care for and with students. However, as discussed throughout this book, exercising mature forms of empathy is also fundamental to attuning to students' needs and interests. It is critical that we do not presume to know what students need to support their learning, but that we use every possible means to determine those needs, prior to making assumptions about their musical capability or their motivation to learn. As illustrated in Chapter 3's vignette with student Amari, such attunement includes seeing students for who they are, and what they really need from the teacher, rather than focusing on any alleged deficits.[31]

In Box 5c, OHCME author Kimberly A. McCord shares an example of a student and teacher experiencing an empathy disconnect, where neither of them appears

Box 5c Learning Guitar, and an Empathy Disconnect between Mr. Roberts and C.J.

C.J. was playing the electric guitar for the first time. He was barring a chord across the adapted guitar with four strings tuned to A, E, A, E with colored stickers that guide musicians to match the color and shape of the notated music to the color and shape of the stickers on their instrument. C.J. understood how to decode the Figurenotes©* music, but the feel of the scratchy guitar strings under his finger was very irritating. "This guitar hurts."

His teacher was becoming exasperated and let out a big sigh. He mumbled to the other music teacher, "These kids complain all the time." C.J. once again said, "This guitar hurts! THIS GUITAR HURTS!" C.J. stood up and started to remove the guitar. Mr. Roberts (Mark), his teacher, replied, "You have to build up calluses and that takes a while. Why are you giving up so soon? We just barely got started."

"I SAID, THIS GUITAR HURTS!"

"C'mon C.J., tough it out! We need to learn this song today so next week we can start on a new one. Can you stick with this a little longer, just for me?"

"NO!" He drops the guitar as he struggles to get the strap off his shoulder.

Both appear to lack empathy for each other. Mark could stop the lesson and brainstorm solutions with C.J. His focus is on getting C.J. to comply long enough to learn the song, his way. C.J. just wants to leave. He no longer cares about learning guitar or playing rock music. He wished Mr. Roberts understood that the feeling of the strings under his fingers bothers him. He was excited about playing the guitar until the combination of the loud sound of all the other students playing badly and the strings rubbing on his fingers overwhelmed him. Mark doesn't understand why C.J. is so upset. He can't ignore the entire class while taking care of C.J. every time he has a complaint. He told Sherrie, the special educator that he needed an aide to come with C.J. because he knew it would be difficult for him to accommodate for a kid like C.J. What was he supposed to do now? He can't have C.J. having outbursts in class and he can't have him dropping his instrument.†

*Figurenotes© is "an adaptive notation that connects to stickers on instruments that are used in rock bands" (McCord, "This Guitar Hurts!," 245).

†McCord, "This Guitar Hurts!," 245–246.

to be attuned to the concerns of the other. C.J., a student with neurodiversity and sensory needs, is in pain from the guitar strings on his fingers and is distracted by the cacophonic sounds of his classmates learning guitar for the first time. These extreme discomforts lead to several loud outbursts, which are met with frustration rather than understanding from Mr. Roberts, his teacher.

McCord offers a different version of this same scenario in Box 5d. Here the teacher cares for, about, and with C.J. by anticipating his needs and making the classroom a

Box 5d C.J. and Mr. Roberts (Mark) Find a Way Forward

The lesson with C.J. was going amazingly well, thought Mark. He picked up how to read the music by matching his finger with the sticker on his guitar. In fact, C.J. seemed to understand Figurenotes© better than Mark! He was glad that teacher from Vermont suggested it in the Facebook group. When C.J. pulled up his finger and frowned at it for a moment Mark asked, "is your finger bothering you?" C.J. nodded his head. Mark asked, "what is making your finger hurt?"

C.J. pointed at the part of his fingers that hurt and put his fingers down close to the strings and said, it hurts my fingers." Mark mirrored what C.J. said and elaborated, "you say the guitar strings are hurting your fingers? That must make it very hard to keep up with the song, plus I bet you want to stop and give your finger a rest too, am I right? I'm going to have to think a bit about how to make the guitar strings feel better for your fingers. While I do that, can you rest your sore fingers and watch and listen to the other musicians playing?" C.J. agrees and lays his guitar in his lap.

"A guitar hurt my finger!" C.J. says looking at Mark. "My fingers hurt!" (C.J. struggles with speech and not only has trouble speaking, but when he does speak, he uses a very loud voice). Mark acknowledges what C.J. says, "I agree, I wouldn't want to play guitar if it hurt my fingers all the time. C.J., I am going to figure out how to fix the guitar, so it won't hurt your fingers." Mark says this while looking at C.J. and smiles. C.J. sits down after carefully picking up the guitar and laying it on his lap. It is a bit difficult to tell but C.J. does seem satisfied.*

*McCord, "This Guitar Hurts!," 246–247.

safe and accepting space. As McCord notes, the teacher "probably would not have been able to anticipate C.J.'s reaction to the guitar strings, but he likely would have known that a chaotic, loud classroom would be a difficult place for C.J. to not only stay calm, but also to focus on learning."[32] She honors how the teacher, too, was also feeling overwhelmed in the first scenario, and how a bit of forethought and accommodations stopped a potential problem from escalating—but most importantly, maintained student wellbeing. This change of approach might presumably keep other students in the class more comfortable as well. (See Reflection Activity 5.8.)

In a different but related scenario, McCord tells the story of Rachel, a young singer with autism, whose musical ear was so refined that she could use her perfect pitch to label multiple notes played at the same time. Rachel described singing with other musicians as "the only time in my life that I truly feel myself,"[33] because it was a time when she was able to communicate reciprocally with others through musical empathy (as defined in Chapter 4). Unfortunately, Rachel's teacher, Mrs. Charles, removed her from multiple music classes—the things in life she loved the most—after she made outbursts in class, such as "How many times do I have to hear F instead of F7? Just add the E♭ PLEASE!!!"[34]

Mrs. Charles was frustrated and embarrassed by Rachel yelling out musical mistakes that she hadn't noticed or hadn't yet been able to fix. She removed Rachel from class despite that the outbursts involved specific suggestions for student improvement. McCord offers a compromise that might have worked in this situation instead, as shown in Box 5e.

Box 5e Rachel and Mrs. Charles Work Out a Compromise

It is important for teachers to be consistent and fair. Rachel and Mrs. Charles could benefit from an objective facilitator to work out a compromise. Rachel may not be allowed to argue and interrupt the choir rehearsal, and Mrs. Charles might not rush to remove her from the group. They might work out a subtle sign (such as Rachel tugging her ear lobe) when Rachel finds herself trying to hold back her urge to correct the mistakes. If Mrs. Charles doesn't respond to the sign because she isn't noticing Rachel, the prearranged quiet spot is an acceptable place for Rachel to go sit and cool down. Rachel can then return whenever she feels ready. [. . .]

Creating strategies for returning choral rehearsal to an ensemble that feels like a community makes it a safe musical environment and an efficient use of everyone's time. Rachel feels cared for because she now has the autonomy to be in the choir rehearsal or not, depending on her tolerance level. Mrs. Charles ends the rehearsal a bit early and goes over the pieces with Rachel and often makes a note of problems based on what Rachel heard. She remembers to thank Rachel for helping and Rachel returns the compliment with "you are welcome!" Both feel that the other values her, and this feeling causes the two to want to try other ways of creating a caring relationship between them. Rachel has an enlarged score for every piece and keeps her notes on this copy. At times Mrs. Charles notices her taking the score with her to the cool-down place. This makes Mrs. Charles feel better about Rachel leaving the class. She is still staying musically engaged.*

*McCord, "This Guitar Hurts!," 251.

Caring with Adult Learners

Development—whether musical, physical, social, emotional, or psychological—continues throughout adulthood to the end of our lives. While I was working on this chapter, I received an unexpected phone call from my mother, who will be turning 90 years old next week. Mom doesn't typically do cold calls (she is a busy woman and prefers to text), so I picked up quickly. It turns out that she called rather than texting simply because she was trying to be efficient and save time and effort, given that she broke her humerus a few weeks ago and her dominant arm is in a cast.

"Not a drama," as she likes to say. She simply called to ask me about kefir, and how best to consume it, because her physician's assistant (PA) recommended it to her after she had asked him about every possible way to expedite her bone regrowth. After we discussed all things probiotic, Mom described her medical visit to me—how most of her doctors and nurses provided detailed answers to her questions. However, Mom told me, calmly yet clearly, that this particular PA tends to treat her like "an old person who doesn't know anything."

It was a remarkable comment to hear from my mother—this woman who has devoted her entire life to the pursuit of knowledge. Mom has spent decades reading voraciously, works regularly at the computer, and is continually looking up information on her phone. Learning is ubiquitous for this nonagenarian. She even published a book with the title, *The School of Life Is Always in Session*—a memoir of her father, who similarly spent his life learning as much as he could until he passed away at 89. Mom has been up on all the latest technologies for decades, such that she is always my first go-to person when I need to learn about new software or a new gadget.

Yet to this physician's assistant, Mom was apparently just an old woman who didn't need to know or wouldn't understand nuanced information that might help her survive and thrive. Only because I know Mom so intimately, I was able to feel the sting permeate through her stoic retelling of the medical visit. I know how incredibly astute and intelligent and insightful she is. She sees things holistically, with wisdom that comes from age and experience, but also from many hardships. Yet for whatever reason—perhaps lack of time, overwhelm, lack of experience working with older patients, perhaps not by choice—this physician's assistant did not connect with Mom personally, to know her in this way. I wish for his sake (as well as hers) that he could have.

As I reflected on this situation, I recalled many years ago when I felt a similar sadness while reading a published guide for private studio instruction. The author cautioned readers from taking adult students into their private studios. The rationale against it had something to do with how adult learners were allegedly set in their ways, less willing to try new things, overly concerned with details that didn't matter, and had sensitive egos.

This is not my experience at all. For me, it has always been a remarkable gift to learn with—and from—adult students. I don't know the background information about this author so I can't judge their situation. I can offer compassion by imagining that they had had some difficult experiences knowing how to connect with adult learners, and that they likely didn't have the resources or supports to work through these challenges. So, instead I envision what a different story might look like for happy teachers of adult students. (See Reflection Activity 5.9.)

Stages of Development in Adulthood

As Mom would remind us, we never stop learning. OHCME authors Lisa J. Lehmberg and C. Victor Fung articulate three theoretical stages of psychological development that may occur among people over 40 years old:

- Adulthood (ages 40–64), in which people may focus their attention and energy on leaving a legacy, or making a lasting impact on the world in ways that will outlive them;
- Old age (ages 65 and older), where people may strive toward wisdom, coherence, ego integrity, and a sense of completeness and closure on their life; and
- Gerotranscendence (ages 80 and older), where people mature away from a focus on materialism and move toward psychospiritual transcendence.[35]

Of course, these stages are general and theoretical. Every person will experience their own unique experience of metamorphosis and maturation, depending on their individual circumstances. However, viewing adult learners through a lens of developmental concerns and priorities may be helpful for music teachers when considering their needs, and how they may differ from those of our students who are in earlier stages of development. Concerns, needs, desires, interests, goals, and developmental and processing speeds may differ from those of other students in any way imaginable; hence, as with students at any stage of development or maturation, it is critical to communicate and clarify on a regular basis how things are coming along, and to make continual adjustments.

Caring with Adult Music Learners: A "Yes, And . . ." Approach

The possibilities for caring *with* are endless with adult music learners. A colleague of mine who led a New Horizons ensemble for many years often commented on how older adults made perfect teacher educators for his university students. He explained these adult students were able to articulate what wasn't working for them in ways the younger students could not do. Although some teachers might consider such direct feedback disrespectful or embarrassing, he considered it a rich and wonderful opportunity for pedagogical improvement. The trick is that such improvement requires humility and a willingness to learn along with, and from, adult students.

Private piano studio teacher Kaitlyn Leahy, who was introduced in the previous chapter for her "compassionate music teaching" approach with adult students, aims to recognize what the students can teach her, based on their life experiences. She considers the questions students ask or the suggestions they make—which some might interpret wrongly as resistance or defiance—as hints about how her teaching might be altered to better support their musical development. For example, Kaitlyn has several adult beginning students who are very successful in their extramusical careers, and whose perfectionistic personalities or low tolerance for mistakes are often expressed through comments such as "Oh no, don't make us do that again!!!" Kaitlyn responds to these expressions with humor and curiosity while also taking cues for redirecting the lesson if needed: "I know not to take those kinds of comments personally and I am perfectly fine laughing it off and carrying on [. . .] doing my best to read the room and keep it light."[36]

For many years, Kaitlyn has observed how adult learning needs and styles can be very different from younger students, but also very different from one another.[37]

To account for these varying needs, she has learned to follow each student's lead and respond to their requests with the same kind of "yes, and . . ." approach used in improvisational comedy.[38] In other words, Kaitlyn accepts students' efforts, suggestions, or requests with a "yes" rather than a "no" and then continues with an "and" rather than a "but." This way, adult learners' concerns and needs are validated, and Kaitlyn can continue to support their growth without dominating the lesson's direction. A "yes, and . . ." approach keeps the learner in control, but the teacher is still able to respond with her own contribution to support the lesson, much like an accompanist would do (see Chapter 7 for more on accompaniment in caring-*with* music teaching approaches). In Box 5f, Kaitlyn describes how things ended up in

Box 5f Kaitlyn's "Yes, and . . ." Approach with Adult Beginning Piano Students

Perhaps some of the most valuable experiences I have had as a teacher have come from following my students' lead and responding to their requests like an improv troupe might: "yes, and . . ." For example, during the holiday season last year, one of my students, a recent retiree, asked if she could bring her mom to her lesson. Apparently her mom "used to play" but her mother's piano had been at her house (for her children when they took lessons) for more than 30 years. I didn't have a great idea of how a lesson with my student and her mother would work, but thought, "why not?" I wasn't sure how to prepare for the lesson since I had virtually no information about her mom other than she used to play, but I said "yes, and" picked out a duet arrangement of a familiar holiday tune.

It ended up being the MOST. FUN. LESSON. The two of them sat side-by-side at the grand piano in my big, beige, community music school classroom, giggling at every mistake, singing along with the song to keep track of where they were, and creating innovative new ways to count themselves in. (My favorite was one was the arhythmic and rushed, "okay, go"). It didn't matter that I needed to take a few minutes to rewrite her mom's part on the spot, or that they didn't play it perfectly by the end of the lesson. I ended up taking a few pictures of them playing and taking a beautifully imperfect video to send to my student, which apparently they showed to everybody over the holidays.

It was a lesson where we did not really work toward accomplishing any of her proximal or distal goals, or develop any new musical skills; and it was also a lesson that I may have never thought of having. Even if I had thought of a "bring your mom" lesson, it is certainly not an idea that would work for every student. I really think that these kinds of lessons only work because the student felt comfortable and confident enough to propose the idea and that I felt comfortable and confident enough to go for it with them. Of course it has everything to do with creating that compassionate connection.*

*Kaitlyn Leahy, personal communication, February 21, 2024 (used with permission).

one particularly joyous "yes, and . . ." experience with an adult beginner. Recalling the opening of this section, I can't imagine what Kaitlyn might have missed if she didn't maintain such a philosophy of welcome to the adult learners in her studio.

Developing as Teachers: Practicing Core Reflection

Our journey to supporting student development reflects our own development as teachers. With each caring-*with* interaction, we have an opportunity to improve as teachers as we learn alongside our students, our co-learners. In this final section, I introduce the concept of core reflection, which can help us check in with ourselves and draw on our own strengths as we support students in developing their own musical selves. According to OHCME author Margaret Berg, core reflection is an approach for teacher self-assessment that extends beyond the typical and commonly evaluated professional characteristics of a teacher (such as our musical skills, behaviors while teaching, etc.)—to also account for our personal characteristics (such as our identities, beliefs, values, and core qualities).[39]

Core qualities are defined as positive character traits, including such aspects as "creativity, curiosity, sense of justice, precision, openness, persistence, decisiveness, flexibility, patience, enthusiasm, courage, caring, sensitivity, and humor, to name a few."[40] Each of us has a unique set of core qualities. Understanding what our personal core qualities are, and then recalling times when we have used these core qualities as successful teachers, can boost our awareness of our teaching potential and help us overcome teaching hardships.

Core qualities are more than competencies; they are part of our unique identity. As such, they work in tandem with competence, autonomy, and relatedness (described earlier) to help us find an effective path toward our own development as music teachers.[41] Just as it is helpful to focus on student potentials rather than deficits, it is similarly more empowering for us to focus on our unique strengths rather than our weaknesses, so that we can draw on those strengths and use them as assets to improve our teaching.

There are five phases to core reflection:

1. Describing a concrete situation or problem;
2. Reflection on the ideal (in a situation) and our core qualities;
3. Reflection on an obstacle (e.g., how do you limit or block yourself);
4. Using the core potential;
5. Trying a new approach.[42]

Another important aspect of core reflection involves having a meta-awareness of the ways in which we process our thoughts and feelings as they occur. The thoughts, feelings, and motivations we experience are called "information channels," whereas our awareness of them is called "presencing" (a combination of being present and sensing). Presencing involves staying in the moment with our thoughts, feelings, and motivations. It stands in contrast to "downloading," where we have an automatic response that lacks mindfulness. As Berg explains, presencing allows us to see ourselves more holistically, and to focus not only on our skills and knowledge, "but also [our] beliefs, identity, mission/ideals/motives, and core qualities to engage in more effective and more fulfilling professional behavior."[43]

Box 5g and 5h, written by Margaret H. Berg, contain the same classroom scenario but with different outcomes. In the first (Box 5g), Ms. Smith reflects on a rehearsal of Mozart's *Eine Kleine Nachtmusik* that she just finished. She is evidently frustrated with the progress of the group and not sure how to help the violinists play more together. Although Ms. Smith admits to herself that she is not a fan of instilling fear in the students by singling them out to play solo in front of the rest of the ensemble, she resigns to considering it for the next rehearsal if the "back to basics" clap-and-count approach doesn't work.

In Box 5h, Ms. Smith uses the five steps of core reflection to consider how she might better support the students in their musical development. Bolded text shows the core reflection that has been added to the previous reflection, whereas brackets highlight core reflection concepts. As shown, Ms. Smith uses core reflection strategies to draw on her professional skills along with her personal core strengths to improve her teaching. Through a process of continual presencing and tuning

Box 5g Ms. Smith's Post-Rehearsal Reflection, Minus Core Reflection

"The first violins still aren't quite together on their eighth-note entrances in the first measure of *Eine Kleine*!," Ms. Smith says to herself as she collapsed into her office desk chair at the end of rehearsal. "I could go back to basics tomorrow, having them clap the rhythm while chanting the eighth-note subdivisions. Maybe I should have them play the measure individually to make the point that they need to practice outside of rehearsal?!" An image of Sam and Katy (who sit in the last stand of the first violin section) flashes across Ms. Smith's mind. Sam and Katy joined the orchestra program in 5th grade. They continue to participate in high school orchestra with limited practice outside of rehearsals and neither student takes private lessons, either by choice or due to family finances. Ms. Smith dismisses the image, returning to her reflection on the rehearsal. "I never liked it when my high school orchestra teacher had us play individually in front of the whole orchestra, but we've got to get *Eine Kleine* to the next level since district festival is only one month away!" Ms. Smith quickly decides to first use the "back-to-basics" approach, and if that doesn't fix the issue, she will then use the "playing individually" approach.*

*Berg, "Fostering Care through Core Reflection," 433.

Box 5h Ms. Smith's Post-Rehearsal Reflection, with Added Core Reflection

"The first violins still aren't quite together on their eighth-note entrances in the first measure of *Eine Kleine*!", [core reflection model-phase 1] Ms. Smith said to herself as she collapsed into her office desk chair at the end of rehearsal, the last period of the day. **Ms. Smith takes three deep breaths, followed by a body scan from her feet to her head. During the body scan, she notices tension at the nape of her neck.** [presencing] **Ms. Smith then asks herself a series of questions, each followed with a response. "What am I thinking right now? Clearly I'm thinking about the first violin entrance in the first measure! What am I feeling? I'm feeling tension and frustration. What do I want in this situation? Well, obviously, I'd love uniform entrances from the first violins in the first measure!"** [information channels] **Instead of thinking about various rehearsal strategies used in previous rehearsals** [downloading], **she next takes a few deep breaths** [presencing], **pausing to think about what went well in today's rehearsal. "It was really great to see the looks in their eyes, especially from the students in the back of the sections, when they heard for the first time how it sounds and feels to have <u>everyone</u> begin together, playing softly at the tip of the bow. It took several tries, but they hung in there with each other, as did I with them, for us to sound like 'one big violin.'" Ms. Smith says to herself "That's what I want."** [ideal; core reflection model-phase 2] **"I'm patient and persistent, and I have a gift for building community in my orchestra classes."** [core qualities; core reflection model-phase 2] **Ms. Smith then returns to thinking about the first violin eighth-note entrances in the first measure.** "I could go back to basics tomorrow, having them clap the rhythm while chanting the eighth-note subdivisions. Maybe I should have them play the measure individually to make the point that they need to practice their orchestra music outside of rehearsal?!" **Ms. Smith feels a shiver run down her spine as her eyes tear up.** [presencing] **"Is this the kind of teacher I want to be, embarrassing some of the students as a way to get them to practice more?"** [core reflection model-phase 3] An image of Sam and Katy (who sit in the last stand of the first violin section) flashes across Ms. Smith's mind. Sam and Katy joined the orchestra program in 5th grade. They continue to participate in high school orchestra—with limited practice outside of rehearsals—and neither student takes private lessons, either by choice or due to family finances. **Ms. Smith continues to focus on this image, smiling as she thinks about how Sam and Katy have grown to be good kids who are fun to chat with after rehearsals, despite their lack of consistent home practice.** [presencing] "I never liked it when my high school orchestra teacher did this (playing individually), but we've got to get *Eine Kleine* to the next level since district festival is only 1 month away!" **Ms. Smith pauses her thinking, noticing that her shoulders raised as she started thinking about district festival.** [presencing] **"Hmm. It seems like I might be**

getting focused on our rating. Perhaps my ego and misguided belief that a rating less than a '1' will lead my colleagues to question my competence and musicianship are getting me off track." [core reflection model-phase 3] **Ms. Smith returns to thinking about her strengths as a teacher** [core qualities], **and what she experienced today during rehearsal, with she and the students focused, working toward a common goal, and having a meaningful musical experience. She also thinks about Sam and Katy, and how her focus on the district festival rating, and her subsequent use of the "playing individually" strategy could create some distance between herself and these students, perhaps leading them to quit orchestra.** [core reflection model-phase 3] **Ms. Smith ponders these questions as she imagines the feeling in her body as draws on her strengths during rehearsals.** [core reflection model-phase 4] **"The 'back-to-basics' and 'playing individually' approaches could be modified" she says to herself. "Tomorrow I'll begin rehearsal by talking honestly with the first violins about why I was frustrated with them today. I will tell them I realized, after reflecting, that I needed to take a step back to think about what was most important—our district festival rating or their improvement and experience as an ensemble and as individuals. I'll also remind them that one of the judges will clinic with us for a few minutes after we perform as way to keep all of us focused on festival as a learning experience. I'll then talk to them about continuing to improve during the next few weeks while experiencing moments of 'brain meltdown' focus and 'orchestra family' support for each other during rehearsals. When we rehearse measure 1, I'll start with the back-to-basics approach, and if this doesn't fix the problem with the first violins, I'll have them play this measure one stand rather than one person at a time. I'll also be sure to engage the rest of the orchestra in 'finding a smile (something their peers did well) and a question (asking a question about something you noticed that could be improved).'"** [core reflection model-phase 5] **Ms. Smith's shoulders lower as a smile comes across her face, accompanied by a twinkle in her eye. "Looking forward to seeing how rehearsal goes tomorrow!" she says to herself as she continues to plan for tomorrow's rehearsal.***

*Berg, "Fostering Care through Core Reflection," 436–438.

into her core qualities, she digs deeper, beyond reactive "downloading," to consider how she might engage more honestly with students and find a way for them to develop stronger rhythm skills and even support their peers in doing so.

Core reflection is a kind of self-care practice that promotes teacher development. By association, it can promote student development as well. Presencing and reflecting on core qualities also fosters teacher self-knowledge, which is related to honesty and openness—elements of trust that can lead to authentic connection.[44] Core reflection moves teacher self-assessment beyond merely caring *about* skills and competencies, to caring *for* ourselves as well as our students. Finally, as we communicate openly with our students, it is possible that such honesty and openness might lead to more opportunities for caring *with* students, in which we learn along with them and work together to find solutions for their (and our) musical development. (See Reflection Activity 5.10.)

Conclusion

Perhaps the most important takeaway from this chapter is that there is no one right way to approach musical development, because every student's background, interests, needs, supports, and so forth, are unique. Biases are a natural part of the human experience. Therefore, it is important for us to become aware of the ways that our stereotypes and assumptions about students might stand in the way of their musical progress. Exercising empathy to attune to students' needs and interests, as well as their responses to our pedagogical approaches, is essential. However, even more critical is communicating openly and regularly with students about what they believe they need from us. Learning to attune to students in this way is itself a journey and a process. Just as we want to focus on student potentials, interests, and requests rather than focusing on their deficits, we can practice core reflection with our own teaching, to look beyond our pedagogical challenges and better draw upon our strengths and improve our caring practices.

Reflection Activities

5.1. I invite you to fill out Figure 5.1, the Differentiated Model of Giftedness and Talent (DMGT), for your own musical journey. What specific characteristics about you are unique? What are some mental and physical traits that you possess? What environmental supports have you received? What environmental supports did you lack, or do you currently seek out? What are certain personality traits that you possess that help (or hinder) your progress? What are some things that occurred by chance in your life, which have helped your musical journey? What are some of your specific musical talents?

5.2. With your students or by yourself, fill out the DMGT for a famous musical artist. What natural abilities do/did they have? What environmental supports did they receive? What interpersonal traits impacted or inhibited their growth as musicians? What life events brought them to where they are today (or at the peak of their career)? What developmental processes did they go through? What are their various musical talents?

5.3. Invite your students to fill out the DMGT for themselves. Ask them to reflect on, and share with you, the kinds of supports they want and need toward their individual musical development.

5.4. Think about some of the common accommodations made for disabled students in music learning settings. How do they continue to favor the perspectives or strengths of nondisabled people?

5.5. What are specific ways that you can foster a student's sense of competence? Autonomy? Relatedness?

5.6. What are different ratios of competence, autonomy, and relatedness that you have had at different points in your life? What are different ratios that you see in some of your students?

5.7. Consider some ways to use peer observations (such as in performance festivals) as an opportunity for students to envision the specific musical capacities that they, too, can develop. How might you limit damaging social comparisons and focus the attention instead on readily attainable skills?

5.8. Considering Boxes 5c–5d: How might things have gone differently in each of these scenarios?

5.9. What are some of the things you have learned from adult music students?

5.10. What are some of your core qualities, as defined in the section on core reflection? How might you draw on these to improve your teaching?

Notes

1. Karin S. Hendricks and Gary E. McPherson, "Reconsidering Musical Ability Development through the Lens of Diversity and Bias," in *The Oxford Handbook of Care in Music Education*, ed. Karin S. Hendricks (New York: Oxford University Press, 2023), 408–420.
2. Adapted from Françoys Gagné, "Building Gifts into Talents: Detailed Overview of the DMGT 2.0," in *Leading Change in Gifted Education: The Festschrift of Dr. Joyce VanTassel-Baska*, ed. Bronwyn MacFarlane (Austin, TX: Prufrock Press, 2009), 61–80; see also Françoys Gagné and Gary E. McPherson, "Analyzing Musical Prodigiousness Using Gagné's Integrative Model of Talent Development," in *Music Prodigies: Interpretations from Psychology, Education, Musicology and Ethnomusicology*, ed. Gary E. McPherson (New York: Oxford University Press, 2016), 3–114; Karin S. Hendricks, *Compassionate Music Teaching: A Framework for Motivation and Engagement in the 21st Century* (Lanham, MD: Rowman & Littlefield, 2018); Gary E. McPherson and Aaron Williamon, "Building Gifts into Musical Talents," in *The Child as Musician: A Handbook of Musical Development*, 2nd ed., ed. Gary E. McPherson (New York: Oxford University Press, 2016), 340–360.
3. Hendricks and McPherson, "Reconsidering Musical Ability Development," 412.
4. Guadalupe López-Íñiguez and Pamela Burnard, "Toward a Nuanced Understanding of Musicians' Professional Learning Pathways: What Does Critical Reflection Contribute?" *Research Studies in Music Education* 44, no. 1 (2021): 127–157, https://doi.org/10.1177/1321103X211025850; Guadalupe López Íñiguez and Heidi Westerlund, "The Politics of Care in the Education of Children Gifted for Music: A Systems View," in *The Oxford Handbook of Care in Music Education*, ed. Karin S. Hendricks (New York: Oxford University Press, 2023), 115–131.
5. Hendricks, *Compassionate Music Teaching*; López-Íñiguez and Westerlund, "The Politics of Care in the Education of Children"; Paul Evans, "Self-Determination Theory: An Approach to Motivation in Music Education," *Musicae Scientiae* 19, no. 1 (2015): 65–83, https://doi.org/10.1177/102986491 4568044.
6. Gabbrielle M. Johnson, "The Psychology of Bias: From Data to Theory," in *An Introduction to Implicit Bias: Knowledge, Justice, and the Social Mind*, ed. Erin Beeghly and Alex Madva (New York: Routledge, 2020), 20–40.
7. Hendricks and McPherson, "Reconsidering Musical Ability Development"; Deejay Robinson and Karin S. Hendricks, "Black Keys on a White Piano: A Negro Narrative of Double-Consciousness in American Music Education," in *Marginalized Voices in Music Education*, ed. Brent C. Talbot (New York: Routledge, 2018), 28–45.
8. David Baker, "Disability, Lifelong Musical Engagement, and Care," in *The Oxford Handbook of Care in Music Education*, ed. Karin S. Hendricks (New York: Oxford University Press, 2023), 91–103.
9. E. Beeghly and A. Madva, "Introducing Implicit Bias," in *An Introduction to Implicit Bias: Knowledge, Justice, and the Social Mind*, ed. E. Beeghly and A. Madva (New York: Routledge, 2020), 1–19; I. X. Kendi, *How to Be an Anti-Racist* (New York: One World, 2019).

10. Beeghly and Madva, "Introducing Implicit Bias"; Karin S. Hendricks, "Counternarratives: Troubling Majoritarian Certainty," *Action, Criticism, and Theory for Music Education* 20, no. 4 (2021): 58–78, https://doi.org/10.22176/act20.4.58.
11. Melissa A. Goetschius and Tawnya D. Smith. "The Identity Reconciliation of Five Elementary Students across Their Landscapes of Musical Practice," *Music Education Research* 25, no. 5 (2023): 485–495.
12. Elizabeth Mitchell, "Music's Relational Imperative: Wellbeing, Music-Making, and the Interconnections between Music Therapy and Music Education," in *The Oxford Handbook of Care in Music Education*, ed. Karin S. Hendricks (New York: Oxford University Press, 2023), 366.
13. Mitchell, "Music's Relational Imperative," 366.
14. Personal communication, February 13, 2024.
15. Personal communication, February 13, 2024.
16. Nel Noddings, *Caring: A Feminine Approach to Ethics and Moral Education* (Berkeley: University of California Press, 1984), 202.
17. Hendricks, *Compassionate Music Teaching*, 165.
18. Klein Cain Orchestra, "About Us," Klein Cain Orchestra, https://www.kleincainorchestra.org/about.html.
19. Edward L. Deci and Richard M. Ryan, *Intrinsic Motivation and Self-Determination in Human Behavior* (New York: Plenum Press 1985).
20. Deci and Ryan, *Intrinsic Motivation and Self-Determination*; Evans, "Self-Determination Theory"; Hendricks and McPherson, "Reconsidering Musical Ability Development," 412–413.
21. Hendricks, *Compassionate Music Teaching.*
22. Evans, "Self-Determination Theory"; Allen R. Legutki, "Self-Determined Music Participation: The Role of Psychological Needs Satisfaction, Intrinsic Motivation, and Self-Regulation in the High School Band Experience" (PhD diss., University of Illinois at Urbana-Champaign, 2010); Hendricks, *Compassionate Music Teaching.*
23. Lucy Green, *How Popular Musicians Learn* (Surrey, UK: Ashgate, 2002); Alexandra Lamont, "The Beat Goes On: Music Education, Identity and Lifelong Learning," *Music Education Research* 13, no. 4 (2011): 369–388.
24. Evans, "Self-Determination Theory."
25. Kaitlyn Leahy and Tawnya D. Smith, "The Self-Directed Learning of Adult Music Students: A Comparison of Teacher Approaches and Student Needs," *International Journal of Music Education* 39, no. 3 (2021): 289–300, https:/www.doi.org/10.1177/0255761421991596; Lisa J. Lehmberg and Victor C. Fung, "Caring Connection, Music Participation, and Quality of Life of Older Adults," in *The Oxford Handbook of Care in Music Education*, ed. Karin S. Hendricks (New York: Oxford University Press, 2023), 395–409.
26. Ryan M. Hourigan, "Music as a Vehicle for Caring for Students with Learning Differences," in *The Oxford Handbook of Care in Music Education*, ed. Karin S. Hendricks (New York: Oxford University Press, 2023), 373–384.
27. Mihaly Csikszentmihalyi, *Flow: The Psychology of Optimal Performance* (New York: Harper & Row, 1990); Legutki, "Self-Determined Music Participation"; Hendricks, *Compassionate Music Teaching.*
28. Csikszentmihalyi, *Flow*; Sean Powell, *The Ideology of Competition* (New York: Oxford University Press, 2023).
29. Karin S. Hendricks, "The Sources of Self-Efficacy: Educational Research and Implications for Music," *Update: Applications of Research in Music Education* 35, no. 1 (2016): 32–38, https://doi.org/10.1177%2F8755123315576535.
30. Rebecca A. Roesler, "Musically Meaningful: The Interpersonal Goals of Performance," *Music Educators Journal* 100, no. 3 (2014): 39–43, https://doi.org/10.1177/00274321135177.
31. Warren Churchill and Clare Hall, "Caring about Deaf Music in Culturally Responsive Music Education," in *The Oxford Handbook of Care in Music Education*, ed. Karin S. Hendricks (New York: Oxford University Press, 2023), 545; David A. Stewart, "Ethics and the Preparation of Teachers of the Deaf," in *Ethics in Deaf Education: The First Six Years*, ed. Rodney G. Beattie (London: Academic Press, 2001), 166; Vicki R. Lind and Constance L. McKoy, *Culturally Responsive Teaching in Music Education: From Understanding to Application* (New York: Routledge, 2022).
32. Kimberly A. McCord, "'This Guitar Hurts!': Empathy and Caring in Inclusive Ensembles," in *The Oxford Handbook of Care in Music Education*, ed. Karin S. Hendricks (New York: Oxford University Press, 2023), 246.
33. McCord, "This Guitar Hurts!," 247.
34. McCord, "This Guitar Hurts!," 250.
35. Lehmberg and Fung, "Caring Connection, Music Participation," 396; see also Erik H. Erikson, and Joan M. Erikson, *The Life Cycle Completed (Extended Version)* (New York: W. W. Norton & Company, 1982/1997); Estelle R. Jorgensen, "On Values and Life's Journey through Music: Reflections on the Eriksons' Life Stages and Music Education," in *Authentic Connection: Music, Spirituality, and Wellbeing*, ed. Karin S. Hendricks and Joyce Boyce-Tillman (New York: Peter Lang, 2021), 67–80; Lars Tornstam, "Maturing into Gerotranscendence," *Journal of Transpersonal Psychology* 43, no. 2 (2011): 166–180.
36. Kaitlyn Leahy, personal communication, February 21, 2024.

37. Kaitlyn Sarah Leahy, "Compassionate Music Teaching with Adults Learning Recreationally in Lessons: A Narrative Inquiry" (PhD diss., Boston University Theses and Dissertations, 2024); Kaitlyn S. Leahy and Tawnya D. Smith, "The Self-Directed Learning of Adult Music Students: A Comparison of Teacher Approaches and Student Needs," *International Journal of Music Education* 39, no. 3 (2021): 289–300.
38. James A. Mourey, "Improv Comedy and Modern Marketing Education: Exploring Consequences for Divergent Thinking, Self-Efficacy, and Collaboration," *Journal of Marketing Education* 42, no. 2 (2020): 134–148.
39. Margaret H. Berg, "Fostering Care through Core Reflection," in *The Oxford Handbook of Care in Music Education*, ed. Karin S. Hendricks (New York: Oxford University Press, 2023), 433–444.
40. Berg, "Fostering Care through Core Reflection," 435.
41. Berg, "Fostering Care through Core Reflection,"; see also Deci and Ryan, *Intrinsic Motivation and Self-Determination*.
42. Berg, "Fostering Care through Core Reflection," 435; see also Frits G. Evelein and Franciscus Aloysius Johannes Korthagen, *Practicing Core Reflection: Activities and Lessons for Teaching and Learning from Within* (New York: Routledge, 2015).
43. Berg, "Fostering Care through Core Reflection," 436; see also Carol R. Rodgers and Miriam B. Raider-Roth, "Presence in Teaching," *Teachers and Teaching: Theory and Practice* 12, no. 3 (2006): 265–287, C.
44. Berg, "Fostering Care through Core Reflection"; see also Hendricks, *Compassionate Music Teaching*; Parker J. Palmer, *The Courage to Teach: Exploring the Inner Landscape of a Teacher's Life* (San Francisco: Jossey-Bass, 1998).

6

What I Learned about Expressive Arts Integration and Culturally Responsive Caring

(Featuring Yank'l Garcia, Co-Authored with Tawnya D. Smith and Karin S. Hendricks)

Chapter Overview

This chapter is a case study written by teacher/therapist Yank'l Garcia, with assistance from Tawnya Smith and Karin Hendricks. Ms. Garcia is a certified music therapist who received a master's degree with preK-12 teaching licensure from Boston University. While working on the degree, Yank'l conducted a self-study to explore ways to integrate music therapy approaches into music education. The case study explores the depth of care a teacher can provide by practicing empathy and authentic care with healthy boundaries. In this chapter, Ms. Garcia writes honestly and openly about what she learned from her students as she tested out a project in which she integrated expressive arts approaches in a community orchestra program. It provides several examples of how to integrate expressive arts practices with educational strategies to foster caring relationships, connection, and a deeper love of music learning. This chapter also offers a model for reflective practice as Ms. Garcia considers how she might better practice culturally responsive caring in the future. It includes pictures from the students' expressive arts activities, with many additional color pictures accessible online.

Introduction: From Karin's Perspective

Our students are often our best teachers. No matter how much teacher preparation coursework or professional development we have completed, no expert can make it "real" for us in the ways our own students can. They aren't afraid to tell it to us like it is, to show us how it is, to *live* it like it is. Their honest feedback can sometimes be brutal, but when we listen and apply their ideas it can be game-changing—sometimes even life-changing. When we gain students' trust, they are more likely to "have our backs" and communicate suggestions to us before we fall flat on our

Daring to Care with Music Education. Karin S. Hendricks, Oxford University Press. © Oxford University Press 2025.
DOI: 10.1093/9780197777589.003.0006

face—or at least they still love us when we fail because they know we are honestly trying to care for, about, and *with* them. (See Reflection Activity 6.1.)

I have included this chapter in the book because of what I learned from my own students, and what they have, in turn, learned from their students. The most poignant (and painful) feedback I received about *Compassionate Music Teaching* came from Janie, a mid-career teacher who was working on a doctorate at Boston University. We read the text for a class she took with me one summer. I'll never forget the punch in my gut when she announced (in front of the entire class), "I can't relate to this book. The teachers featured in this book are all perfect, and I'm not perfect. I need a book that shows the realities, failures, strivings of real teachers with real problems." I winced, but I knew she was right. I committed to myself in that moment to make my next book even more "real." (I will leave it up to you, dear readers, to let me know what "real" means for you, and whether or not I've captured it this time.)

This chapter is an illustration of students teaching teachers, on multiple levels. Yank'l Garcia was also a student I taught—a certified music therapist who came to Boston University to get a master's degree with preK-12 teaching licensure. Yank'l came to our program already with a teacher/therapist mind and heart. She taught me, by example, about the depth of care one can offer to others by practicing empathy with healthy boundaries. The way she integrates therapy principles with educational strategies is a powerful model of care for all students, not just students with trauma histories.

In this chapter Yank'l provides several examples of how to integrate expressive arts practices with educational strategies to foster caring relationships, connection, and a deeper love of music learning. She writes openly about her realities, strivings, vulnerabilities, and failures—as well as the many things she learned from her own students—as she tested out a project in which she integrated expressive arts approaches in a community orchestra program. Most of the chapter is written in Yank'l's own voice but co-authored by my colleague and partner Tawnya Smith, who provided a reflective space for Yank'l as they wrote together about Yank'l's experience, and about engaging in practices of culturally responsive caring in the future.[1]

A brief note about music education and music therapy: Anyone who has spent time in a music learning space—especially in recent years—knows that the boundaries between music education and therapy are often blurred. It is critical to maintain those boundaries, however, as educators and therapists each receive different training to prepare them for specific challenges that may arise.[2] Therapists are trained to work safely and ethically with certain therapeutic techniques, and it is important for music educators who have not received such training to not overstep in ways that might—while well-intended—cause more harm to students or to themselves.

With that caveat in mind, there is much in music education that can be informed by music therapy practices. *Oxford Handbook of Care in Music Education*

(OHCME) author Elizabeth Mitchell, who is a trained music therapist and music therapy educator, describes how principles of learning and wellness are shared by both fields. She argues that care is critical for both therapy and education, and that care can predict the success of both.[3] Reciprocal and responsive relationships are also at the heart of both. Mitchell writes, "Similar to clients in therapy, students too are better able to meet their goals and to thrive when educators skillfully and safely prioritize the student–teacher alliance [and what] better way to explore and embody relationality than through music?"[4]

Creative arts therapies can also inform the work that we do as music educators.[5] According to Mitchell, creative approaches to musical engagement can help foster resilience and adaptability within reciprocal and responsive music-making relationships.[6] Yet, whether engaged in music therapy or education, there is a real potential to do harm when people's lives, needs, and identities are not considered. In this chapter and the one that follows, I argue that caring approaches in music education require that music teachers be culturally responsive (Chapter 6), and identity-responsive and identity-affirming (Chapter 7).

Integrating Music Therapy and Music Education in Teaching Practice: From Yank'l's Perspective

As a board-certified music therapist, I (Yank'l) have engaged in music therapy with school-aged clients in many settings. I have had the opportunity to work one-on-one and in groups with children and adolescents displaying various learning differences. Music therapy is a way to improve communication, motor skills, cognition, and social/emotional health[7] while simultaneously cultivating creativity to foster individual wellbeing.[8]

I decided to pursue my graduate degree in music education while working in Florida as a teaching artist in an El Sistema–inspired not-for-profit organization that supported students from underserved communities. In this work, I found that my teaching style was naturally informed by my music therapy understandings. I observed, listened, adapted, and learned from the students in the classroom. This was key for me to gauge how to structure the material in a meaningful manner. I often used original songs, just as with my music therapy clients, to help transition to the next activity or aid students to learn and recall information. I used visuals with motor movements to support the learning of new concepts, and I encouraged socialization for students to practice executive functioning skills, improve self-esteem, and build leadership opportunities.

While working in the El Sistema program, my teaching philosophy was rooted in a desire to provide a positive environment for students to learn music, but also to learn about themselves in relation to classroom activities. Because of my music therapy experience, I had been exposed to the impacts of trauma and other challenges to the early development of children. I was sensitized to the need for shaping a caring classroom that did not exacerbate or ignore these issues, but instead created a safe space for learning.[9] In addition, I was aware of the need to avoid acknowledging such issues through a deficit approach[10] that could further marginalize students in the learning process.

As a master's student, I decided to conduct my own teacher-research case study to further investigate ways that I could integrate music therapy and music education as a future music educator. Some researchers suggest that music therapy and education lie on a continuum.[11] Elizabeth Mitchell, for example, observed that between therapy and education "there is very little that distinguishes one point from another,"[12] and that a combination of education with therapy might "maximize" the potential for both.[13] I desired to better understand how therapy could inform my education practice, especially given the current movement within education to create trauma-informed classrooms and curricula,[14] engage in mindfulness education,[15] and promote general health and wellbeing.[16]

One way that music educators might adapt our practice would be to consider carefully how we might integrate knowledge from the fields of music and arts therapies—while maintaining our primary aim to educate. I sought not to inappropriately attempt to "heal" students through such a therapy-informed teaching approach, but rather to craft a learning environment that supported healthy development and individual student growth in addition to academic and musical achievement. As the three of us describe at the end of this chapter, the blend of therapy and education approaches I tried out was in many ways successful in promoting the students' psycho-social wellbeing and creating a community of belonging. However, I also learned a lot about how to improve in the future, including with what Geneva Gay[17] refers to as "culturally responsive caring."

The Workshops

When I decided to conduct this project, I was already working in an orchestra program with students from a low-income community in a predominantly Haitian neighborhood outside of Boston. I taught first- and second-generation Haitian American students who were all fluent in English, spanned the ages of 7–17, and had been playing their instrument for three or more years. The students shared with me that they often learned music by rote and had modest music literacy skills.

I created a series of expressive arts-informed orchestral workshops for beginning string players whom I already knew because I gave private lessons for the program. I arranged for five 2-hour workshops for a group of students who participated in the 3rd year orchestra, from 7 to 17 years of age. The activities I designed provided opportunities for students to be creative, and for their contributions to be shared and valued by others in the group. It was my aim to create a culturally caring environment that would account for the learner's interests and allow for their imagination and creativity to flourish. I included visual art journaling experiences to connect a specific theme in the music rehearsed that week in the workshop. I incorporated expressive arts into these workshops as a space to reflect, build on prior learning, and freely create, and for students to explore their own perspectives and thoughts.

From a culturally responsive perspective, it was my intention to offer familiar music of the student's culture to blend it with the European orchestral repertoire they were studying in the program. (We will return later, in retrospect, to what I learned through error.) I designed the expressive arts activities in conjunction with a grade 2 piece that aligned with the playing level of the students and had a title that I hoped would resonate with the student's cultural heritage. This piece has a repetitive melody, and the musical form allowed for the addition of a rhythm section so students could add percussion elements as they wished. Admittedly, as I will discuss later, I didn't do much research into the song prior to introducing it to the students. I also programmed the Haitian Konpa as I thought it would be a familiar genre on which to build a relationship for future collaboration between the students and myself.

Introducing a New Song

The first day of the workshop I tried to calm my nerves by repeating to myself that I had carefully organized all my materials and reviewed my plans and sequencing more than a handful of times. I knew patience and flexibility would be important given that the first workshop had been scheduled the weekend after a week-long break. Because the students weren't required to attend, I was nervous about them arriving on time or coming at all. For the next five weeks, I would be sharing a room in an old church basement that was equipped with an altar covered by a mantle, a bookcase containing a few children's books, two upright pianos—neither quite in tune—several chairs, and two toddler-sized tables. This was a familiar space for the students who made music here every Sunday. As I saw them begin to pile up the tables with their instruments and belongings, I requested they place their items in a different spot so that we could all start by sitting together around the tables.

Once I welcomed the students to the space, we began our first topic: melody. Our first expressive arts exploration included two listening examples; the first was the grade 2 piece that we would rehearse the following weeks, and the second, the rhythmic instrumentation of a Haitian Kompa. After giving each student a piece of paper and coloring markers, I prompted them to listen to the music and interpret what they heard. Pressing play, I intentionally looked anywhere in the room other than at the students, or their work, hoping they would feel more at ease to create.

Yank'l: So, what did you hear?
Jonathan (9): Someone on a journey through rain and sun, then like fighting and battling villains.
Ann (10): It was mysterious [...] and it had something more to tell us.

In my journal from the first workshop, I noted, "the younger students in the group were much more open-minded to the activities than the older students; their drawing and writings represented this." However, while reflecting on their artwork, I realized that was beyond the point. Though I had expected the students to draw a picture and freely write their thoughts, I noticed that their images shared more about themselves, and I learned this through student commentary that accompanied the expressive arts activity. Whether the students drew a lot or a little had much more to do with feeling comfortable to create.

Chris: I thought it was easy, because in music, I think it's easy to picture something. [. . .] it's easy to close your eyes and picture what happens, and this, I just drew what I thought was happening.

Ann: I was looking around to see how to make it about myself and make it about me and nobody else.

Mike: Well, I didn't know those musics, so I didn't know what to write about [. . .] I don't really think about the mood, you know, or the picture, and that was difficult for me to draw a picture . . . like, I can't draw a picture of, like, background music, or what it feels . . . I'm not used to sitting down and listen to music like that.

When rehearsing the grade 2 piece for this session, we focused on the melody of the piece. I asked questions, such as: "What does the melody sound like? Can someone sing it back? What instruments play the melody?" In this workshop, the students would sing the melody together on a neutral syllable of their choice, learning the melody at first by rote, and then by note name and fingering number. Due to the array of music literacy levels among the students I often implemented scaffolding when learning new music passages. The first level of practice always included singing a phrase while being accompanied by another student or myself, playing the part on a string instrument. Singing became the building block for learning this piece and what was practiced prior to playing on the instrument.

Overall, in this first session, the issue of comfort continued to emerge. I wondered how these activities might shed light on how these students can learn and perceive themselves as musicians. As the weeks went by, I gave the students several activities to question, reflect, and share their feelings.

Challenging What I've Been Taught

As the students came into the room in the second week, the first step in our class was to define rhythm.

Tessa: Rhythm is a beat in music.

Nina: Rhythm is when you use the sounds of music and make it into a beat.

It was in all their definitions—rhythm is a beat. I wanted the students to experience these beats in several ways: recreating Kompa rhythms, making their own rhythms, and finally, at the end of this workshop, to create a visual representation from their written and kinetic expressions. I envisioned shaping these two areas, melody and rhythm, throughout the five workshops. I wanted the students to have full control over how they perceived and improvised rhythms. By having a dedicated workshop on this topic, I could scaffold and guide their thinking, if needed, which would evolve in the weeks to come.

Our first task was for students to make their own beat by exploring how they could create new sounds on their stringed instruments (beyond traditional bowing or plucking). I made the obvious comment, in a joking manner, that harming their instruments was possibly not the greatest of ideas and asked them to be mindful when exploring. Our youngest student Nina, age 7, had difficulty controlling her explorations and hit her violin on the music stand.

I asked students later about their experience in this workshop. Nina reported that she remembered this workshop as the time she "hit [her] violin on the stand." And then there was a very long pause. Nina smiled after she said this, her eyes peering over her glasses at me—grinning with a closed mouth. I have observed how Nina was often reprimanded by adults and students, in and out of class, for her overly curious behavior. This long pause, I imagined, was Nina waiting for me to say something about her actions. That didn't happen though, which is why there was a long pause. I am certain I must have smiled back at her before asking, "Are there any other ones you did?" On the other hand, Mike, our oldest student, shared, "Well, I was taught not to hit the instrument. Nah, like, make a beat on the instrument. I thought, where do I make a beat where I won't hurt it?"

I tried not to show hesitation when presenting this activity, as it was important to allow the students to create without a list of limitations, only possibilities. I wanted them to know I trusted them in how they would make these discoveries, and that I would be there to guide them if they needed help. The students began with just simple quiet tinkering, and I remember walking around the room, trying to create a more informal experience where there would be no wrong or right answer.

Sara: I was trying to make sounds around the bridge and see how that sounds.
Breanne: I tapped on my instrument... like with my bow on the curved side.

For some students, this was easily achieved:

Chris: I'm always banging on stuff, and I like that in that activity, I could do that freely.
Regina: I felt comfortable about it. I liked how we did it with each section and not a random thing for each person so it was more controlled and organized.

For others, the support of their peers helped them to create in the environment.

Tessa: I heard and I saw people playing on the backs on their instruments, so I drew that and I also drew like the noise of how loud or how soft rhythm is.

Jonathan: We just tapped our instruments and made like a different rhythm out of everyone else.

Students now had an opportunity to use their new playing technique to the various rhythmic components of a traditional Haitian Kompa percussion section. Everyone learned the basic rhythm assigned to the conga, bell, and drum rhythms, and then we proceeded to divide the class in half, one half playing either their own rhythms or the Konpa rhythms, while the other half created a visual representation through drawing. Reviewing these drawings during that workshop was surprising to me because all the students drew a similar image with very few variations. They were drawing the beat, as how many would observe a heartbeat appearing on an electrocardiogram (ECG). Nina's and Ann's drawings from Workshop 2 are shown in Figures 6.1–6.2.

When we learned the next section of the grade 2 piece, I had the students take two minutes to learn the notes in the next passage with their stand partner. I observed so I could learn how students worked together, and to gauge who needed extra support. We continued with the theme of rhythms by practicing how to chant them. I chose the *ta, ti-ti* syllabic system simply because students shared that it was the most familiar to them. Each section took a turn chanting as the rest of the orchestra supported them by keeping a steady pulse. Then we began layering each of their passages using pizzicato, as the other sections chanted their rhythms. This

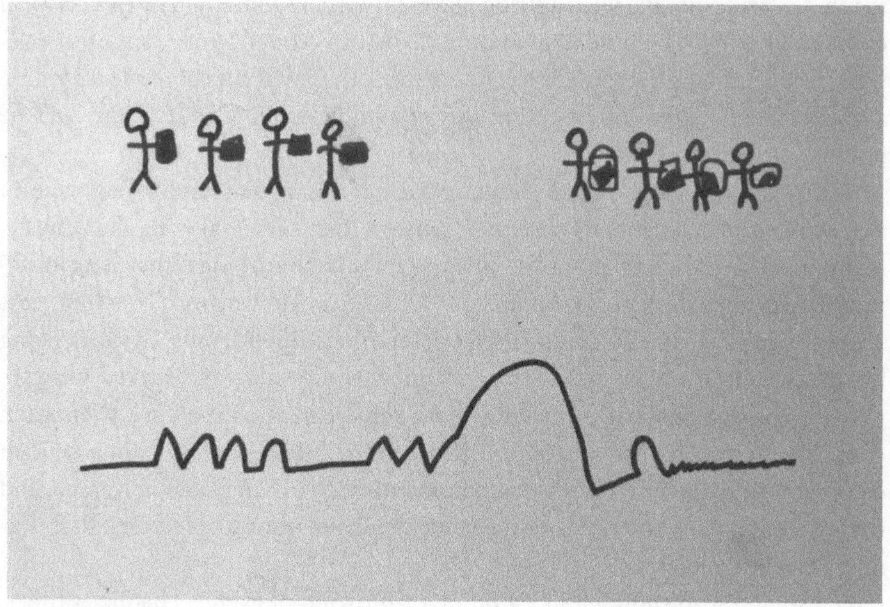

Figure 6.1 Nina's Drawing, Workshop 2, "It Sounded Like a Festival!"

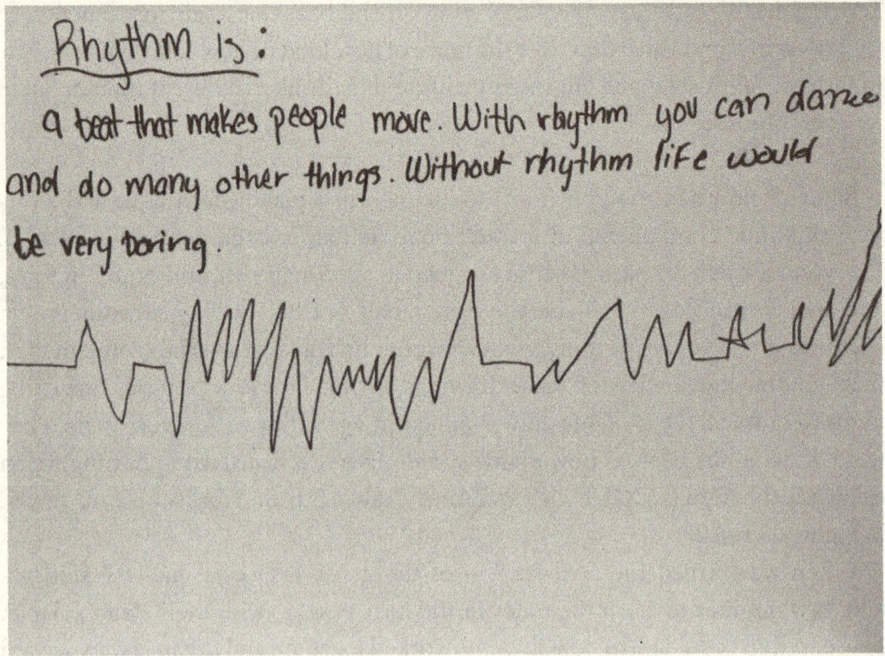

Figure 6.2 Ann's Drawing, Workshop 2.

scaffolding gave multiple opportunities for the students to practice their rhythms, while also understanding how they connected, related, or unified with their own part.

Looking back on my personal reflection of this workshop, I sense this session left the students questioning what a string player is typically allowed to do in a classical orchestral setting. The hesitation and re-asking of "What do you want us to do?" when first beginning the sound exploration made the environment feel tense for me as the teacher. This tension heightened when a student shouted out, "Why can't we just play our instruments?"

At this point, students began shouting back to this student and telling them to stop. I asked the students to raise their hands if they were enjoying the activity; many, if not all, raised their hands. This was followed by asking if they felt embarrassed. Almost all the hands went up. Finally, I asked, "How many of you think this is making music?" The students were hesitant to raise their hands. By challenging the manner in which we play string instruments the students believed we were possibly not making music, which was not a response I was expecting. Even when doing the Kompa rhythms I realized that coming into a predominantly Haitian community did not mean they would know and enjoy playing Haitian Kompa, and having sensitivity to the needs of the students was more valuable to me than fulfilling my own interests.

The second workshop felt like a bit of a whirlwind of events, chaotic at times, but I have some of my favorite memories from this workshop because the students began to have a sense for taking musical risks in the class. From the post-interviews they all said it was "fun," "cool." One student said, "I felt good. I felt it, like, it was part of how music was supposed to be.

Yank'l: So, what did you think of the class that day?
Mike: Okay... it comes together [...] it was fun creating our own music, it was like, as I say "out of the line" of musically, like, having fun with music instead of being professional with it. It was a really good idea to make a beat off of it.

Listening to Oneself and Others

By our third workshop, the students knew to sit around the table together to learn the session's topic. The activities in the third workshop would include beginning and ending with the creative arts project and dedicating the bulk of the class to rehearsing the canon section of the grade 2 piece. At the start of the class, many students looked excited and smiled at the sight of colorful tissue paper layered around the table, appearing to wonder what we were going to create. We reviewed the topics from our previous weeks: melody and rhythm. Students selected a color that would represent how they saw the melody, and a color to represent the rhythm. During this workshop the students constructed a tissue paper collage where they united both melody and rhythm to represent the piece as a whole. This collage would be revisited once more at the end of the session when I asked the students to reflect what different parts of themselves make them as a musician. Robert's colorful collage for Workshop 3 can be viewed online (use QR code in Figure 6.3).

Unlike our other expressive arts activities, in this one, the students were completely quiet, if not whispering; focused on the task at hand. Most verbalizations came from students commenting on each other's work or helping each other to pass the needed supplies. I believe the subdued energy happened simply because of the focus required to complete the activity. The students needed to plan where to place the tissue paper in order to bleed onto the main paper underneath and attend to the amount of water brushed over the tissue paper to achieve the color bleeding.

One student, Liam, worked very quickly and grabbed all the green and blue paper near him before the start of the activity. He proceeded to pile layer after layer, and then brushed water on top of the tissue paper. Liam continued this process, and as I watched him, scrunching my face in uncertainty, he pulled away the tissue paper to reveal that no color had transferred onto his main paper. Liam complained about this, saying how "it didn't work right," and how he probably "didn't use enough water." He then continued by placing two sheets of full tissue paper over the entire paper and poured water from the cup all around. It was really messy at this point, and the sounds of shrills of discomfort, scattered laughter, and shouts of his name filled the air.

Figure 6.3 QR Code for Robert's Collage, Workshop 3.

Liam greeted his onlookers with a shrug and a simple pleading "what?"

Tessa, who had been sitting right next to Liam when it happened, did not mention his name in the post-interview, but said, "Yeah, so like, when people were spilling water on the table, I didn't really like that." I remember Liam sharing how much he disliked his image because of how much color had taken over the page (see Figure 6.4 for a QR code linking to this artwork). To me, the intensity of the green and blue was very much like Liam himself—bold, curious to do things his own way. When I shared this with him, he was reluctant to agree, but smiled. I hoped he understood in his own way that I was complimenting him for his bravery.

As the students completed the first half of the project, we set off to rehearse the passage in the piece that contained the melody as a canon. In prior weeks we had learned the melody to the point of it becoming an earworm, and we had worked to learn how to chant rhythms as an orchestra. And so, this rehearsal was spent on understanding the role of the canon and how to weave a conversation between upper and lower strings. To help the students learn how the melody was being echoed, I asked the orchestra to play only when they saw moving eighth notes. This turned into a fun game for everyone and was repeated several times due to the overwhelming requests. One this interplay was understood, we shifted to brainstorming about how to add their original rhythms using the percussion techniques learned in the prior week. I asked the students to create a rhythm that we would insert as what I knew as a descarda, or an improvised jam session.

Teamwork and collaboration did not come easily to the instrument sections. This was particularly the case for the cello section, which needed more of my support to learn how to compromise and show patience toward one another. One student wanted everyone to agree to his rhythm loop and rejected all the other choices because he was the "section leader." The two other cellists tried to get him to listen, and instead he just played his pattern when it was someone else's turn to share. When each section presented their rhythm, the cellos were still not quite on the same page, and presented two different rhythms, the one the two students worked on together, and the one that the section leader had selected. This discord in the cello section continued in future sessions.

Figure 6.4 QR Code for Liam's Artwork, Workshop 3.

At the last half of the workshop, we turned our attention once more to the artwork, which was now dry and ready for us to write onto it. The students were asked to free write their responses to the following question: "What are the different parts of you that make you a musician?"

Nina: I wrote, "I am a [violinist]," and "I am awesome," and "I am the dreamer who wishes to play better," and "my goal is to have better sounding and better [position]" (see Figure 6.5 for a QR code to view this collage online).

Yank'l: What are some things you enjoyed about this activity?

Nina: I enjoyed talking about myself. About me as a musician.

Jonathan: Well, I like to play violin, play in my free time because, like, it helps me stay calm and focused when I'm trying to do something (see Figure 6.6 to view this collage online).

Have you ever thought about the different parts that make you a musician?

Jonathan: No. I've never thought about that. But it was fun, and it was exciting to just jot down my thoughts about myself.

In this activity, 13 out of 15 students shared something positive; two did not write a response, saying they did not know what to write; and out of the 15, only one student noted something negative about themselves by writing they were "a lazy player," which was followed by, "I am a Good player." For this beginner group, made up predominantly of teens, I was surprised at the number of positive associations to their identity as a musician. It was welcoming to hear as I reread their responses.

Remembering my own experiences playing in orchestra as a teen, I was extremely self-conscious about how I played. I never wanted to warm-up before orchestra, feeling a great amount of fear of what someone would say about my playing. I often sat in the first stand, but this never made me feel like a confident player growing up. As an adult, I feel that if I had had more experiences that made me feel comfortable about making mistakes and having fun playing, I would have better self-esteem as a violist. Given this same assignment as a teen, my response in describing myself as a musician would have included words like, "okay violist," or "hard-working," or "shy." In asking this question, I was not aiming for any particular answer, and my

Figure 6.5 QR Code for Nina's Collage, Workshop 3.

Figure 6.6 QR Code for Jonathan's Collage, Workshop 3.

intent was to learn more about how these students perceived themselves. Reading all the positivity in these drawings was great because, to me, their positive relationship to their musicianship was something to celebrate.

A "Dischord" among Fellow Cello-Mates—Or an Opportunity for Connection?

Musical goals were the topic of the fourth workshop. We took some time to reflect on what we had accomplished in our time together, and I mentioned that the following week would be one of closure, as it would be our last meeting. Many students shared their sadness, and that they had enjoyed coming to orchestra each week because of the activities. I started the workshop by asking the students to write one goal and to create an image to accompany that goal. QR codes to view Breanne's and Jonathan's painting for Workshop 4 are shown in Figures 6.7 and 6.8, respectively.

Chris: Have a better understanding of the certain rhythms I could create and stuff and kinda expressing myself in that sort of way.

Robert: I never really set a musical goal in an orchestra environment. It's kinda always been one-on-one like I'm going to finish this book and then move on to the next one.

Figure 6.7 QR Code for Breanne's Painting, Workshop 4.

Figure 6.8 QR Code for Jonathan's Painting, Workshop 4.

In this workshop, we needed to decide where in the music to add our improvised rhythms. I asked students to turn to their neighbors and share their ideas. This part of the class turned out to be completely chaotic to me, which was something I did not anticipate. Students screamed back and forth across the room, sharing what they thought, arguing, and challenging others' ideas. There was no structure to the talking. I did redirect comments that seemed to alter the environment to one of negativity. As I stood in the front of the class, I panicked, not knowing how to stop what seemed, to me, like an out-of-control classroom. I remember raising my hand without speaking—waiting—before some students began quieting each other and saying to stop. We took a moment to learn how to listen and when I suggested that we play through each of the suggestions instead, students agreed. At the end we took a vote and talked about what we liked and disliked about each possibility.

Regina: Well . . . some people wanted to do it at the beginning, some people in the middle more so, and skip some of the parts of the middle, or at the end. I thought it would go best at the end. That way we don't skip anything from the original piece and we can add our little something to it.

Chris: I liked it, but some other people in the orchestra didn't. In the cello section there were a few people who said they didn't like the rhythm. There was someone in the violin section that wanted to take it out completely. I didn't even want to move it, I liked where it was. I was on the opposing side.

Finding a place for the rhythms was meant to be an opportunity to have the students have ownership over their rhythmic composition. It truly became an argument among many students. What was amazing was how the students never asked for my help in swaying a student or providing my opinion; they worked hard together to solve it. Only one student in the post-interview used the word "arguing" to describe that day. Yet for this student, seemed normal to communicate in such a manner, as the activity allowed them a chance to debate and each offer their voice:

Ann: I think it was nice that everyone was kinda arguing about where to put it. It shows that they really care about where they want it to be.

In contrast, as Paul described, in orchestra they were simply taught to sit there and wait their turn to play.

Paul: Well, usually the orchestra director tells us to play this song, and then yells at us if we do something wrong, or just works with one section the entire time, and then after that, work on everyone else the next week, so when we get to the performance it doesn't even sound good.

As students, it seemed that previously that they had never been asked to give their opinion or decide on anything pertaining to how they engaged in music in the orchestra:

Jonathan: Well, it's usually [what] the teacher says.
Regina: Yeah, in my past experiences in orchestra it has always been [the] conductor [that] chose what to do, when to do with the music, so it was different that you let us choose that.

Students shared how in contrast to their past orchestra experiences, these workshops had caused them to view the time they spent making music together more like that of spending time with family.

Chris: Yes, because we did a lot of group work and in the other orchestra we don't get to do that. 'Cause, it really felt like a family.
Robert: I definitely felt that I had more opportunities to work with my fellow cello mates than I did with any other teacher I've ever had.

Based on these student responses, maybe this is how making decisions felt comfortable to them, and I was being sensitive to how I believed a discussion should look and sound like. The students were certainly engaged with the music, and with one another.

Orchestrating a New Music Community

On the last day of the workshops, I could not wait to see the students, share our last class together, and have the opportunity to record the piece. I intended for the workshop to be a day for the students to reflect on what they learned and enjoyed, as well as what they would like to share with other teachers if they were to do something similar in their orchestra class. For this workshop, students free-wrote around a picture of their faces while adding different thoughts they had about the workshop. I want to honor the students' privacy, and for that reason, I have not shared pictures from that week. Instead, I want to share an art-based representation of the data with a picture of myself instead to represent this last workshop (see Figure 6.9; Figure 6.10 contains a QR code for the color version online).

Yank'l: Well, what was your favorite part about the workshops?

Breanne: I liked how all of these activities corresponded with [the grade 2 piece], and I liked the art part, and being able to release your creativity.

Paul: I kinda took away thinking of how to mix art with music together since I also make paintings too.

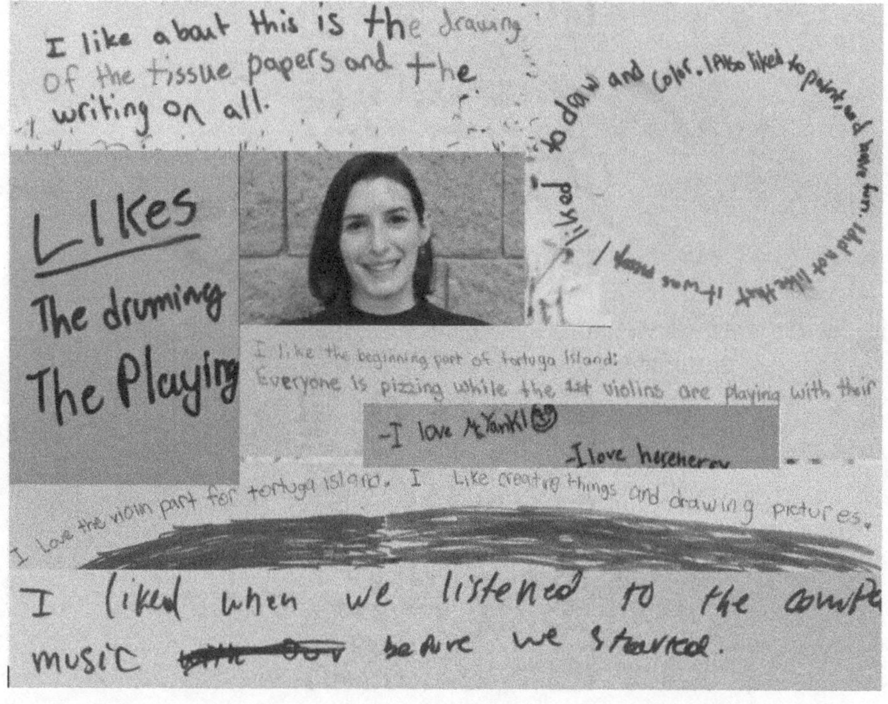

Figure 6.9 Yank'l's Art-Based Representation of the Final Workshop (b/w version).

Regina: I've been saying it a lot, but I'm better with rhythms now. How to distinguish them from different parts in the music.

Robert: I thought it was something really new cause I've never had a teacher, or an orchestra group leader, to come up with that idea of expressing yourself through music like that.

Yank'l: What would you tell teachers doing this in their orchestra class?

Ann: To think about what music is to them, and like, different definitions of music.

Robert: I'd probably say umm . . . just help them have fun with it. You know, try not to limit them [the students] too much. Try not to keep the kids off to a corner or anything like that, let them go wild, go free.

Regina: I think I'd be a positive thing to mix different types of activities in the orchestra class.

Just like that, the end of the day came quickly, as if time sped up. My shared experiences with the students in this last session seemed shortened, and limited. As I think back to the last day, I remember snapshots. Smiling, laughter, pouting faces, high-fives, thank-yous, and of course hugs—lots and lots of hugs.

Rather than the reader continuing to read my thoughts to finalize this section, it would only be fitting to insert this quotation from our bass player to conclude our workshop reading journey.

Figure 6.10 QR Code for Yank'l's Representation in Color.

Figure 6.11 QR Code for Mike's Painting, Workshop 4.

Yank'l: What was your favorite part about the whole experience?

Mike: Oh, it's coming in last. 'Cause the rhythm . . . when I play in music, I mean, when I play in orchestra, I usually follow where I come in, like in one sound. I don't count 1, 2, 3, 4. 'Cause you do that thing [cueing in conducting] where the cello goes first, then the viola, then violin first, violin [second]. Then I come last . . . now it's my turn . . . E! (see Mike's painting online using the QR code in Figure 6.11).

Reflections on Teaching (from the Perspective of Yank'l, Tawnya, and Karin)

As we reflect on the extent to which an expressive arts approach was helpful for creating an environment that supported the social and emotional health of learners, we can say that it allowed Yank'l to make the orchestra learning environment more student-centered and student-led. Because Yank'l most often played the role of facilitator, she created a space where the students could reflect beyond the notes and the demands of a conductor. She asked the students to think critically about how they perceived music, their role in the orchestra, and their own individual identity as a musician. The expressive arts therapy activities helped students to freely explore their creativity and convey their thinking. (See Reflection Activity 6.2.)

Finally, the ways in which Yank'l connected with the students and saw the dignity and possibility in each of them demonstrated her care *for*, *about*, and *with* them as fellow music-makers and co-learners. She also showed care *through* music and expressive arts, and modeled care for melody, rhythm, and for others in the classroom. In reflection, we celebrate all that Yank'l did to facilitate a place of belonging for and with her students, while considering below what she might further do in the future to foster an even greater sense of culturally responsive care. The rest of this chapter revisits Yank'l's workshops from that perspective.

Culturally Responsive Caring

Culturally responsive teaching is becoming a more popular topic in music education.[18] Part of implementing culturally responsive approaches in our teaching includes transforming outdated teaching practices that may be less relevant to today's learners and replacing them with approaches that are more meaningful and relevant to students' lives, identities, and the communities in which they live. Yank'l wished to integrate her knowledge as a therapist and educator to integrate an expressive arts curriculum in an orchestra class. She tested out her curriculum in an after-school program that served first and second-generation Haitian immigrant students from a low socioeconomic background. As she did so, she recognized that the traditional orchestra rehearsal method she had learned might not fully align with the aims of a culturally responsive approach with the students in her care. She believed that principles from her music therapy background might allow her to engage in a culturally responsive caring informed curriculum and teaching practice.

According to Geneva Gay, author of *Culturally Responsive Teaching*, teachers who embody culturally responsive caring hold high expectations, relate genuinely with their students, and are relentless in facilitating positive learning experiences.[19] Gay also noted the difference between *caring about* and *caring for* the needs of ethnically diverse students, stressing the importance of attending to the psychoemotional wellbeing of learners. Yank'l sought to integrate expressive arts principles to her orchestra teaching which, in her previous experience as a therapist, had been beneficial in promoting the psychoemotional wellbeing of her clients.

To study the transformation of her teaching practice, we applied Geneva Gay's attributes of caring as criteria for teacher self-reflection. These attributes are as follows:

1. *Caring is attending to person and performance* is exemplified by teachers who hold positive beliefs about their students' potential and demonstrate concern beyond academic progress. These teachers also care for student's "emotional, physical, economic, and interpersonal conditions"[20] to create a consistently caring environment.
2. *Caring is action-provoking* is demonstrated by teachers who act on the concerns listed above, to take concrete actions that afford students opportunities for empowerment. These teachers speak and act in ways that legitimize student voice and make them visible both in and outside of the classroom. Such teachers convey respect and individual concern for students through listening and acknowledging them, offering them choices, and taking efforts to make content relevant to all students.
3. *Caring prompts effort and achievement* is shown by teachers who hold students to very high expectations while simultaneously engaging in "emotionally warm, personally caring, and interpersonally supportive instructional styles."[21]
4. *Caring is multidimensional responsiveness* acknowledges that culturally responsive educators have sufficient cultural competence to be responsive to learners in context.[22] (See Reflection Activity 6.3.)

We chose to reflect on these four attributes in Yank'l's teaching experiment as a way for all three of us to consider how we might transform and interrupt traditional practices and habits in our own teaching that may not be culturally caring teaching practice. There is some evidence, as mentioned above, that the expressive arts approach created a place and medium for students to express cultural values and individual identity. However, after further reflection, the framework has helped to identify additional ways that a more culturally responsive classroom could be fostered.

Ideas for Growth (from Yank'l's Perspective)

Although my intentions were good, I erred in terms of piece selection. I made a huge assumption that coming into a Haitian community that I would be culturally responsive by performing a grade 2 piece that had a title I thought the students would resonate with. This issue alone could span the bulk of this chapter, honestly. This piece of music was not written by a Haitian composer, but by a Caucasian male whose inspiration came from historical reference to pirates in the 17th century. I was not celebrating the Haitian culture in this way, which was my intent. I must honestly admit this was a poor choice in regard to culturally responsive teaching.

I made one more assumption in regard to my planning, which was having Kompa music as a means to bridge and introduce rhythms and rhythm exploration. The students were not Kompa listeners—their parents were—and it was odd to them that I would share this music when it was something they associated with the adults in their lives not in their own music listening. After this discovery, I changed the "jam session" to include only original rhythms to loop for the final piece.

As a music therapist and educator, care is at the forefront of my teaching. Gay's first attribute of care, *caring is concern with person and performance*, is strongly evident. Being an active observer and listener, I know that I learn best about my students from my students. As a group, we learned about listening to others, being patient, how to compromise, working together, being confident and brave, and leading your section from every seat in the orchestra. Students were constantly reminded about trying their best, and how if they did not understand, that they had each other for help.

Gay's second attribute, *care is action-provoking*, was evident when I had students take ownership over their original rhythm loops, and supported them when they wanted to express them percussively on their instrument. They also collaborated on the placement of their jam session within the music. Students felt comfortable to come into our space and talk before our workshops began, and I always wanted to know something about their week so I could check in about how they were doing. Also, I did my best, given my previous mistakes on repertoire, to make the content relevant after adapting to student responses.

Caring prompts effort and achievement is the area I could have more fully embraced in my teaching. When arguments arose, my role as an educator attempting to implement culturally responsive teaching needed to include not just empathy but also clear responses from me in a manner that required accountability to arise from the students. Our united goal was to complete the full piece, add the rhythmic section, and have an expressive arts experience in a total of 10 hours. This in itself shows how high my expectations for achievement were for these students. Going into this study, the students were aware that we had only five weeks to learn, rehearse, and polish this piece for a recording. Students knew they were expected to practice on a regular basis and be ready for each rehearsal. It is with this understanding that our last caring attribute comes into play—*caring is multidimensional responsiveness.*

Throughout this entire experience (planning the workshops, engaging the students, looking back at the artwork, and listening to the interviews), Gay's fourth attribute of caring is the one I feel I am walking away with, as resonating the most deeply, for a number of reasons. I learned so much from the students about their home lives, how they came to join this community music program, and how the program as a whole was a larger family unit. These students came together each week not because they all went to the same school, but because they were all part of the surrounding community, and many students expressed how critical the larger Sunday music program was to their lives.

Being the best teacher I could be for these students required multidimensional understandings. It is not enough for me to come in for five weeks, assuming anything about students before taking time to listen and learn. Only after getting to know their students can a teacher can begin to shape, form, and co-create an appropriate curriculum and experience with their class. During those five weeks, students in turn questioned how orchestral music can be multidimensional, how diversity exists (or doesn't) within the orchestral world, and how their individual role was valuable in the orchestra's collective musical effort.

What I Will Do in the Future

When applying the expressive arts through the lens of the attributes of caring, I would build my curriculum beginning from a place of learning. For me, I learned that this process should have begun with the fourth attribute of culturally responsive caring: understanding the multidimensionality of your students, their families, and the community at large. This would then, in turn, provide information to create a meaningful learning space that translates to cultural competence and responsiveness to the learners. Shaping the expressive arts into this space would then encourage the learner to further learn and explore about themselves through a medium that is unrestrictive and personal, and can transform into a valuable process for the students to engage in critical thinking. The role of the teacher as facilitator allows modeling of personal values through creative arts endeavors, while holding students to a high expectation that enables accountability and empowers students' voices.

I look forward to future explorations, learning how an expressive arts classroom using culturally responsive teaching could function as a year-round curriculum rather than a short five-week project. I want to learn more about how the expressive arts and a culturally responsive teaching classroom can affect the socioemotional growth of students. I wonder: How does participating in such a classroom transfer to other areas of a students' day-to-day life?

Finally, I hope to continue to learn how other educators are breaking the mold of the traditional orchestra classroom to include the expressive arts. I wonder how adding the expressive arts to an orchestra classroom could change the focus from teacher centered to student centered, in a way that better fits the needs of the ever-transforming learner. Learning and pedagogical transformation will be a journey throughout my career, one that I'm excited to take.

Conclusion

This chapter is a case study of music teacher/therapist Yank'l Garcia, who tested out a project in which she integrated expressive arts approaches in a community orchestra program. An expressive arts approach was helpful for creating an environment that supported the social and emotional health of learners, and it appears to have made the orchestra learning environment more student-centered and student-led. Because Yank'l most often played the role of facilitator, she created a space where the students could come together more as a "family" and offer their own ideas for expression beyond what might have been afforded through a more traditional conductor-led approach. Students engaged in expressive arts activities to reflect more deeply about their own musicianship, the music they played, and their musical identity. The expressive arts therapy activities also helped students explore multiple avenues for creativity and convey their thinking about their music learning.

Finally, expressive arts approaches afforded ways in which Yank'l could care *for*, *about*, and *with* the students. It helped her to see the dignity and possibility in each student as a fellow music-maker and co-learner. She also showed care *through* music and expressive arts, and modeled care for melody, rhythm, and other learners in the classroom. In reflection, Yank'l recognized her success in facilitating a place of belonging for and with her students, while also considering what she might do to foster an even greater sense of culturally responsive care in the future. In the next chapter, I draw on additional ideas from OHCME authors to envision identity-responsive and identity-affirming approaches to care in music education.

Reflection Activities

6.1. What feedback have you received from your own students that was difficult to hear? How did your acceptance of this feedback change the way you teach?

6.2. With your own students, try out some of the expressive arts integration activities described in this chapter. How do students respond? What changes? Note: Because expressive arts activities may be new to your students (especially in more traditional or teacher-directed music education settings), you may find that it takes a time or two for students to feel ready to take expressive risks. We invite you to practice patience, curiosity, and creating a no-pressure, nonjudgmental space.

6.3. Which of Geneva Gay's principles of culturally responsive caring (caring is attending to person and performance, caring is action-provoking, caring prompts effort and achievement, caring is multidimensional responsiveness) resonates most with you? Which principle is something you can improve in your own teaching?

Notes

1. Yank'l Garcia received a research grant for this project through the Boston University Arts Initiative and invited BU faculty member Tawnya Smith to advise her project. Tawnya was not involved with any teaching or pedagogical decisions but assisted Yank'l in the expressive arts data collection, post-teaching reflection using the principles of culturally responsive caring, and with writing her reflections in the chapter. This study was cleared through the Boston University Institutional Review Board. All student names are pseudonyms.
2. Elizabeth Mitchell, "Music's Relational Imperative: Wellbeing, Music-Making, and the Interconnections between Music Therapy and Music Education," in *The Oxford Handbook of Care in Music Education*, ed. Karin S. Hendricks (New York: Oxford University Press, 2023), 361–372.
3. Mitchell, "Music's Relational Imperative," 364.
4. Mitchell, "Music's Relational Imperative," 365.
5. Tawnya D. Smith, "Building a Bridge between the Improvisational Expressive Arts and Music Education," in *Applied Arts and Health: Building Bridges across Arts, Therapy, Health, Education, and Community*, ed. Ross W. Prior, Mitchell Kossak, and Teresa A. Fisher (Chicago: University of Chicago Press, 2022), 119–132.
6. Mitchell, "Music's Relational Imperative," 366.
7. Michael H. Thaut and Barbara L. Wheeler, "Music Therapy," in *Handbook of Music and Emotion: Theory, Research, Applications*, ed. Patrick Juslin and John Sloboda, Series in Affective Science (Oxford: Oxford University Press, 2010), 819–848.
8. Barbara L. Wheeler, ed., *Music Therapy Handbook* (New York: Guilford Publications, 2015).
9. Karin S. Hendricks, Tawnya D. Smith, and Jennifer Stanuch, "Creating Safe Spaces for Music Learning," *Music Educators Journal* 101, no. 1 (2014): 35–40.
10. Manu Sharma, "Seeping Deficit Thinking Assumptions Maintain the Neoliberal Education Agenda: Exploring Three Conceptual Frameworks of Deficit Thinking in Inner-City Schools," *Education and Urban Society* 50, no. 2 (2018): 136–154.
11. Elizabeth Mitchell, "Therapeutic Music Education: An Emerging Model Linking Philosophies and Experiences of Music Education with Music Therapy," *Canadian Journal of Music Therapy* 22, no. 1 (2016): 19–41; Mitchell, "Music's Relational Imperative"; James Robertson, "An Educational Model for Music Therapy: The Case for a Continuum," *British Journal of Music Therapy (London, England: 1995)* 14, no. 1 (2000): 41–46.
12. Mitchell, "Therapeutic Music Education," 20.
13. Mitchell, "Therapeutic Music Education," 37.
14. Susan Craig, *Reaching and Teaching Children Who Hurt: Strategies for Your Classroom* (Baltimore: Paul H. Brookes Publishing Co., 2008); Susan Craig, *Trauma-Sensitive Schools: Learning Communities Transforming Children's Lives K-5* (New York: Teacher's College Press, 2016); Patricia A. Jennings, *The Trauma-Sensitive Classroom: Building Resilience with Compassionate Teaching* (New York: W. W. Norton & Company Inc., 2019); Barbara Sorrels, *Reaching and Teaching Children Exposed to Trauma* (Boston: Gryphon House, 2015).
15. Patricia A. Jennings, *Mindfulness for Teachers: Simple Skills for Peace and Productivity in the Classroom* (New York: W. W. Norton & Company Inc., 2015); Frank M. Diaz, "Mindfulness, Attention, and Flow during Music Listening: An Empirical Investigation," *Psychology of Music* 41, no. 1 (2013): 42–58; Frank M. Diaz, "Relationships among Meditation, Perfectionism, Mindfulness, and Performance Anxiety among Collegiate Music Students," *Journal of Research in Music Education* 66, no. 2 (2018): 150–167; Daniel Rechtschaffen, *The Way of Mindful Education: Cultivating Well-Being in Teachers and Students* (New York: WW Norton & Company, 2014).
16. Karin S. Hendricks, *Compassionate Music Teaching: A Framework for Motivation and Engagement in the 21st Century* (Lanham, MD: Rowman & Littlefield, 2018); Katrina McFerran, Derrington Philippa, and Saarikallio Suvi, *Handbook of Music, Adolescents, and Wellbeing*, 1st ed. (Oxford: Oxford University Press, 2019).

17. Geneva Gay, *Culturally Responsive Teaching* (New York: Teachers College Press, 2020).
18. Gay, *Culturally Responsive Teaching*; Constance L. McKoy and Vicki R. Lind, *Culturally Responsive Teaching in Music Education: From Understanding to Application* (New York: Routledge, 2023).
19. Gay, *Culturally Responsive Teaching.*
20. Gay, *Culturally Responsive Teaching*, 53.
21. Gay, *Culturally Responsive Teaching*, 57
22. Gay, *Culturally Responsive Teaching.*

7

Identity-Responsive and Identity-Affirming Pedagogies

Chapter Overview

In addition to experiencing safety from harm, music students need a space where they can be who they are, without a need to change or conform to fit with anyone else's expectations of rightness. Brave spaces of belonging in music education are those in which co-learners are free to fully express their unique identities. Although it may be impossible for music teachers to create a perfectly brave space for students, they can help students envision their own expressive possibilities by exercising an awareness of, and responsiveness to, student identities. This chapter considers various topics related to identity-responsive (caring-*for*) and identity-affirming (caring-*with*) pedagogies. Topics include intersectionality and holistic acceptance; co-creating the learning space; "living alongside cringe" and learning from mistakes through compassionate self-reflection; creating brave spaces of belonging and radical welcome; fostering a culture rich in microaffirmations; practicing microinterventions; cultural responsiveness (broadly defined); evaluating our own identities, assumptions, and practices; caring through unconditional love; and exercising wonder, curiosity, improvisation, and accompaniment.

Introduction

Think, for a moment, about someone in your life whom you know very well, and whom you love deeply: Perhaps a child, a spouse, a sibling, a forever friend—whoever comes to mind for you. What is it that you love about this person? Likely it is a blend of many things, ranging from their sense of humor to their adorable smile, the cute way their eyebrows curl when they concentrate, their endless creativity, perhaps their exquisite listening skills. I imagine that this person causes an electric lift inside of you when you hear their voice, when they walk in the room, or when you see a text notification with their name on it. Perhaps you are so connected that you think of them or sense their presence even *before* they walk in the room or text you.

Daring to Care with Music Education. Karin S. Hendricks, Oxford University Press. © Oxford University Press 2025.
DOI: 10.1093/9780197777589.003.0007

How did this relationship form? I assume that it developed over time, and as you got to know this person more and more, you began to love more things about them. Of course, no human is perfect, so there are likely things about this person that also drive you up the wall (we don't need to recall those things here). Yet despite those imperfections, you can see their holistic self, their multifaceted nature, their intersectional layers of identity—all their complexity and wholeness—and that makes them beautiful to you.

Each music learner also has a complex and colorful array of identity characteristics, woven together to construct the person they are. Some aspects of their identities are very visible to us, whereas there are other parts of them that we may never know. It is impossible to know every aspect of the students we teach, no matter how much time we may spend with them in school or lessons, in extracurricular activities, day after day and year after year. Furthermore, no matter the age or ability level of a student, aspects of their personal identity—the way they define themselves as people and navigate within their world[1]—are constantly evolving, as is the case with every human.

Add to this conundrum the constantly evolving state of musical identities and expressions in contemporary society. With nearly ubiquitous access to virtually any kind of music through streaming services (combined with the ever-increasing ease of music creation and production), people from all walks of life—from do-it-yourself musicians to Grammy-winning artists—are stretching and expanding across genres to create eclectic, innovative, and multidimensional musical expressions.[2] As music education researcher Anand Sukumaran writes in a study of multidimensional and multi-musical identities:

> The ways people pursue knowledge, make social sense of their worlds, and connect with others are less bound by geography, culture or localized identity than in past times. The constant access to distributed, multi-located sources of knowledge acquisition has become a key feature in global youth culture and has many implications for how young people construct their musical identities.[3]

This is the pluralistic musical world in which we live—where genres, styles, and cultures overlap, and where we and our students can access, enjoy, and create nearly any eclectic musical mix in a way that expresses our unique identities.[4]

Our personal identities shape and are shaped by our musical identities—which, in turn, shape and are shaped by the multidimensional music with which we engage.[5] Music, identity, and wellbeing are interrelated; music-making that aligns with our identity can enhance connections to self and to others.[6] It is critical for students' (and our own) sense of wellbeing and authentic connection that we honor the broad array of identities in music learning spaces.

What an exciting technicolor era in which to learn and teach music, when students' music playlists, interests, and skill sets are as multiplicitous and dynamic as are their own human identities. It is simultaneously thrilling and daunting to think about negotiating all these various and unique music learners, with all their various and unique identity characteristics, with all their various and unique musical goals, interests, dreams, and so forth—which, then again, we may never fully get to know due to their continual evolution, coupled with our limits in space and time. Yet from a lens of care, it is our business to connect with these identities because they are the very stuff from which learners form their interests, their motivations, their musical expression—virtually everything that matters in caring-*with* musical relationships. How do we navigate this tension? I'm grateful for the contributors to the *Oxford Handbook of Care in Music Education* (OHCME), who have inspired several ideas.

I propose that music educators might conceptualize *identity-responsive pedagogy* as a form of caring *for* students, and *identity affirming pedagogy* as a form of caring *with* co-learners. Through these lenses, teachers look not just at one aspect of a student (such as culture), but they embrace and offer care for, about, and with students' full and complex selves. Both approaches factor in students' culture, background, musical tastes, personality, dispositions, skills, and so forth—all the things that make up their identity. Identity-responsive pedagogy provides space for teachers to assess students' needs and care for their learning through a holistic lens, with awareness of students' many intersectional identities. Identity-affirming pedagogy opens the lens further to how we might support and sustain music learners through a continual, iterative process of identity transformation. Through such caring-*with* interactions with our co-learners, it is inevitable that we, too, will be continually transformed.

In this chapter I examine several concepts related to identity-responsive and identity-affirming pedagogies, in the context of caring for and with music learners. I first address intersectionality and holistic acceptance and offer several suggestions for seeing and embracing students' dynamic and multidimensional identities. I then offer suggestions for engaging in learner-attuned and learner-affirming approaches.

Embracing Intersectional Identities

As music teachers, we have the opportunity and privilege to get to know our students deeply and meaningfully, often far more than our colleagues who teach other subjects. We forge deep and meaningful connections because of the extended amount of time we might spend together (days, months, years of instruction, plus time spent in extracurricular performances and other events). Additionally, as described in Chapter 2, we also forge bonds through the connective potential of music itself.[7] As a result, we are able to visualize what Nicole R. Robinson has described as music classrooms that are "not just spaces for imparting musical skills [but also] vibrant ecosystems where diverse identities, experiences, and perspectives converge."[8] Although it is impossible to ever know all aspects of co-learners' identities fully, we can practice an awareness of, and responsiveness to, student identities to help learners envision their own expressive potential. Specifically, we can embrace who they are as humans and musicians by practicing holistic acceptance, creating brave spaces for belonging through radical welcome, and curating spaces filled with microaffirmations.

Intersectionality and Holistic Acceptance

As noted in Chapter 3, care is only care when it is received as such.[9] OHCME author Latasha Thomas-Durrell argues further that care is only care when the one-caring accounts for, and affirms, every intersectional aspect of the cared-for: "If one does not embrace the whole picture of a person, then one is not embracing the person at all."[10] Thomas-Durrell puts care at the foundation of *intersectionality*, a term coined by Kimberlé Crenshaw in the early 1990s to illustrate the multiple intersecting experiences that a person may have, due to how all aspects of their identity characteristics (race, gender, class, ability, etc.) interweave and overlap with one another.[11] For example, understanding societal aggressions against Black women is not as simple as just adding together issues of power and privilege related to race plus gender. Instead, intersectionality invites more careful awareness of how multiple aspects of sexism intersect with multiple aspects of racial discrimination, so that oppression of Black women is recognized as much more than a sum of its parts.[12]

Continuing with the math analogy, we might view intersectional aspects of a student's identity not as addition, but as exponential algebra. Every aspect intersects with other aspects—much like a matrix[13]—yet some of these aspects may have a greater impact or weight that produces an even more profound impact (see Figure 7.1). For example, a person may have various identity aspects that influence how they engage in music learning and in life. Being Black in a predominantly White school will have numerous impacts, as will being female in a school system where feminine behavior is viewed and rewarded differently than masculine behavior. If one has a learning disability or a trauma history, these things will also impact a student's experience, but differently depending on the ways they have learned resilience or have other provisional supports to get them through difficult times.[14] Each additional layer of a person adds intersecting aspects of their identity.

I find it difficult to express the magnitude of these identity intersections as I have witnessed them in various students I have taught. My own experience has been one of tremendous privilege; I grew up with plenty of money and with parents and siblings who taught me how to advocate for what I needed—and because of the way I looked, no one questioned that advocacy. I learned to assume that I would get what I wanted when I asked for it, and I entered countless interactions with that confidence, which I am certain held sway. I have also been able to smile my way through conflict and assume that people who held powerful positions would

Figure 7.1 Hypothetical Intersectional Identity Matrix with Weighted Characteristics.

trust what I said. I have made false assumptions that others would have these same benefits, and that is not at all the case. For example, interacting with first-generation college students has helped me recognize how many social and academic strategies I learned over the course of my life that propelled me ahead of others at school—strategies I simply picked up from being at a dinner table every day with other college graduates. To use a baseball analogy, I can't truly celebrate having slid across home plate in my academic career without also recognizing that I started life on third base.[15] (See Reflection Activities 7.2 and 7.3.)

Understanding intersectionality invites holistic acceptance. Holistic acceptance in music education involves recognizing the ways in which a student's various identity characteristics intersect with one another to create a beautifully complex uniqueness. It also requires providing a kind of individualized, nonuniversal form of care that honors this intersectionality.[16] The outdated, "one size fits all" approach to musical development (see Chapter 5) certainly does not apply to intersectional care.

Holistic acceptance requires a level of care beyond recognizing and honoring a student's culture, even when broadly defined (as described later in this chapter). First, culture, although important, is only one aspect of a person's identity. Second, culture means something different to every person because of how various aspects of their identity intersect with it. Here is where caring *with* is critical, as it involves a dialogical and dynamic form of co-learning in which teachers attune to, and communicate with, learners about identity-related musical aims. Thomas-Durrell reminds us that this kind of care takes dedication, as it requires space and time "for connections to grow and flourish."[17]

Co-Creating the Learning Space

In addition to creating time and space for meaningful relationships to grow, holistic acceptance also requires music teachers to facilitate a caring-*with* co-created learning space, built on trust and empathy. Thomas-Durrell recommends four aspects for fostering such a space: (a) embracing dissent, (b) fostering critical thinking and autonomy, (c) each person getting what they need, and (d) acceptance of the whole person.[18] She cautions us against turning these four components into a simple formula—after all, holistic acceptance is the opposite of "one-size-fits-all"—but she offers these concepts as a way of envisioning the kinds of dispositions and approaches that we might foster as we strive toward holistic acceptance with the co-learners in our care.

Embracing dissent involves teachers being open to students expressing different or opposing opinions or ideas. Students may offer perspectives verbally or in other ways such as through expressions of lived experience, such as "In my experience/culture/family, we . . ."[19] Each time that a student is heard while speaking their truth, and their voice uplifted or amplified without harm being done to them, trust can build between the student and the teacher. I mention in *Compassionate Music Teaching* that, as trust grows, students may begin to "feel confident enough in their own abilities and potential so that they are willing and interested in seeing their peers succeed as well."[20]

As trust is built over time and students begin to recognize that differences of opinion and identity expressions are welcome in the space, students and teachers alike may feel more open to engage in critical thinking. Then, students and teachers may work together as co-learners to interrogate power structures (both in the classroom and in society) that oppress or marginalize some voices. Thomas-Durrell writes:

> The acceptance and centering of people who have been downtrodden can demonstrate to students that even when society has deemed one unworthy of acknowledgment, the teacher and everyone in that collective space lavishes care on those rejected people even more. This is a supreme act of care, compassion, and empathy that embraces the notion that when one rises, everyone rises.[21]

This level of care, built on trust, empowers individual voices to rise in a collective space—affording *autonomy* within a balanced power structure where students may be more invested in learning, more productive, and more open to trusting and connecting with others.[22]

Each person getting what they need is, for Thomas-Durrell, the definition of equity. It involves two things: (a) an acknowledgment of the ways in which each person has different needs and experiences, and (b) making changes to policy and practice so that these various needs can be met. It may at first seem daunting for a busy and already-overwhelmed teacher to have to consider how everyone can get what they need. However, this is where the power of a co-created learning space comes in: Teachers and students, as co-learners, can communicate and work together to determine what these provisions might be, and how to create them together.

Finally, *acceptance of the whole person* brings us back full circle to the concept of intersectionality—which, by definition, is seeing students as more than the sum of their parts. Thomas-Durrell cautions against "additive" practices to preset curricula (for example, keeping the standard songs in the published method book but throwing in some Mariachi because one happens to teach a large Hispanic population). It is not wise to presume that students will enjoy a particular kind of music or learning style because they happen to have ties to a particular culture. The previous chapter offers an example of how such an approach went awry for one teacher, who introduced Kompa music to students with Haitian backgrounds, only to realize that the students didn't relate to it. As Thomas-Durrell writes, "Picking apart the pieces of one's identity, highlighting single components, is not caring for the person as a whole."[23] Instead, we can learn to better understand how to care for, about, and with the whole person through a process of increasing trust, as we embrace dissent, make space for and uplift student voices, encourage critical thinking and autonomy, and communicate with students to co-create what they need.

A Story about Holistic Acceptance

One of the most gratifying experiences of writing a book is hearing from music teachers whom I may have never met before but who are kindred spirits. These people often entrust me with their thoughts, wonderings, hopes, and successes in practicing compassion—especially when they dare to practice the kind of slow, deep care that seems out of fashion in a "higher, better, faster, stronger" world. They also often share stories of their own musical journeys. I share one such story in Box 7a, with permission. I invite you to consider some of her intersectional experiences as you read this story, written in the teacher's own words. Please note the ways that she did, and did not, receive holistic acceptance.

"Living alongside Cringe" and Learning from Mistakes: Compassionate Self-Reflection

The story in Box 7a gives me tremendous hope. After several trials in her personal life and in band, this student-now-teacher was seen, heard, and embraced holistically. She was welcomed back to the community she left, embraced as a teenage mother, invited to play with the group, and fitted with a uniform just for her. She was given opportunities to thrive musically and socially, just as she was. She was given a second chance not only in music but in life.

At the same time, this story reminds me of the countless times that I have failed to be so compassionate with my own students. It would be easy for me to share inspirational stories like this and conveniently forget about the times I made mistakes as a teacher—to keep those mistakes to myself, thereby taking on a public persona that isn't quite accurate and doesn't demonstrate an openness to learning from trial and error. As I described in the previous chapter, one of the criticisms I've received from

Box 7a A Story of Holistic Acceptance

No one in my family experienced formal music education during their school years, but my parents took a chance on me. I began piano lessons when I was eight and began band and chorus in 6th grade. My mom worked for a school district that had a reputation as an amazing school system. We lived on the other side of that district line because it was cheaper, but I was able to attend a higher-ranked high school (RHS) due to my mom's employment with the amazing school system.

By the time I was 13 years old, I knew I wanted to be a music teacher. I wanted to share the joy and belongingness that I felt from participating in the music program. I earned first chair flute in the district honor band in 8th grade and continued earning a spot in the district honor band in 9th grade. I also began playing bassoon that year. While at the district honor band in 9th grade, I met the band kids and band director of the school that I would have attended had I gone to my home high school (HHS). They were awesome.

I also found out that the HHS band director had close ties to the Amazing University (AU). I wanted to go to AU, because it had a reputation as having a great school of music and I needed to be able to commute to the college as my parents could not afford housing on campus.

Their band director expressed interest in having me join the HHS program and said he'd even order a new bassoon that I could play. Their band program was much stronger than RHS and because of the AU connection, I made the move to HHS during my sophomore year. This is where the story starts to turn.

Close to the beginning of that school year, I started dating . . . and the guy I had started dating had a history of trauma in his childhood and I felt sorry for him. Needless to say, I overlooked a lot of unhealthy behaviors—he was narcissistic and abusive. I was just a naive 15-year-old. That summer I was checked into an institution for suicidal thoughts. I never thought I would be able to break free. The institution helped, but he still pushed for us to be together—I'm convinced that trying to break up with a narcissist is one of the hardest things to accomplish.

At the beginning of my junior year, I found out that I was pregnant. Weird to say, but the pregnancy saved me. I didn't want the child that I was carrying to be treated the way I was being treated—my eyes had finally been opened. It took a restraining order against my boyfriend, but I was finally free.

My therapist recommended that I not do marching band and take additional time for self-care. Between being pregnant and not marching, the HHS band director became a totally different teacher. I was no longer allowed to participate in the ensemble. I was allowed to practice alone in the uniform closet during his planning period, which I did for one semester.

Music was so important, but I was no longer allowed to be a part of the group. My family met with the principal and superintendent, but the HHS band director had such a sway in this small rural county that they didn't buck him. We could have sued but chose to move on. At one point, I wasn't sure that my formal music education and dream to become a music teacher would come to fruition.

I chose to transfer back to RHS during the second semester of my junior year. The RHS band director could have treated me poorly, as I had left his band to join a stronger one. Instead, he welcomed me back with open arms, he fitted me for a concert uniform that would fit a pregnant woman, and I began fully participating in the ensembles. I was treated as one of his own. I had my daughter in May of my junior year—she even had a few visits to the band room before school was out. I marched (yay!) during the fall of my senior year and then began college during the second semester of that year.

I had amazing, supportive parents and a band director who allowed me to continue my passion. I did get into AU and became the first person on both sides of my family to earn a college degree. I'm not gonna lie—being a parent, being a music education major, and working 20–30 hours a week was a very difficult period, part of why I still have such a drive to work hard. And more happy endings . . . my husband adopted my daughter not long after we were married.

Today, 25 years later, I am still in contact with my RHS band director. He saved my dreams. These experiences are also why I strive to be as inclusive, empathetic, and caring in my own music classroom. I will never be perfect, but I do my best to create an inviting and safe space for our students. This is my why.*

*Anonymous, used with permission.

Compassionate Music Teaching is that I focused primarily on all the good things that music teachers did, which made the text less relatable to some teachers who knew they would never be perfect. I also think about how one of the principal messages of *Daring to Care* is the importance of opening ourselves up to vulnerability and connecting authentically with others.

With these things in mind—and with Taylor Swift's advice from her New York University commencement address to "live alongside cringe"[24] as we look back on our lives and learn from past mistakes—I feel compelled to reflect openly about how I sometimes failed to see or support the full humans in my music classes. For example, it was all too easy to enforce a "no missed rehearsal" policy without fully listening to students about why they might have missed class, and what supports they might have needed in their lives—musically and otherwise. Furthermore, I wasn't always consistent in enforcing that policy depending on how much a student's attendance at the performance would "improve" the sound. In these times, I neglected to see the whole of the person or to consider the multiple pathways to musical development, instead seeing only how they would benefit the performance in the short term.

I can have self-compassion while reflecting on better options for the future. Of course, as music teachers we have limited time and space, and it is impossible to support all students, with all their concerns, all the time. But the story above, juxtaposed with Thomas-Durrell's concept of holistic acceptance, causes me to reflect on the ways that I could have better built trust (rather than fear of punishment), practiced empathy, embraced dissent, and co-created workable solutions with the learners themselves—the true experts in their intersectional identities and associated music learning needs. What reflections or stories do you have to share? (See Reflection Activity 7.4.)

Reconceptualizing Social Emotional Learning (SEL) through a Caring-With Lens

As I am writing this book, Social Emotional Learning (SEL), a program intended to teach students interpersonal and social skills,[25] has, quite remarkably, found itself in the line of fire between opposing political forces. Some factions suggest that teachers' SEL-informed practices are overly controlling of students, used as a mechanism for erasing students' unique and intersectional identities, or directed only toward students that teachers deem "difficult" rather than used to support all students' growth and support of one another.[26] On the other hand, other factions have connected SEL to other initiatives that put the student in front of the content and—quite oppositely from the previous opinion—claim that SEL emphasizes too much about a student's individual identity.[27] Those in this second group desire to maintain students' attention on course content only (what I have termed caring *about*) and claim that SEL programs might lead to political indoctrination.

The relationship between education and politics is as old as public education,[28] and the current positioning of SEL as a political landmine could provide enough material for a book all on its own. However, here I focus on the ways in which OHCME authors Scott N. Edgar, Kara Ireland D'Ambrosio, and Elise Hackl-Blumstein revisit concepts of SEL through a lens of compassionate, caring-*with* music teaching.[29] Through such a lens, they suggest that SEL must be situated as a collaborative venture between teachers and co-learners, so that students' needs and challenges are not dictated, but rather explored. They transform SEL concepts of *self* (self-awareness, self-management); *others* (social awareness and relationship skills); and *decision-making* to a more collaborative and equitable conceptualization of *identity*, *belonging*, and *agency*.

In a caring-*with* environment, the SEL competencies related to "self" are replaced by "identity," as co-learners make space to explore various aspects of who they are, and how these parts of themselves influence beliefs, biases, and mindsets. The competencies associated with "others" are replaced with "belonging," as co-learners work together to create spaces where students can be vulnerable to take musical risks, collaborate on problem-solving, engage creatively and empathically together, and communicate effectively with others. Finally, the SEL competency of "decision-making" is replaced with "agency," reflecting how co-learners make space to hear and amplify one another's voices and work together toward positive social change. In "agency," co-learners practice ethical responsibility and practices to support one another's wellbeing. Box 7b contains examples for each of these revised

Box 7b SEL Competencies Revisited through a Compassionate, Caring-With Lens

Self → IDENTITY

- Musical creation fosters self-awareness and allows for students to develop a greater sense of identity, autonomy, and emotional vocabulary.
- Musicians learn the necessity of personal goal-setting, self-assessment, and accountability for artmaking and themselves.

Others → BELONGING

- The relationship built between teachers and students over multiple years of instruction fosters the caring environment necessary to help build school connectedness, foster empathy, and provide a sense of belonging.
- Collaborative music classrooms build connections between students, facilitate community engagement, and uplift and celebrate the cultural assets of students.
- Music classrooms necessitate vulnerability and facilitate a space where students can explore, tinker, envision, and grow.

Decision-Making → AGENCY

- The collaborative community developed in the music classroom welcomes discussions and an awareness of acceptance and embracing diversity, resulting in a greater sense of agency and effecting meaningful change.
- Student voice is amplified through the musical process, providing an experience to develop personal and musical efficacy.
- The musical process necessitates editing of the product. This process builds student capacity to hone their beliefs and become flexible to represent themselves in concise and meaningful ways.*

*Edgar, D'Ambrosio, and Hackl-Blumstein, "Compassion and Care," 195–196.

concepts within a music education context, recalling how an emphasis on relational skills can support and enhance musical artistry.

Creating Brave Spaces of Belonging and Radical Welcome

As noted in Chapters 3 and 4, "brave spaces" differ from "safe spaces" in that they go beyond merely protecting learners from physical or emotional harm, to providing learners with a sense of authentic belonging. Brave spaces allow learners to be who they are without need to conform, to have their voice silenced, or without fear of oppression.[30] The co-created spaces described in the previous section on holistic acceptance are brave spaces, in that dissent and difference are welcome; student voices are lifted and amplified; and learners co-create environments in which they feel a sense of trust, empathy, and mutual empowerment.

Brave spaces shift conversations of diversity and inclusion to practices of radical welcome. First, note that I have clarified between "conversations" and "practices." Safe spaces often leave ideas at the level of conversation, and sometimes even restrict ideas and voices for the sake of protecting feelings.[31] Brave spaces, however, evoke deep levels of caring action that elicit real change—sometimes even without the need to waste precious time talking and talking when people are attuned to one another's needs and can get up and get going, for and with one another.[32] Second, instead of merely "making space for" or "allowing" minoritized individuals to the table (practices that keep the power with the powerful), *radical welcome* is embodied in a truly diverse community where a collective range of individuals not only learn from and celebrate one another but also work toward one another's liberation and empowerment.

There is strength in community, and strength in diversity. Uniformity makes a music learning community weak and redundant, as only certain strengths are celebrated whereas other creativities and innovations are devalued. Uniformity overlooks the ways in which learners' multidimensional contributions might benefit others.[33] Yet music education has for a very long time been formed by a master-apprentice model that serves only the people who fit with pre-established norms, protocols, and musical genres presumed to be superior over others.[34] Historically, the music education welcome has not truly been for everyone, but rather for those who identify with a certain kind of music and certain music learning style. In contrast, radical welcome can provide space for music teachers to engage student creativities to solve musical problems in ways they had never imagined nor anticipated.

The simultaneously frightening and emancipatory truth about radical welcome is that it requires us as music teachers to be open to continual evolution and transformation ourselves.[35] If we are truly open to dissenting views and to co-learning with our students, we will invariably change as a result.[36] When we co-create brave spaces with co-learners, we encourage and model positive risk-taking as we dialogue together and learn together. Modeling positive risk-taking can be win-win. Not only do we grow in musical, pedagogical, and life knowledge, but we can help students (a) become better attuned to their individual needs, interests, and values; (b) learn how to assert and express those needs; (c) listen to and respect the expressions of others; and (d) forge authentic connections with others and with the music they make. (See Reflection Activity 7.5.)

Fostering a Culture Rich in Microaffirmations

Box 7c contains portions of a Facebook post written by the inimitable Bruce Walker, a professor of music at Columbia Basin College. Bruce is a sought-after

Box 7c Microaggressions at the Grocery Store

So my next Facebook post was going to be a review of my lovely time at the 2023 NAfME Northwest Division Professional Development Conference; however, I have to write about what just transpired at Winco foods here in Richland. I was in self-checkout scanning my small amount of groceries (because I'll be flying down to do a workshop with some wonderful kiddos) and this older gentleman stops me and wants to chat. Now, anyone that knows me knows I appreciate and will do things for folks in the older generation without hesitation (grandparents were always important to me).

The conversation goes something like this:

MAN: "Oh wow, how tall are you?"

ME: "I'm six foot six, sir."

MAN: "You must play basketball and use that height somehow."

ME: "Actually, I'm quite clumsy; however, I am a college professor and professional musician."

MAN: *his posture changes with intrigue* "I see. *scans me up and down* Let me guess . . . saxophone."

ME: "Actually, I'm a cellist, orchestra conductor, and researcher."

I continue to smile while he puts his phone down

MAN: "Conductor? Wow, they let you on stage being that tall? *chuckles* Where have you conducted?"

ME: "I just came back from Alabama doing the Alabama All-State Orchestra and I also conduct the Columbia Basin College Orchestra where I am a professor and the Walla Walla Symphony Youth Orchestra where I am the music director and conductor."

MAN: "Oh really, you really do all of that? I would think you'd just be a construction worker or something."

ME: "Well when I'm not working, I enjoy changing lightbulbs for people."

both of us laugh . . . albeit mine is mostly an attempt to neutralize the conversation

We continue to exchange conversation about my parents, how the cello is a relaxing instrument, and what he does for a living. I gather my groceries and say goodbye.

Now, why am I writing this? Many are curious about what I am passionate about in regards to my academic research. Towards the end of my doctoral coursework, I stumbled upon a term that resonated with me so loudly because I was typically "the only" or a part of "the few" in almost every activity I chose to be in. Microaggressions are essentially everyday slights and insults that people experience in daily interactions, some of which are well-intentioned, but have harmful consequences. Although I do not believe this gentleman was malicious in his curious attempt to converse with a Black man in a predominately White town (approximately 76% of the population identifies as White), it does cause me to view the conversation critically. Microaggressions can easily deteriorate an individual's self-esteem, create feelings of isolation, and contribute to a larger culture of bias and discrimination.

I am very aware of my height, race, and profession. On the surface, they have not traditionally mixed (meaning at first glance, one would assume something completely different); however, I have a right to do what I do just as everyone else. Am I mad about this interaction? No. Will I be able to write and/or commiserate with folks that know me and extract the subtle thematic elements that can be drawn from all of this? Absolutely!

At the end of the day, I will be BIG, BLACK, and BEAUTIFUL and I am PROUD of what I have accomplished so far. I choose to be visible to inspire others, not only because it is the right thing to do, but those that look like me can know that YOU can do this too. "Microaggressions in music education" is a topic that does not have enough conversation surrounding it. Fortunately, I will do my best to contribute something scholarly to the field to get this ball rolling.*

*Bruce Walker, Facebook post, used with permission.

orchestra conductor who traverses the world from musical engagement to musical engagement spreading warmth, love, and musical artistry wherever he goes. My comment in Chapter 1 that "we do not have to choose between kindness and quality" is embodied in Bruce's pedagogy. I have had the sheer joy and privilege of working with Bruce during his doctoral coursework at Boston University. He and I have had many conversations about the roles that race and racism play in music education, from classrooms to professional associations. I have learned a great deal from him—and his Facebook post was no exception. He has offered his permission and blessing to share the post.

Upon reading the material in Box 7c, one could, I suppose, downplay the situation and assert that nothing was wrong, that the man at the grocery store was merely striking up a friendly conversation. But the problem comes in the way that Bruce wasn't seen or believed for who he was, in all his exquisite intersectionality. Rather, he was judged wrongly about his person and questioned about his merit to belong where he was in his career, based on only a few external features. For example, the man not only expressed surprise, but he offered a suggestion for a different, blue-collar job when Bruce asserted that he was a professional classical musician—an area of employment historically reserved for elite members of society.[37] Furthermore, he questioned how well Bruce would be received on an orchestral stage given his large stature.

Bruce describes the kinds of microaggressions that minoritized people endure every day. I've witnessed these myself when hanging out with friends and colleagues of color—the way they are subtly (and sometimes not so subtly) treated differently than I am as a white woman when we are in predominantly white spaces together. Even in casual settings I have seen my friends checked up on more frequently, asked to refill someone's drink on their way back to the restroom when we are out for dinner together, skipped over when waiting in line, told that people "like them" probably aren't interested in going to the symphony, complimented on the way they speak so well, asked if someone can touch their hair (or just having someone touch it without asking), and so forth. I could keep going. On the other hand, each of these instances reminds me of the small and simple ways that my privilege adds up over time to get me ahead of others in life, just because of the way I look.

Any of these small comments or events could be discounted or perhaps even ignored if it happened once. But when they occur continually and repeatedly day after day, it can, as Bruce described, "easily deteriorate an individual's self-esteem, create feelings of isolation, and contribute to a larger culture of bias and discrimination." Research tells us that being told or presumed to be less capable by others can wear one down and have a tangible effect on one's capability and achievement.[38] This is the case in music learning spaces as well as exchanges at the grocery store.

Microaggressions are defined as "brief, everyday exchanges that send denigrating messages to certain individuals because of their group membership."[39] They are small insults or put-downs that can sometimes seem innocent enough, but that compile to the point of serious damage to a person's sense of wellbeing, focus, achievement, and prosperity.[40] Microaggressions can happen to anyone who is minoritized in some way, whether due to race, religious difference, cultural background, sexual orientation, gender, disability, and so forth.[41] For example, I've witnessed a friend of mine become "invisible" when she uses a wheelchair in public, with people refusing to look her in the eyes or even cutting in line in front of her. I've seen parents gather their children closer when a gay couple walks by them. I've seen people glared down by strangers when praying over their meal in a restaurant. And so forth.

Looking again at Figure 7.1, the exponential impact of microaggressions becomes even clearer from an intersectionality standpoint. Given the ways that microaggressions wear people down, and given how identities intersect with all aspects of our lives, it becomes clear that microaggressions aren't just one person's problem. They promote an unsafe and distrusting culture for all of us.

Offering Care through Microaffirmations

In contrast, a compassionate and caring music learning space is filled with *microaffirmations*. OHCME authors Alice A. Tsui, Juliet Hess, and I define microaffirmations as instances "where teachers and other co-learners engage in small acts of identity recognition to disrupt hurtful and/or insensitive practices and discourse."[42] Microaggressions wear people down over time, whereas microaffirmations can build up over time to nurture an atmosphere of care in which all co-learners are embraced and encouraged for being who they are.[43]

Microaffirmations can be simple but potentially deeply impactful. Examples of microaffirmations might include: smiling at a student, asking them how their day went (with no expectations for certain responses except to listen), remembering something they like to do outside of class and asking about it, nodding and gesturing that you see their hand raised while another student is finishing a thought, telling them you hear them when they express frustration, providing space for dissenting voices (as described above), using students' preferred pronouns, using students' preferred names, asking students what kinds of support they prefer you give them, telling students what they have taught you, giving students a chance to try again, apologizing for mistakes with specific plans to do better, not jumping to fix things when students are simply asking to be heard, and so forth.[44] (See Reflection Activity 7.6).

One example of a simple and easy act of affirmation that may have a macro effect on connection, is learning to pronounce students' names correctly. For example, it has been a common practice for many United States educators to Americanize Asian students' names (such as changing a name like "Xianjun"[45] to a Western name such as "June") simply because it is easier for the teacher to remember and pronounce. OHCME author Kính T. Vũ describes getting to know Asian students' names as a form of intercultural sensitivity, whereby teachers recognize and see all learners as human beings, not merely producers of musical notes.[46]

I have learned (from some very caring colleagues) to reach out to students prior to the beginning of a new class, and to ask students whose names I struggle to pronounce, to email a recording of themselves saying their name before the first class meeting. Or, rather than requiring extra work from students who are already very busy adjusting to a new culture, I often ask permission to record students pronouncing their names on the first day of class when they introduce themselves to one another. Then I practice it over and over before the next class meeting until I can say it with ease. Students are usually grateful for the effort and very willing to help me learn.

Teachers can also offer microaffirmations to minoritized students by highlighting successful stories of people who look like them—again taking care while doing so, such as by offering a multidimensional curriculum that celebrates a variety of perspectives and identities rather than adding on to an otherwise unaffirming curriculum in ways that further single students out. OHCME author Amy Lewis emphasizes the importance of providing students with positive images and role models that counter harmful ideas and stereotypes.[47] Lewis also recommends the importance of teachers using self-reflection to check for our own biases, and to model vulnerability and a willingness to learn—which are also microaffirmations of students' value to us, as tangible demonstrations of the ways in which we desire to learn from and with them.

Offering Microaffirmations with Care

Remembering that care is only care when it is received as such, it is important to offer microaffirmations with care, so that they are not received unintentionally as microaggressions. For example, I'll never forget walking into a classroom of a well-meaning music teacher who had taken the time to put up a poster of "Women Composers." How wonderful that this teacher spent time and money to put up a poster to help his female students visualize a composer as one of their possible selves. The problem, however, was that this poster hung right next to a second poster, titled "The Great Composers," with pictures of all male composers. This well-meaning attempt at a microaffirmation became potentially microaggressive when women were separated from a list of composers who were allegedly the "great" ones.

Pointing out distinctive features of a person's identity in front of others can be another way to emphasize their difference rather than foster a sense of belonging. For example, if I made a big deal out of pronouncing a student's name in front of the entire class, that could put them on the spot while relegating to them a status of "other" in that space. As mentioned previously, another example might be selecting music that we believe represents a students' culture, without asking students' input about what music they enjoy, which could show stereotypical beliefs or a lack of care for the many and varied aspects of their identity.

It feels important to pause here, lest this section (or any other) create a "call-out" culture where everyone becomes afraid to try anything for fear of someone else's judgment. I'd rather we create a "call-in" culture where we remember that we are all trying, that we are all "living alongside cringe" in one way or another, and that we are all continually learning. (I address "call-in" versus "call-out" culture further in Chapter 9.) These examples are just to offer ideas of how to exercise care. I hope you, the reader, can see these examples as an invitation to join me as I try, fail, and try again, to turn mistakes into better and wonderful opportunities for connection.

Affirming Identities through Music

Microaffirmations are a fundamental piece of elementary music teacher Alice Tsui's anti-oppression curricula at New Bridges School in New York City. Alice's emphasis is, first and foremost, on affirming students' identities and creations through music, and centering joy in what each student brings to the classroom. Students are taught to affirm one another through music that they co-create, such as "Be the Light," a rap written by New Bridges Elementary students and alumni:

> [W]e see the power in each other So why don't we help one another . . . Be true to yourself cause our joy is revolutionary . . . Be the light Stand strong with all of your might . . . Follow your heart to do what's right.[48]

Some of the remarkably affirming work by New Bridges Elementary can be viewed by scanning the QR code in Figure 7.2 below.

Figure 7.2 QR Code for New Bridges Elementary Performance of "Be the Light."

Practicing Microinterventions

Part of "following our heart to do what's right" might include microaffirmations of a person's identity by standing up against microaggressions—through what Derald Wing Sue calls *microinterventions*.[49] Because microaggressions are often unintended expressions of a person's implicit bias, it can sometimes be helpful to point out the microaggression. Box 7d includes some examples of microinterventions, adapted for music education. These strategies can apply in any situation where there is bias—which, as noted in Chapter 5, is nearly everywhere.

Learner-Attuned and Learner-Affirming Approaches

This chapter focuses on practicing *identity-responsive pedagogy* as a form of caring *for* students, and *identity-affirming pedagogy* as a form of caring *with* co-learners. These two pedagogies are difficult to separate because they can happen simultaneously and overlap in many ways. As explained in the first part of the chapter, these pedagogies involve embracing intersectionality (through holistic acceptance; brave spaces, belonging, and radical welcome; and creating a culture of microaffirmations). Additionally, identity-responsive and identity-affirming pedagogies may be recognized through learner-attuned and learner-affirming approaches, such as: cultural responsiveness (broadly defined); unconditional love; and embracing curiosity, wonder, and improvisation.

Cultural Responsiveness (Broadly Defined)

In his groundbreaking book on reality pedagogy,[50] science teacher Chris Emdin tells a story of when he mentored a novice teacher who simply could not keep the attention of his students. The teacher had been touted as a "model educator" by administrators, despite having taught only a few years. He had been placed in a lead teacher capacity for reasons that Emdin could not understand, given how

Box 7d Microinterventions Adapted for Music Education

- Helping people recognize a different perspective ("Can you see how that comment might have come across?");
- Naming the microaggression ("That's a stereotype");
- Undermining the hidden message ("Actually, I know plenty of Asian people who aren't interested in playing the violin");
- Making the hidden message explicit ("Are you suggesting that she is so good at the violin simply because she is Asian?")
- Challenging the stereotype ("I think he's in show choir because he works really hard and sings really well, not because he is attracted to boys");
- Broadening the judgment beyond that identity characteristic ("A lot of people find it hard to practice when they're exhausted or have to work multiple jobs");
- Asking for clarification ("Can you explain what you mean by that?");
- Reverse the statement ("Thanks, as a person from Massachusetts you sing Schubert well too.")
- Describe the problem without naming a specific perpetrator ("I'd love to hear everyone's opinions about this improvisation. Can we make sure everyone has a chance to talk?").*

*Adapted from Sue et al., *Microintervention Strategies*.

he did not appear to connect with his students. But Emdin began to understand the administrators' thinking when he reviewed the teacher's lesson plans and discovered the impeccable detail in each of them. To the administrators it must have seemed that the novice teacher was a genius for anticipating every student need and every turn of the lesson in advance. But to Emdin, the excessive detail in the plan was a red flag about the teacher's lack of responsiveness to students, something that mere caring-*about* lesson plans could not afford.

Emdin next observed the teacher in action, noting how the teacher did, in fact, stay right on track with the lesson, no matter what was happening around him. The classroom might as well have been a video with a green screen. Students were quiet and appeared to be well behaved, not talking out of turn (something that likely also captured the admiration of administrators). However, Emdin observed signs of boredom, frustration, and confusion on the faces of the students—something the teacher did not appear to notice.

There was no doubt that this new teacher cared deeply about what he was doing. He may have even felt that he was caring deeply *for* the students by putting so much effort into his planning. Yet he lacked the kind of responsiveness and attunement to the students that might have facilitated a much stronger level of engagement and commitment to learning. Using *Daring to Care* terminology, the teacher missed opportunities for authentic connection.

As the teacher's mentor, Emdin spent an extensive amount of time helping him step into the lives, contexts, and cultures of the students, which were rich with influences from the Black Pentecostal church and Hip-Hop. By observing the approach taken by Pentecostal preachers and Hip-Hop MCs (guided by Emdin's care and encouragement), the teacher came to understand the ways that he might improve engagement in his classroom by "connecting with them emotionally, balancing structure and improvisation, utilizing knowledge about students' backgrounds and interests to present material in meaningful ways, and fostering a sense of community."[51]

With great efforts, Emdin was able to help the teacher recognize the power of letting the students in—into his line of vision, into his wonderings, into his planning, into his pacing, into his risk taking, into his (and their) power. With each brave step the teacher took, he gradually recognized that he would not, in fact, lose control of the classroom as he had feared. He learned through each step that he could keep protocols and routines in place, but in a free-flowing and improvisatory way that allowed for rich, even electric, engagement with the students. To use *Daring to Care* terminology, he could enjoy a reciprocal and responsive classroom as he learned to care *for* and *with* the students he taught.

Emdin's "reality pedagogy" is a type of culturally responsive pedagogy, but it focuses on the inside-out rather than the outside-in. In other words, Emdin encourages teachers to immerse themselves in the intersectional and vibrant lives of the students rather than labeling isolated features of students' cultures and adding on to the curriculum. This approach recognizes and honors the uniqueness of each student within an array of individual, intersecting cultures in which they live their lives.

Culture, broadly defined, is far more than race, ethnicity, or geography. I invite you to think of the various worlds in which you live, work, interact, and make music. Who are your friends and associates in each of these worlds? How does your language change in each different world? What topics do you share in each world? How do you relate with members of this world? Each of these is a kind of culture in itself. As illustrated in the opening "movie scene" in Chapter 2, each of our students lives within their own set of micro-cultures that shape who they are, how they learn, and how they engage with music.

OHCME authors Warren Churchill and Clare Hall call for music educators to consider a broader definition of culture, which might include any group that shares common customs, beliefs, and values.[52] Cultures have *concrete* aspects, such as musical products or events; *behavioral* aspects, such as mannerisms and language; and *symbolic* aspects, such as shared meanings and beliefs.[53] Churchill and Hall offer an example of Deaf culture, where members of the community share concrete expressions of poetry and art, behavioral practices for communication in different contexts, and symbolic dimensions of shared beliefs and values reflected through the subtle nuances of sign language. As described in the vignette about Amari in Chapter 3 (Box 3a), Amari's teachers saw Amari through their own cultures (broadly defined), and recognized how Amari was different or had deficits rather than considering the nuances of culture in which Amari lived. A more culturally responsive, caring-*with* approach might have involved shaping music learning in dialogue with the student and others in the student's community.

Interrogating Our Own Identities, Assumptions, and Practices

For music teachers, one way to mitigate cultural insensitivity (such as in the instance of Amari) is to self-reflect on our own identities and the intersectional cultures that influence the decisions we make.[54] We might ask ourselves: How do our own identities influence our judgments? As Juliet Hess suggests, "culturally responsive teaching [broadly defined] centers the student and takes a strengths-based approach to pedagogy that acknowledges the strengths and assets students bring."[55]

An identity-affirming pedagogy would allow for a caring-*with* approach instead of imposing deficit or one-size-fits all models.[56] It would also include self-reflection into the ways that our intersectional identities might influence our judgments about students, and what we deem to be "good" or "bad" based on our own traditions, communication styles, and beliefs. I invite you to visit or revisit the Core Reflection activity in Boxes 5g and 5h (Chapter 5), and take a preview of the Analysis and Inquiry of Current Practices (Boxes 9a–9c, Chapter 9) to engage in self-reflection about how your own intersectional identities influence your teaching practices.

Caring through Unconditional Love

I began this chapter by inviting you to think about someone you love deeply. Now, I'd like to flip that request, and ask you to think of someone—perhaps a student—who is challenging for you to get along with. What parts of their identity do you know well? What parts of them are you less familiar with? It is possible that the parts of these students that we don't get along with most, happen to clash with the parts of our own intersectional identities that are most pronounced in us (as addressed in Figure 7.1). In many cases, music teachers are positioned to have long-term relationships with people whom they don't choose, or with whom they struggle to connect in positive ways. In such instances, identity-responsive and identity-affirming pedagogies may require that we care for and with them through practices of unconditional love.

To OHCME author Marissa Silverman and other care scholars, caring is loving: "To say, 'I care for you' means 'I love you.' [. . .] A music teacher who practices love-as-care engages with students as persons who are in the process of developing toward full personhood."[57] As I discuss in Chapter 5, we can sustain and affirm students' musical selves as we support them as *they* envision that ideal self, and then we provide the things that they want and need to work toward that ideal. Of course, their ideal self will morph along the way, so this target is at best only loosely and temporarily defined. However, the role of identity-affirming pedagogy is to affirm the movement toward an ideal self, whatever it is in each moment—and, most importantly, in the form that students communicate it to us.

On the other hand, OHCME author Brandi Waller-Pace suggests that caring for our students is only one aspect of loving.[58] She asserts that love is broader than caring for and about students—as teachers may view as merely caring for the classroom's physical space, for students' technical development, and offering "discipline and critique based on their concept of how students should be."[59] We might even attempt to care for students but not truly care in reciprocal and responsive ways, not without honoring the intersectionality of their identities.

In contrast, Waller-Pace draws on the work of bell hooks to define genuine love as "a combination of care, commitment, trust, knowledge, responsibility, and respect."[60] These elements of love are, to me, qualities of caring *with*.[61] For Waller-Pace, authentic love through caring *for* and caring *with* involves honoring "the full humanity of children"[62] and resisting approaches where we show power or domination over them. She explains:

> We cannot truly care for students from the position of a kind dictator, "nicely" enacting an autocracy that denies their agency and humanity, and prohibits authentic connections and trust. [. . .] When we tell our students we love them without embedding in our practices a deep ethic of love that includes justice, we are simply perpetuating a surface-level understanding of what love is.[63]

Unconditional love, like radical welcome, requires our own willingness as music teachers to be vulnerable, genuinely listen, learn, act, and to transform.

Offering Unconditional Love—Unconditionally

We do not have to share or agree with all the customs, traditions, and languages of our students to offer them genuine love. I'd like to offer a personal example, if I may. I am a member of the LGBTQ+ community but I come from a family with very devout practices within a conservative religion that does not affirm my marriage. Because of the love I share with my family, we have agreed—through intentional and thoughtful conversations—to love one another and honor each other's identities despite these differences.

We connect through our own family culture, through concrete aspects that make our family what it is (music, food, travel, sports, board games, family celebrations, writing books, etc.). We speak with a common language (including through spontaneous outbursts of parodied songs, but also through that Intermountain West accent that I just can't shake). We draw on the symbolic values we share (the importance of human connection, loving others, hope for good things, a desire to make the world a better place) as we attempt understand how such love, hope, and desire for action might resonate in one another's lives.

Most members of my family will not likely ever go to a Pride parade (although some certainly will), and I will likely not attend their denominational meetings. However, we still listen openly to one another, focus on common ground, and practice cognitive empathy to understand how valuable these events might be for the other. As Juliet Hess and I note about the limitations of empathy (see Chapter 2), we will never fully understand one another—but that is not the goal. The goal is also not to change one another. The goal is to love unconditionally.

The same can be true for musical co-learners. No matter our efforts to connect with students, we will never resonate with every aspect of their multifarious and intersecting identities. As described previously, doing so is virtually impossible due to time, space, and continual evolution of those identities. However, we can find common ground through the micro-cultures that we share. We can start with the micro-culture of our shared music learning space, where we are all learning new things together. From there, we can consider how various intersectional aspects of co-learners shape the decisions, ideas, and motivations they bring to our shared music-making experiences, and then connect those intersectional aspects of their identity with various intersectional aspects of our teaching.

Unconditional love, like caring *with*, moves beyond superficial notions of love that equate to pity and thereby maintain harmful power-over relationships.[64] Part of the symbiotic relationship in caring-*with* music education is, for OHCME author Martin Urbach, in the process of loving students "deeper, wider, louder, and quieter" (see Box 7e). The kind of vulnerability, honesty, and an openness to learn from and with our students that Urbach describes, requires that we embrace wonder, curiosity, and a spirit of improvisation—which is the final aspect of identity-responsive and identity-affirming pedagogies.

Exercising Wonder, Curiosity, Improvisation, and Accompaniment

Without trust in a relationship, the ways that we are different from others can cause us to experience fear. With trust, these same differences can instead cause us to experience wonder and amazement. OHCME author June Boyce-Tillman argues that teaching music through a philosophy of wonder can transform a learning space that limited by stereotypes and prejudice, to one that embraces students' dignity and humanity. In the spirit of caring *with*, she suggests that music teachers can learn the art of wonder by observing young children, who are experts in wonderment. In the spirit of radical welcome, Boyce-Tillman explains that the act of

Box 7e Loving Deeper, Wider, Louder, and Quieter

I say "love deeper" because we might have students who are easy to love, and thus strengthening those relationships as a foundation for an education, combats oppression, and points toward liberation. I say "love wider" because we might have students who at the first sight of a loving interaction, push us away and [. . .] we must try a little harder to care, communicate, and commit to those students as well. [. . .] I say "love louder" because love is as love does, merging intention with action and outcomes [. . .] and letting students know we are there for them, through thick or thin, as comrades and not allies, as adults who will put something on the line to center, cherish, and care with them.

Finally, I say I must learn how to love quieter because trust and care need space, time, and privacy. Gentle and patient interactions that do not draw attention to oneself. [. . .] Maybe it is a private message on Zoom, checking in sans prying about the student's week; perhaps it is a piece of constructive and critical feedback that is not "You did so well, *but* . . . ." Loving quieter involves nontransactional relationship building, aimed toward musical collaboration, composition, performance, and analysis, but most importantly for the sake of getting to know each other [. . .], which requires vulnerability and honesty with others if we are going to learn, not from but alongside, and with, one another.*

*Martin Urbach, as quoted in G Smith, Waller-Pace, Urbach, and Powell, "Love, Care, Revolution, and Justice," 501.

wonder—"characterized by a very particular attitude of special attentiveness"[65]—can lead to transformation as we open ourselves to this new awareness.

Such "special attentiveness" is reminiscent of the caring attention I described earlier about Martin Urbach, in his interactions with his students. It is also reminiscent of the curiosity involved in supporting a student in their unique pathways toward musical development and expression. Finally, this special attentiveness is practiced by any music teacher who, in the process of reciprocal and responsive caring-*with*, engages in the process of improvisation every day—whether teaching jazz, composition, or virtually any form of music-making. Caring-*with* music education requires improvisation, no matter the content.

Daring to care with music education requires a willingness to be curious, to learn, to be vulnerable, to improvise, to transform. We cannot presume to be responsive in our caring if we are unwilling to improvise. As knowledge is changing rapidly and musics are becoming more and more multidimensional, our role will need to change from "teacher" to "facilitator" and "co-learner." Our aims can no longer be centered around teaching isolated skills that lead to specific, targeted outcomes to prepare students for jobs—especially when the kind of jobs music learners may eventually take may not even exist. We need, instead, to prepare them to be curious, engaged, responsible learners who can adapt with care and caring to an ever-changing world.[66]

There is so much more richness that music learning spaces can have when we open ourselves up to learning—along with our students—new and expanding ways of music-making. Embracing the many intersectional identities in each music learning space can open us up to a wealth of knowledge and ideas about music we never could have imagined. As music education philosopher Randall Allsup has articulated, however, it is impossible for teachers to be prepared with all the ways that music education might turn in this increasingly pluralistic world. Instead, it is important to be open, flexible, and ready to learn and embrace "what might be"[67]—in other words, to improvise, and to accompany.

Caring-With as Accompaniment

Drawing on the musical concept of accompaniment, OHCME authors Justin McManus and Bruce Carter envision what music teaching might look like if it shifted focus from "aiding" or "fixing," to a focus on "accompanying"—where music teachers practice curiosity, openness, empathy, and trust, to follow and support the student on the student's learning journey.[68] Using the support of LGBTQIA+ students as their vantage point, McManus and Carter explain that accompaniment affords teachers the opportunity to learn alongside students' own identity explorations. Further, as music teachers we can learn from our own mistakes as we build partnerships with co-learners. For example, when teaching a transgender student, we might accompany the student on their journey through practicing (possibly multiple) changes in pronouns and names without judgment, but with curiosity and openness. Accompanist-teachers are open to wonder, curiosity, and improvisation, demonstrated by their willingness to listen, learn, adjust, attune, practice flexibility, and apologize openly when we make mistakes.

Accompaniment can take four steps: critical listening, adaptability, communication, and feedback. *Critical listening* in musical accompaniment involves careful attunement to the lead performer's phrasing, style, tempo, and so forth. In terms of affirming identities, critical listening involves careful attention to the cues of the student in terms of what might be helpful versus harmful. Taking the same example of a transgender student, it might involve careful listening to the ways they refer to themselves, and in which contexts they feel safe to express their full identity, so we do not overstep or put the student in a potentially hurtful situation.

Critical listening is more than merely careful listening, however. OHCME author Kelly Bylica explains that critical listening involves critical self-reflection, including reflecting on how the ways we make meaning of what we hear or see may be influenced by our own backgrounds, assumptions, and identities.[69] Critical listening involves an openness to exploring and engaging with diverse perspectives—much like having an openness to dissenting voices, as described earlier. As explained in Chapter 2, such listening involves resisting the urge to hear a "right" or "best" answer, and instead embracing multiple perspectives that may be true or right for different students at different times.

According to Bylica, we can practice, teach, and model critical listening as a radical form of care when we support students to become the agents and authors of their own meanings and interpretations—in other words, as we listen to accompany students on their own music learning journeys. We can teach critical listening through relationships as well as through music, by encouraging musical risk-taking, improvisatory dialogue, creative compositions, and performance as we reimagine musical works "not as objects of which to make sense, but as opportunities to explore musical imaginings inquisitively in an ongoing manner."[70]

Adaptability for a musical accompanist involves the ability to adjust when things go awry.[71] In the case of identity affirmation, a music teacher will stay attuned to change as music students' needs and desires change. *Communication* is key here. It involves a willingness to reach out and build trust over time (as described in Chapter 2), as well as an awareness of the way our body language and other communicative cues show support for, and connection with, our students. Just as a musical accompanist is continually engaged in eye contact and subtle gestures to connect with a lead performer, the ways we carry ourselves matter as much as what we say. (See Reflection Activity 7.7.)

Finally, musical accompanists seek *feedback* after a rehearsal or performance to ensure that they are on track with the lead performer. Similarly, it is critical for accompanist-teachers to be open to learning and changing as a result of the feedback students give us. McManus and Carter advocate for feedback in all aspects of teaching, from rehearsal language to students' name change procedures. Simply making space for feedback, whether through direct questions or providing anonymous avenues (such as surveys, suggestion boxes, or student representatives) can build trust and connection among students.

Conclusion

It's thrilling to think about all the ways that each human expresses themselves, and how they connect with and make meaning of the world. Each of us has a unique set of experiences and identities, which makes it very challenging to know our students intimately—even for music teachers who spend countless hours with students over a long period of time. Our students' identities are constantly evolving, and as we open ourselves to learning along with our students, we too will enjoy a perpetual state of transformation. Identity-responsive and identity-affirming pedagogies are means for caring *for*, and caring *with*, students in ways that embrace their dynamic and uniquely wonder-full, wonder-promoting identities. Holistic acceptance does not mean that we will understand or agree with everything about our students. On the contrary, holistic acceptance is a way of practicing unconditional love while creating spaces of belonging and affirmation, and exercising wonder, curiosity, improvisation, and accompaniment.

Reflection Activities

7.1. This chapter has a lot of different ideas that overlap and intersect, and they may require a bit of digestion and self-reflection time. If you haven't already done so, I invite you to put the book down for a bit, go on a walk or some other movement activity, and let the ideas percolate. Then when you're ready, please return to the rest of the reflection activities. Honestly, please rest for a moment—I trust you'll come back when the time is right.

7.2. Fill out a version of Figure 7.1 for yourself. Make a matrix with as many cells as you need. Which aspects of your identity have more weight than others? How has this changed over time?

7.3. Invite your students to fill out a version of Figure 7.1 and, as they are willing, to share it with you and/or with other co-learners.

7.4. Do you have a "living alongside cringe" teacher experience to share after reading the story about holistic acceptance in Box 7a?

7.5. What are some examples you have seen or practiced for creating safe spaces, versus brave spaces, versus radical welcome?

7.6. What are some microaffirmations that you have received in your life? What are some microaffirmations you can offer to your students?

7.7. Record yourself teaching a music lesson and then watch it. What subtle nonverbal cues and gestures do you notice about the ways you affirm (or don't affirm) certain students?

Notes

1. Alexandra Lamont, "Musical Identity, Interest, and Involvement," in *Handbook of Musical Identities*, ed. Raymond MacDonald, David J. Hargreaves, and Dorothy Miell (New York: Oxford University Press, 2017), 176–196.
2. Auh Myung-Sook and Robert Walker, "Musical Identities in Australia and South Korea and New Identities Emerging through Social Media and Digital Technology," in *Handbook of Musical Identities*, ed. Raymond MacDonald, David J. Hargreaves, and Dorothy Miell (New York: Oxford University Press, 2017), 789–805; Anand Raj Sukumaran, "Many Streams, One River: Multimusical Educators in the K-12 Music Classroom" (PhD diss., University of Michigan, 2022); Nicholas Patrick Quigley and Tawnya D. Smith. "The Educational Backgrounds of DIY Musicians," *Journal of Popular Music Education* 5, no. 3 (2021): 397–417.
3. Sukumaran, "Many Streams, One River," 7–8.
4. Auh and Walker, "Musical Identities"; David J. Hargreaves, Raymond Macdonald, and Dorothy Miell, "The Changing Identity of Musical Identities," in *Handbook of Musical Identities*, ed. Raymond MacDonald, David J. Hargreaves, and Dorothy Miell (New York: Oxford University Press, 2017), 3–23; Alexandra Lamont and David J. Hargreaves, "Musical Preference and Social Identity in Adolescence," in *Handbook of Music, Adolescents, and Wellbeing*, ed. Katrina McFerran, Philippa Derrington, and Suvi Saarikallio (New York: Oxford University Press, 2019), 109–118.
5. David J. Elliott and Marissa Silverman, "Identities and Musics: Reclaiming Personhood," in *Handbook of Musical Identities*, ed. Raymond MacDonald, David J. Hargreaves, and Dorothy Miell (New York: Oxford University Press, 2017), 27–45; David Hargreaves and Alexandra Lamont, *The*

Psychology of Musical Development (Cambridge: Cambridge University Press, 2017); Andy McKinlay and Chris McVittie, "'Will the Real Slim Shady Please Stand Up?': Identity in Popular Music," in *Handbook of Musical Identities*, ed. Raymond MacDonald, David J. Hargreaves, and Dorothy Miell (New York: Oxford University Press, 2017), 137–152; Kristen Pellegrino, "Becoming Music-Making Music Teachers: Connecting Music Making, Identity, Wellbeing, and Teaching for Four Student Teachers," *Research Studies in Music Education* 37, no. 2 (2015): 175–194.

6. Karin S. Hendricks and June Boyce-Tillman, eds., *Authentic Connection: Music, Spirituality, and Wellbeing* (Bern, Switzerland: Peter Lang, 2021); Pellegrino, "Becoming Music-Making Music Teachers."
7. See Chapter 2 for a more extensive discussion of the connective power of music.
8. Nicole R. Robinson, "Intersectionality in the Music Classroom," *Southwest Musician* 92, no. 6 (2024): 36.
9. Nel Noddings, *Caring: A Relational Approach to Ethics and Moral Education*, 2nd ed. (Berkeley: University of California Press, 2013).
10. Latasha Thomas-Durrell, "(Re)Imagining Intersectionality: Holistic Acceptance in Music Education," in *The Oxford Handbook of Care in Music Education*, ed. Karin S. Hendricks (New York: Oxford University Press, 2023), 169.
11. Kimberlé Crenshaw, "Demarginalizing the Intersection of Race and Sex: A Black Feminist Critique of Antidiscrimination Doctrine, Feminist Theory and Antiracist Politics," *University of Chicago Legal Forum* 140 (1989): 139–167; Kimberlé Crenshaw, "Mapping the Margins: Intersectionality, Identity Politics, and Violence against Women of Color," *Stanford Law Review* 43, no. 6 (1991): 1241–1299, https://doi.org/10.2307/1229039.
12. Crenshaw, "Demarginalizing the Intersection of Race and Sex"; Thomas-Durrell, "(Re)Imagining Intersectionality."
13. Thomas-Durrell, "(Re)Imagining Intersectionality." See also Tawnya Smith's treatment of the ecofeminist "matrix of oppression" in "An Ecofeminist Vision of Music Education: Resisting the Intertwining Logics of Domination," in *The Oxford Handbook of Feminism in Music Education*, ed. Marissa Silverman and Nasim Niknafs (New York: Oxford University Press, in press).
14. Deborah Bradley and Juliet Hess, *Trauma and Resilience in Music Education* (Routledge, 2022).
15. I heard this analogy somewhere in a conversation, but I cannot remember or find the source. In a spirit of feminist ethics, I want to thank the person for the idea rather than suggest that it is my own original analogy.
16. Kevin Shorner-Johnson et al., "*Convivencias* and a Web of Care," in *The Oxford Handbook of Care in Music Education*, ed. Karin S. Hendricks (New York: Oxford University Press, 2023), 69–78.
17. Thomas-Durrell, "(Re)Imagining Intersectionality," 169.
18. Thomas-Durrell, "(Re)Imagining Intersectionality," 169–170.
19. Thomas-Durrell, "(Re)Imagining Intersectionality," 169–171.
20. Karin S. Hendricks, *Compassionate Music Teaching: A Framework for Motivation and Engagement in the 21st Century* (Lanham, MD: Rowman & Littlefield, 2018), 152.
21. Thomas-Durrell, "(Re)Imagining Intersectionality," 172.
22. Thomas-Durrell, "(Re)Imagining Intersectionality"; Marian Mahat and Mollie Dollinger, "Mind the Gap: Co-Created Learning Spaces in Higher Education," in *The Translational Design of Universities: An Evidence-Based Approach*, ed. Kenn Fisher (Boston: Sense Publishers, 2019), 245–258; Megan Tschannen-Moran *Trust Matters: Leadership for Successful Schools* (Hoboken, NJ: Jossey-Bass, 2014).
23. Thomas-Durrell, "(Re)Imagining Intersectionality," 174.
24. Hannah Dailey, "Taylor Swift's NYU Commencement Speech: Read the Full Transcript," Billboard, May 18, 2022, https://www.billboard.com/music/music-news/taylor-swift-nyu-commencement-speech-full-transcript-1235072824/.
25. Scott N. Edgar, Kara Ireland D'Ambrosio, and Elise Hackl-Blumstein, "Compassion and Care through Musical Social Emotional Learning," in *The Oxford Handbook of Care in Music Education*, ed. Karin S. Hendricks (New York: Oxford University Press, 2023); Judit Váradi, "A Review of the Literature on the Relationship of Music Education to the Development of Socio-Emotional Learning," *SAGE Open* 12, no. 1 (2022): online first.
26. Caroline T. Clark, Alyssa Chrisman, and Suzanne G. Lewis. "(Un) Standardizing Emotions: An Ethical Critique of Social and Emotional Learning Standards," *Teachers College Record* 124, no. 7 (2022): 131–149; see also Gareth Dylan Smith, Brandi Waller-Pace, Martin Urbach, and Bryan Powell, "Love, Care, Revolution, and Justice: Loving Oneself and Loving One's Students," in *The Oxford Handbook of Care in Music Education*, ed. Karin S. Hendricks (New York: Oxford University Press, 2023), 494–503.
27. Zara Abrams, "Teaching Social-Emotional Learning is Under Attack," American Psychological Association, September 1, 2023, https://www.apa.org/monitor/2023/09/social-emotional-learning-under-fire, 192–204.
28. Patrick Slattery, *Curriculum Development in the Postmodern Era: Teaching and Learning in an Age of Accountability* (New York: Routledge, 2012).
29. Edgar, D'Ambrosio, and Hackl-Blumstein, "Compassion and Care," 192–204.
30. Brian Arao, and Kristi Clemens, "From Safe Spaces to Brave Spaces," in *The Art of Effective Facilitation: Reflections from Social Justice Educators*, ed. Lisa Landreman (Sterling, VA: Stylus Publishing, 2013), 135–150; Karin S. Hendricks, "Compassionate Pedagogies for LGBTQ+ Student

Visibility, Radical Welcome, and Authentic Expressions of Music and Personhood," in *The Oxford Handbook of Gender and Queer Studies in Music Education*, ed. Nick McBride and Colleen Sears (New York, Oxford University Press, in press); Karin S. Hendricks, Cheryl Freeze, and Yi, "Spaces and Facets of Trust for Secondary School LGBTQ+ Music Students," in *The Oxford Handbook of Gender and Queer Studies in Music Education*, ed. Nick McBride and Colleen Sears (New York: Oxford University Press, in press).

31. Robin D'Angelo, *White Fragility* (Boston: Beacon Press: 2018).
32. Hendricks, *Compassionate Music Teaching.*
33. Tawnya D. Smith, "Caring with the Earth, Community, and Co-Learners for the Health of Biological, Social, and Musical Ecosystems," in *The Oxford Handbook of Care in Music Education*, ed. Karin S. Hendricks (New York: Oxford University Press, 2023), 141–152.
34. Randall Allsup, *Remixing the Classroom: Toward an Open Philosophy of Music Education* (Bloomington: Indiana University Press, 2016).
35. Stephanie Spellers, *Radical Welcome: Embracing God, the Other, and the Spirit of Transformation* (New York: Church Publishing, Inc., 2021).
36. Karin S. Hendricks, "A Call for Care and Compassion in Music Education," in *The Oxford Handbook of Care in Music Education*, ed. Karin S. Hendricks (New York: Oxford University Press, 2023), 5–21.
37. Tawnya D. Smith and Karin S. Hendricks, "Diversity, Inclusion, and Access," in *The Oxford Handbook of Musical Performance*, ed. Gary E. McPherson (New York: Oxford University Press, 2022), 528–549.
38. Karin S. Hendricks, "The Sources of Self-Efficacy: Educational Research and Implications for Music," *Update* 35, no. 1 (2016): 32–38, https://hdl.handle.net/2144/26744.
39. Derald Wing Sue, *Microaggressions in Everyday Life: Race, Gender, and Sexual Orientation* (Hoboken, NJ: John Wiley & Sons, 2010), 24.
40. Derald Wing Sue, Christina M. Capodilupo, Gian C. Torino, Jennifer M. Bucceri, Aisha M. B. Holder, A, Kevin L. Nadal, and Marta Esquilin, "Racial Microaggressions in Everyday Life: Implications for Clinical Practice," *American Psychologist* 62, no. 4 (2007): 271–286, https://doi.org/10.1037/0003-066X.62.4.271.
41. Juliet Hess, "How Does That Apply to Me?" The Gross Injustice of Having to Translate," *Bulletin of the Council for Research in Music Education* 207–208 (2016): 81–100, https://doi.org/http://www.jstor.org/stable/10.5406/bulcouresmusedu.207-208.0081; Justin McManus and Bruce Carter, "Accompanying LGBTQIA+ Students in the Music Classroom," in *The Oxford Handbook of Care in Music Education*, ed. Karin S. Hendricks (New York: Oxford University Press, 2023), 179–192; Tawnya D. Smith, "Microaggressive Stress and Identity Trauma: The Work-Related Mental Health Risks of LGBTQ+ Music Teachers," *Bulletin of the Council for Research in Music Education* 238 (2023): 7–22.
42. Alice A. Tsui, Juliet Hess, and Karin S. Hendricks, "'I Just Wanna Live My Life Like It's Gold': Prioritizing Anti-Racist Music Education," in *The Oxford Handbook of Care in Music Education*, ed. Karin S. Hendricks (New York: Oxford University Press, 2023), 514.
43. See also Hendricks, *Compassionate Music Teaching*, 116; Derald Wing Sue, Cassandra Z. Calle, Narolyn Mendez, Sarah Alsaidi, and Elizabeth Glaeser, *Microintervention Strategies: What You Can Do to Disarm and Dismantle Individual and Systemic Racism and Bias* (Medford MA: John Wiley & Sons, 2020).
44. Karin S. Hendricks, "Compassionate Pedagogies for LGBTQ+ Student Visibility, Radical Welcome, and Authentic Expressions of Music and Personhood," in *The Oxford Handbook of Gender and Queer Studies in Music Education*, ed. Nick McBride and Colleen Sears (New York: Oxford University Press, in press).
45. Boston University student Xianjun Yu has kindly volunteered this example for the book. At her request, I have also included an Anglicized description of her name's pronunciation here in the footnotes. Based on our collaborative work, we have agreed to describe the pronunciation of her name as "see-ee-AAN? JwEEN. yÜ?" (for Ü, form a "u" with the mouth but pronounce an E)
46. Kính T. Vũ, "Call Me by MY Name: Knowing Our Students' Names as Intercultural Sensitivity," in *The Oxford Handbook of Care in Music Education*, ed. Karin S. Hendricks (New York: Oxford University Press, 2023), 471–482.
47. Amy Lewis, "Critical Race Theory and Care in Music Education," in *The Oxford Handbook of Care in Music Education*, ed. Karin S. Hendricks (New York: Oxford University Press, 2023), 463–471.
48. "Be the Light" is an original song produced by the Class of 2020 and Class of 2021 of New Bridges Elementary. See https://youtu.be/p1OSZVCnDJI for the song that includes footage of the songwriters and producers, as well as the entire New Bridges community through the pandemic.
49. Sue et al., *Microintervention Strategies.*
50. Christopher Emdin, *For White Folks Who Teach in the Hood . . . and the Rest of Y'all Too* (Boston, MA: Beacon Press, 2016).
51. Tawnya D. Smith, Karin S. Hendricks, and Deejay Robinson, "Pentecostal Pedagogy and Musical Engagement: A Narrative Portrait," *Bulletin of the Council for Research in Music Education* 237 (2023): 7.
52. Warren N. Churchill and Clare Hall, "Caring about Deaf Music in Culturally Responsive Music Education," in *The Oxford Handbook of Care in Music Education*, ed. Karin S. Hendricks (New York: Oxford University Press, 2023), 542–554.
53. Nitza M. Hidalgo, "Multicultural Teacher Introspection," in *Freedom's Plow: Teaching in the Multicultural Classroom*, ed. Theresa Perry and James W. Fraser (New York: Routledge, 1993), 99–106; Vicki R. Lind and Constance L. McKoy, *Culturally Responsive Teaching in Music Education: From Understanding to Application* (New York: Routledge, 2016).

54. Juliet Hess, "Cultural Competence or the Mapping of Racialized Space: Cartographies of Music Education," *Bulletin of the Council for Research in Music Education* 227 (2021): 7–28, https://doi.org/10.5406/bulcouresmusedu.227.0007.
55. Hess, "Cultural Competence," 15, as quoted in Churchill and Hall, "Caring about Deaf Music," 547.
56. David Baker, "Disability, Lifelong Musical Engagement, and Care," in *The Oxford Handbook of Care in Music Education*, ed. Karin S. Hendricks (New York: Oxford University Press, 2023), 91–102.
57. Marissa Silverman, "Caring about Caring for Music Education," in *The Oxford Handbook of Care in Music Education*, ed. Karin S. Hendricks (New York: Oxford University Press, 2023), 39.
58. Gareth Smith et al., "Love, Care, Revolution, and Justice."
59. Gareth Smith et al., "Love, Care, Revolution, and Justice," 499.
60. bell hooks, *All about Love: New Visions* (New York: William Morrow, 2001), 7, as cited in Gareth Smith et al., "Love, Care, Revolution, and Justice," 499.
61. Hendricks, *Compassionate Music Teaching*; Karin S. Hendricks, "Authentic Connection in Music Education: A Chiastic Essay," in *Authentic Connection: Music, Spirituality, and Wellbeing*, ed. Karin S. Hendricks and Joyce Boyce-Tillman (New York: Peter Lang, 2021), 237–253.
62. Gareth Smith et al., "Love, Care, Revolution, and Justice," 499.
63. Gareth Smith et al., "Love, Care, Revolution, and Justice."
64. Hendricks, *Compassionate Music Teaching*; Hendricks, "Authentic Connection in Music Education."
65. June Boyce-Tillman, "The Hospitality of Wonder and Its Relation to Care and Compassion in Music Education," in *The Oxford Handbook of Care in Music Education*, ed. Karin S. Hendricks (New York: Oxford University Press, 2023), 80.
66. Kari Smith, Siv Måseidvåg Gamlem, Ann Karin Sandal, and Knut Steinar Engelsen, "Educating for the Future: A Conceptual Framework of Responsive Pedagogy," *Cogent Education* 3, no. 1 (2016): online first.
67. Allsup, *Remixing the Classroom*, 19.
68. McManus and Carter, "Accompanying LGBTQIA+ Students."
69. Kelly Bylica, "Critical Listening and Authorial Agency as Radical Practices of Care," in *The Oxford Handbook of Care in Music Education*, ed. Karin S. Hendricks (New York: Oxford University Press, 2023), 482–494.
70. Kelly Bylica, "Critical Listening and Authorial Agency," 487.
71. McManus and Carter, "Accompanying LGBTQIA+ Students."

8

Caring for Wellbeing and Mutual Flourishing

Chapter Overview

As music teachers foster caring relationships with co-learners, it is possible to become so caught up in the experiences, feelings, and/or needs of another that we could lose our own sense of self and become unable to facilitate learning in effective or appropriate ways. As Nel Noddings cautioned, "there is a characteristic and appropriate mode of consciousness in caring."[1] This chapter offers insights for practicing appropriate personal and professional boundaries—along with no-guilt self-care approaches—to maintain healthy levels of caring. Topics include work-related stress, practical self-care (vocal hygiene, hearing health, musculoskeletal health, psychological health), mindfulness, boundary setting, and co-creating a culture for mutual flourishing. The chapter contains specific practices for readers to try on their own, including do-what-you-can-when-you-can practices for mindfulness, body awareness, breathing, and micro-moment check-ins to assess one's state of wellbeing. It ends with a call to band together, to create a culture that promotes mutual flourishing.

Introduction

There is not much I find as soul-deflating as when a supervisor tells me to "be sure to take time for self-care." Granted, those of us with supervisors who say these things are very fortunate to have such kindness directed our way. Yet these gestures often come after the supervisor has also given us a list of all the things that are due by such-and-such date, and of course reminded us of the obvious fact that "our students need an extra special amount of care these days." Even when well-intended, it can feel like adding insult to injury—especially when we're already doing all we can do just to keep up with the pressures of our job, let alone take the extra time to meet the holistic needs of our students, let alone care for ourselves.

If you're lucky, you have been given ample resources to help your students—and even luckier if you are given tangible, usable supports (rather than vacuous reminders) for your own self-care. But in most cases, the concerns and issues we and our students are facing right now are so unprecedented that no amount of training, professional development workshop, or theory du jour can fully prepare us for the

Daring to Care with Music Education. Karin S. Hendricks, Oxford University Press. © Oxford University Press 2025.
DOI: 10.1093/9780197777589.003.0008

work of caring for our students or ourselves.[2] Unfortunately most political and educational systems are not set up to give us that support, either. As you may know from direct experience, these systems often work in direct opposition to what we need. Many of us dream of a different universe where politicians and policymakers simply leave us alone and let us use our expertise and energy to care with students in the way we do best, rather than sowing public distrust for personal gain.

Yet here we are—and as frustrating as it feels at times, it is true that we can't fully care for, about, and with our students unless we have the nurturance *we* need to keep up with the pace. We can certainly rely on a spike of adrenaline to make it through short-term bursts of heightened activity; after all, our bodies were programmed to do unimaginable things when we need to save ourselves or rescue someone else from danger. But as I discussed in Chapter 1, it is neither healthy nor helpful for music teachers to live like superheroes. Living in hyperdrive day after day, year after year, just isn't sustainable—no matter how much we may love what we do. But recognizing our superpowers and banding together with others whose strengths complement ours can be life-giving.

Understanding Work-Related Stress

Work-related stress and associated burnout have been serious problems in music education for decades—and things have gotten exponentially worse for teachers in recent years. In her chapter in the *Oxford Handbook of Care in Music Education* (OHCME) Bridget Sweet explains how stressful it has been for music teachers to be "expected to go back to 'business as usual' despite extreme circumstances"[3] in a teaching profession that may be very different than the one we signed up for. There is certainly much stress in our job that is beyond our control—and Sweet quotes Jessica Nápoles to suggest that music teachers "cannot assume all responsibility or work harder and harder to solve problems that they have no agency to solve."[4] However, knowing and understanding the various sources of our stresses can be helpful for recognizing what we *can* control, and to make changes in any ways possible.

In *Trauma and Resilience in Music Education*,[5] Tawnya D. Smith also bemoans how the culture in which music teachers work has been detrimental to our sense of resilience, as teachers have received little support for, or accurate information about, the various stressors that we face.[6] Smith describes how terms such as "burnout" and "compassion fatigue" have been misunderstood and have often promoted false and problematic assumptions such as "that teachers have adequate personal, community, and health care supports."[7] Some narratives about burnout even suggest that teachers "simply get tired of working with challenging students"[8] rather than recognizing the complicated layers of stress on us.

Further, Smith notes how most music education literature up to this point has played into the negative stigma associated with mental health and has focused on encouraging teachers to merely push through their challenges by maintaining a good attitude, with an approach "akin to blaming the victim."[9] In contrast, Smith explains how teacher stresses are real and often complex, and come from a variety of external (e.g., social, systemic) and internal (e.g., mental, emotional, physical) sources—and therefore need to be understood rather than easily dismissed as a teacher's weakness or lack of care for students. An acute awareness of such stresses can help teachers understand and advocate for the support they need.

Smith distinguishes between several different stressors that music teachers face, including workplace stress, compassion fatigue, burnout, traumatization, vicarious traumatization, and secondary traumatic stress. These terms overlap quite a bit in the research literature; however, Smith defines them broadly as follows:

- ***Workplace stress***: Occurs when someone's skills and/or knowledge do not align with their workplace assignments, and they are not given the supports or control they need to be successful.
- ***Compassion fatigue***: A global term for care-related exhaustion and despair that encompasses both burnout and secondary traumatic stress.
- ***Burnout***: Feelings of despair, fatigue, and hopelessness at work.[10] Smith draws on prior research[11] to describe how teacher burnout develops over time, in three phases. First, teachers experience *emotional exhaustion* as they are overwhelmed and unsupported in work-related demands. Next, they may experience *depersonalization* as they lose their sense of care for/about the students and become reactive, cynical, or indifferent to the stresses that students themselves face. Third, as stresses mount and teachers lose their sense of how to improve their circumstances, they may experience a *lack of self-efficacy belief*, in which they feel unable to cope with work-related stressors, which then creates a self-perpetuating downward spiral of stress and feelings of inadequacy.[12]
- ***Traumatization***: When someone has a powerfully negative experience and they lack a sense of safety and control. For a deeper look into trauma, please revisit Chapter 3.
- ***Vicarious traumatization***: When someone witnesses or hears the disclosure of another person's trauma and takes on many of the same feelings of that trauma into their own mind and body.
- ***Secondary traumatic stress (STS)***: The stress that results from someone experiencing vicarious traumatization. Depending on the person, STS can run on a spectrum from minor (experiencing virtually no symptoms) to extreme (to the point that the person might be diagnosed with post-traumatic stress disorder or PTSD).[13] Smith explains that the severity of STS is related to such factors as: a person's capacity for empathy, their own prior exposure to trauma, and their lack of sufficient supports to healthfully process the shock of witnessing someone else's trauma. She writes, "Given the inherently emotional

nature of music teaching, the potential experiences of affective empathy [may] put music teachers at higher risk."[14] (See Reflection Activity 8.1.)

Considering the variety of external and internal stressors that a music teacher might face—and further noting the continuum of responses that are possible in each of these potential stressors—Smith asks music teachers and administrators to do the following: (a) consider the complexity of stress, (b) challenge narratives that suggest teachers just aren't doing enough, and (c) advocate for more compassionate care for teachers that honors their individual and collective stresses. Some of the specific supports that Smith proposes for music teachers include: mentorship or collaboration with mental health professionals; professional development to learn trauma-informed approaches (such as those addressed in Chapter 3); and professional resilience education (including opportunities to learn coping strategies, self-regulation, and self-advocating forms of mindfulness). These supports might come in the form of top-down, administrative initiatives; however, they can also happen on micro levels with each of us choosing an approach that works for each of us, as time and opportunities allow. (See Reflection Activity 8.2.)

It is important to restate that there are some things we can change, and some things we cannot. Knowing what we can change—and knowing how to change it—can afford us a tremendous sense of power and agency. Chapter 9 addresses some of the ways to make changes in music learning settings, from the micro (self) to the macro (society) level. The rest of this current chapter provides ideas for self-compassionate, realistic, no-guilt, do-when-and-how-you-can self-care practices to support us along our journey toward mutual flourishing.

Daring to Care for Ourselves

Most of us haven't been taught or encouraged to engage in healthy forms of self-care. In fact, most of us were raised and trained to teach in a culture where it was considered selfish to think of ourselves first—presuming, falsely, that doing so might mean that we would have nothing left to give to anyone else. This kind of extremist thinking is cut from the same cloth as the idea that more is always better—and both ideas feed into a system where workers are conditioned and rewarded for overworking. In fact, our "faster, stronger, higher, better" world has taken to celebrating workaholism rather than recognizing it as a harmful pathology. As journalist Arthur C. Brooks writes, "No one says, 'Wow, an entire bottle of gin in one night? You are an outstanding drinker.' But work 16 hours a day, and you'll probably get a promotion."[15]

Although most of us would really love to do less work or at least have more control over the work we do, there is still a faction of us that find excessive amounts of work much more comfortable than facing quiet times when we might have to face parts of ourselves that we'd rather leave unseen or unheard. Bridget Sweet notes the difficulty of changing behaviors, even when changes will be helpful to us, in part because of the vulnerability involved in "taking stock of one's own wellness."[16] She confesses—and I concur—that self-care does not come naturally for some of us and may require continual mindful effort throughout one's life.[17] Sweet describes how her sister calls her a "burnt toast eater" because, she writes, "I will sacrifice my own wellbeing to prevent someone else from experiencing something unpleasant."[18]

No matter the reason for our lack of self-care—whether imposed by challenging work demands, or because we've been conditioned to do anything else than care for ourselves, or maybe because we simply don't know where to start—doing so is essential for any teacher who wishes to fully care for, about, and with their students for the long run. Self-care is not selfishness; it is a matter of health and longevity. So, in the spirit of mindfulness and of each of us just doing what we can, perhaps you might consider one thing in the following section to simply become more attentive about—and then, without judgment or shame, see where the road takes you as you let the details work themselves out naturally.

Four Starting Places

Bridget Sweet offers four starting places for music teacher self-care: vocal hygiene, hearing health, musculoskeletal health, and psychological health.[19] These research-based recommendations come from the Health Promotion in Schools of Music (HPSM) Project, the Performing Arts Medicine Association (PAMA), and the National Association of Schools of Music (NASM). I offer a brief overview below, but I invite you to read Sweet's full OHCME chapter for more detail and encouragement.

Vocal hygiene isn't just for voice or choir teachers, as we all need to keep our voice in excellent shape for the sake of longevity. Sweet encourages music teachers to consider not only the ways we use our voice (e.g., shouting over students making music, vs. getting technological or acoustical voice amplification), but also to be mindful of the way that certain medications, foods, and drinks might impact our voice. She offers this motivational strategy:

> Think of all voice use as Monopoly money. Each day brings a new, but limited, stack of money representing allotted voice use for that day only. Consider when and where that money is "spent" and where it might be "saved," such as singing along with students, talking over students while they play instruments, singing with the radio in the car, talking through lunch, meetings in noisy locations, or general volume of voice in the music classroom. Ultimately, we each have only one voice and it deserves protection.[20]

Hearing health is a much more serious concern than many music educators realize or want to admit, according to Sweet's review of research. Risk of noise-induced hearing loss (NIHL) varies according to the level of sound intensity and length of exposure, but it is wise for music teachers to monitor noise levels and use ear protection in settings where exposure is above 85 decibels.[21] Sweet recommends that we check out various options for earplugs, as well as a palette of technological tools (e.g., apps to monitor sound levels, smartwatches to monitor sound exposure, online hearing loss simulation tools to encourage healthful sound), and of course regular hearing tests—which I recognize (from my own experience) might be inconvenient or even scary. However, as Sweet points out, it's better to know the truth than to deal with "frightening 'unknowns' and assumptions."[22]

Musculoskeletal health is another thing that a lot of musicians tend to put on the back burner (no pun intended). As a former conservatory student and regular orchestra clinician, I've noticed that high-intensity, fast-paced ensemble rehearsals and studio lessons seem to be places where attention to musculoskeletal health is most easily neglected but most desperately needed. I know countless musicians who carve their reeds like masterpieces, or monitor humidity daily in their violin cases, or dote over their collection of guitars as if they were their children—yet neglect to care for their own body-instrument until it screams at them in pain or injury. I am admittedly one of those people. I often get so caught up in the moment and the magic (and the grind) that I forget how much more efficient and effective my practice will be when I am in the best possible condition. Especially when practice time is limited, taking time for musculoskeletal awareness is time saved and *bought.*

Playing-related musculoskeletal disorders (PRMDs) are exceptionally common in music performing, with some statistics suggesting that as much as 62%–93% of professional musicians experience PRMDs.[23] "Pain is the body's way of communicating that something is wrong," Sweet reminds us, "be it an unsuitable fit between the body and the instrument, the way one holds the body, tension or constriction in places where there should be none, or many other possibilities.[24] When we engage in healthful musculoskeletal practices we not only learn to alleviate our own immediate pain and stiffness, but we also model for our students how to promote injury prevention, foster expressiveness, and enjoy lifelong music-making.[25]

There are several excellent techniques for musicians and teachers to improve musculoskeletal health, including Alexander Technique,[26] body mapping,[27] and/or Feldenkrais[28] approaches.[29] These three techniques are each aimed at fostering internal awareness of the way the body is working (or not working), thereby allowing the body to open to greater levels of ease. Even a lesson or two with one of these approaches can be game-changing—not just for music-making but for life.[30] I provide more information about these approaches later in the chapter.

Psychological health for music educators might involve feelings and beliefs related to our capability as teachers. According to Sweet, music teachers might deal with music performance anxiety or imposter syndrome, or more general depression or anxiety. Earlier in this chapter I described several work-related stressors outlined by Tawnya Smith, including vicarious traumatization and secondary traumatic stress, which can also have an impact on a teacher's psychological health. No matter the concern or mix of concerns we might have in terms of psychological health, it is imperative for us to remove stigmas and normalize this kind of care. It is no different than caring for our voice, muscles, bones, or musical instruments. In *Performance Anxiety Strategies*[31] my co-authors and I offer several different approaches to managing stage fright, while also calling on each of us to change the culture of performance to one that is more caring and accepting of everyone's unique journeys.

What we each need for psychological health is individual and personal; however, self-care practices (such as those offered in the section below) can help us center ourselves and become more attuned to what we need to thrive. Some psychological concerns require the help of a licensed professional, and that is also time and money well spent. Sweet encourages music teachers to engage in continual self-care to allow ourselves to feel natural emotions and foster self-acceptance. She reminds us that a lifetime of committing (and recommitting) to self-care can empower us "to navigate the music education profession more on our own terms by putting aside the burnt toast and continually re-filling our cups and vessels along the way."[32] (See Reflection Activity 8.3.)

Guilt-Free, Do-What-You-Can-When-You-Can Approaches to Wellness

For music teachers, there are countless stressors beyond our control, and we are often left with little time, energy, or control to make big changes in our lives. There are, however, some things that we can do to break free from overwhelming patterns and create more time and energy for the long run. Making our work more sustainable requires individual and collective action—which, of course, can seem like piling on even more work. But even when we are taxed to the max, we can still make subtle but powerful changes in our own lives with committed and often simple (yes, often these truly are simple!) self-care practices. Below, I address a few, including mindfulness, movement and body awareness, breathing, and finding micro-moments for wellness practice.

The Subtle Strength of Mindfulness

My personal experiences with holistic approaches such as Alexander Technique, Feldenkrais, and body mapping[33] remind me of the ways that powerful transformations can happen over time when one takes on a continual practice of simply noticing. Just as small but persistent drops of water can erode rock over time,[34] so a mindfulness practice can change the way we see the world—with thoughts changing actions, and actions impacting the world around us. Although such practices can often make us feel emotionally or physically vulnerable, such openness to vulnerability is part of welcoming important changes in our lives. If you haven't considered these approaches, they're worth a try; there's nothing to lose and potentially much to gain!

Mindfulness is defined as "attention-based, regulatory, and self-inquiry regimes"[35] that help us view our life experiences with nonjudgmental awareness. In his OHCME chapter on mindfulness, self-compassion, and gratitude, author Frank M. Diaz asks us to notice how our students might pick up (even intuitively) on how we feel, and then reciprocate or mimic our nonverbal expressions back to us.[36] Just like two partners dancing, our moods and feelings can affect the moods and feelings of students, and vice versa—to the point that our expressions are created mutually. When everything is in a good place, this kind of reciprocity with co-learners can foster positive, authentic connections between co-learners.[37] However, the opposite is also true—hence the importance of mindfulness to become aware of the impact we have on others, as well as the impact they have on us. Mindfulness can also help musicians and teachers deal with performance anxiety, foster a positive outlook, and be more self-accepting.[38]

Mindfulness means a lot of different things and can be practiced in many ways. But in general, it involves activities in which we check in with ourselves, our behaviors, our feelings, our words, and so forth—and then regulate to a state that promotes wellbeing. Even when schedules are tight, one way to benefit from mindfulness is an in-the-moment activity called STOP, which Diaz offers to help us practice nonjudgmental self-inquiry any time we might benefit from a mood reset or outlook recalibration.[39] More explanation is available in Diaz's OHCME chapter, but the activity is shown in Box 8a.

Meditation is another way to practice mindfulness. There are a variety of meditation practices out there, and I personally have found every one that I've tried to be helpful in some way. Currently, I meditate 20 minutes twice a day and find that it centers me and clears my head so that I am better able to function. Almost every day I think to myself, "I don't have time for this!" However, once I'm finished, I say, "I'm so grateful I did this" because my mind and body are so much more focused and able to take on whatever the day demands.

In *Compassionate Music Teaching* I tell the story of a time when I walked into a class so frazzled that I told the students twice, with increasing exasperation, that I needed to meditate. One of the students looked at me calmly and invited me to do just that—so I led the whole class in a quick centering and mindfulness activity.[40] I believe this change of pace and activity happened smoothly enough because we had built a climate of wellness and trust—together, gradually—so that they felt comfortable asking and knew I would consider the request a valuable use of class time. (Plus, I'm sure they also knew that I was going to be of no help to them whatsoever unless we did so!) I'm grateful that they felt comfortable asking, and I'm grateful they were open enough to vulnerability to go on that journey with me.

Box 8a The STOP Exercise

(S) Stop what we are doing. Because our minds are usually on autopilot, physically pausing helps us to create a space in which we can bring awareness to our feelings, thoughts, and emotions before acting on them in way that may be misaligned with our deepest values and intentions.

(T) Take deep breaths. Deep breathing helps to slow down our physiological and somatic state. For this stage of the process, I usually recommend breathing into your abdomen for four counts, exhaling slowly for eight counts, and then pausing briefly between each cycle to allow your breathing to return to normal. To keep this process grounded in our senses, I usually put my hand on my belly for the added physical sensation.

(O) Observe with curiosity. Before transitioning to your next class, lesson, or rehearsal, scan your mind and body for any thoughts, feelings, or sensations that may be present in that moment. Is your heart racing? Are you feeling tension or physical pain? Can you locate that tension and physical pain? What emotions are you feeling in this moment? What story is your mind creating about the present situation? Rather than judging any of these experiences as positive or negative, try to notice them with a sense of curiosity or direct some self-compassion at these feelings [...] Often, simply enacting a state of non-judgmental awareness is enough to take us out of autopilot and into a more caring state of mind and behavior.

(P) Proceed with intention. Anchor your awareness in your body, assume a kind and dignified presence, and recall the kind of attitude and disposition that you would like to bring into your next interaction. Remember that mindfulness is not about disowning or invalidating our experiences, but about noticing them and when possible, dealing with them in a way that minimizes harm to ourselves and others.*

*Diaz, "Mindfulness, Self-Compassion, and Gratitude," 330–331.

Body Awareness: Mindfulness Isn't All in Your Head

Learning to know our bodies and felt sensations does not just have to be a fallback in times of stress. Instead, it can (and arguably should) become a way of life to help us live in healthier, more sustainable ways all the time—whether in the classroom, at the grocery store, or driving in traffic. OHCME author Stephen Paparo, a Certified Feldenkrais Practitioner, draws on the Feldenkrais Method to help people develop a life full of rich, embodied self-awareness.[41] He notes how music teachers have become tremendously skilled at sensing many things outside of ourselves (being aware of our environment, catching onto the vibe of a class, resonating with the music we are making, anticipating and attending to the needs of our students, etc.)—so much so, that we often neglect to sense what is *inside* of us. He argues, however, that knowing and feeling what is going on inside of us is not only healthy for our bodies, but also an effective way to attune to students and others as we tune into the messages that our own body is telling us. Box 8b includes questions that we might ask ourselves to recognize how we are feeling in the presence of others.

The Feldenkrais Method and other somatic education[42] approaches are natural complements to the six qualities of compassionate music teaching.[43] Through somatic self-care we learn to *trust* our senses, which enables us to make healthy choices in our activities and interactions that then fosters more trust in ourselves and others. *Empathy* is also enhanced as we practice presence within ourselves, and then can attune more authentically with the experiences of others. Such attunement with self and others is helpful for maintaining healthy boundaries, as described later in the chapter.

Somatic education also helps us learn the mechanisms for *patience* in teaching and learning. According to Paparo, it involves learning bodily movements through "successive approximations toward a goal with the understanding that there is always room for continued improvement."[44] It is a mirror toward *inclusion* as each lesson offers numerous and individualized pathways for learning about our holistic selves, with the goal "to restore each person to their human dignity."[45]

Somatic education promotes *community* by inviting learners to embody "curiosity, playfulness, vulnerability, and authenticity"—all important aspects of co-creating caring relationships, as discussed in Chapter 2. Finally, somatic self-care works similarly to the kind of mindfulness check-ins we have addressed thus far, to help us foster *authentic connection* with ourselves and others. As we tune inward to know ourselves, we are better able to make conscious choices that align with our own values and beliefs, and to act with integrity in our interactions with others.

Box 8b Listening to our Body to Attune to Others

Am I tense or do I move with ease?
Is my breathing restricted or full?
Are my eyes strained or relaxed?
Is my abdomen contracted or released?
Am I feeling hungry or tired?
Am I emotionally content or agitated?
Am I thinking clearly or chaotically?
Are my actions congruent with my intentions?
Am I being productive or do I need to take a break?
What does my gut tell me about my student(s)?
What do I say or do in a difficult or stressful situation?
How do certain situations or interactions resonate with me?
Are my interactions mindful and compassionate?
How does my self-understanding help me to appreciate what my student(s) might be experiencing?*

*Paparo, "Somatic Self-Care for Music Educators," 351.

Box 8c contains a gift to you from Paparo: a self-directed awareness through movement (ATM) exercise. This 20-minute experience is intended to help you understand the felt sensations of turning your head. Although self-exercises such as this do not replace the work you might do with a certified practitioner, it can give you a small taste of what it might feel like to learn somatic self-care practices.

Box 8c Awareness through Movement (ATM) Exercise

Please sit in a chair with a firm, flat surface (as opposed to an office chair with padding and wheels). Read each step of the lesson one at a time, then close your eyes and observe yourself as you move. Repeat for each step until you come to the end of the lesson. Remember to follow the conditions for learning discussed earlier. As a result of doing the lesson, you may notice that you turn your head more smoothly, sit more erect in your chair, breathe more expansively, and feel calmer and more centered. Whatever you notice will provide useful information about yourself.

1. Sit comfortably toward the front of your chair. Have both feet flat on the floor and spread about hip-width apart so your knees are above your ankles. Rest your hands in your lap. Take a few moments to observe how you are sitting. Observe the contact of your pelvis and buttocks with the chair. Observe all along your spine, feeling the back of your pelvis, lower back, middle and upper back, neck, and head. Observe your shoulders and your arms. Finally, observe your breathing. What moves as you inhale and exhale?
2. Slowly turn your upper body, as if to look to the right a very small amount. Then return to facing forward. Repeat this a few times slowly and gently, pausing between each repetition. Make a mental note of exactly how far to the right you can see, without any strain. Stop for a moment.
3. Focus your eyes on an object or spot straight ahead. Keep your eyes still, looking straight ahead, while slowly turning your head and upper body to the right. Then return to facing forward. Repeat this a few times, seeing where you can reduce the effort in your neck, shoulders, chest, and legs. Do not stretch or strain. Notice that your upper body does not turn as far to the right because your eyes are not moving. Stop for a moment.
4. Once again, slowly turn your entire upper body to the right, including your eyes. Turn gently and easily. Can you see a little farther to the right? Stop for a moment.
5. Keep your head and eyes facing forward and slowly turn your shoulders and upper body to the right. Exhale as you turn. Repeat this a few times. Relax your jaw, neck, chest, and shoulders. Notice that your right shoulder

is moving back and your left shoulder is moving forward. Stop for a moment.

6. Again, slowly turn your entire upper body to the right, including your head and eyes. Then return to the starting position. Is it becoming easier and more comfortable to turn to the right than before? Stop and rest. Feel the difference between your left and right shoulder. Feel how your left side is relaxing.
7. Keeping your left foot still and flat on the floor, move your left knee forward very slightly and return to the starting position. This is a very small movement. Repeat this a few times. Relax your left leg and foot as much as possible. Notice that your lower back, shoulders, and head are turning slightly to the right.
8. Simultaneously, move your left knee forward slowly, while turning your entire upper body to the right. Repeat this a few times. Notice that you get a little taller as your turn. Exhale as you turn so your chest can be flexible. Feel how your pelvis moves a little as you turn and how moving your left knee forward improves your ability to turn. Stop and rest. Feel how your left shoulder and left side of your neck and lower back are more relaxed.
9. Repeat steps two through eight, turning to the left. When reading the directions, switch "right" for "left" and "left" for "right." After completing this, continue with the rest of the lesson.
10. Move your left knee forward very slightly, while slowly turning your entire upper body to the right. Then return—go through the starting position—and move your right knee forward, while slowly turning your entire upper body to the left. Repeat this action a few times. Make the movement smooth and continuous. Let your hands slide on your thighs as you turn from side to side. Relax your legs as much as possible. Stop for a moment.
11. Keep your head and eyes still, facing forward, and continue turning the rest of your upper body to the right a little and then to the left a little. Repeat this action a few times. Relax your face, neck, and shoulders. Keep your feet flat on the floor. Breathe freely. Stop for a moment.
12. Turn your entire upper body to the right and then to the left. As you turn to the right, notice that your left shoulder moves forward and your right shoulder moves back. As you turn to the left, notice that your right shoulder moves forward and your left shoulder moves back. Feel how much more easily you can turn. Stop for a moment.
13. Alternately, turn your upper body and pelvis to the right, while turning your head and eyes to the left—and slowly turn your upper body and pelvis to the left, while turning your head and eyes to the right. Repeat this action a few times. Go slowly so the movement is smooth and easy. Do not stretch or strain. Relax your jaw, neck, shoulders, and legs as much as you can. Breathe freely. Stop for a moment.

14. Now move your left knee forward while turning your entire upper body to the right as far as you can, without any strain. Then move your right knee forward while turning your entire upper body to the left as far as you can, without any strain. Notice how easily you are turning and how much farther to the right and left you can see.
15. Now rest. Observe how you are sitting. Are you sitting more comfortably? Is your weight more evenly balanced on your pelvis? Do you feel a slight arch in your lower back? Do you feel taller? What changes do you notice? Do you feel more connected to yourself? Do you feel you are more open to observe and interact with others?
16. Continue to observe any change in yourself throughout the rest of the day.*

*Paparo, "Somatic Self-Care for Music Educators," 354–355.

Breathing and Movement

Breathing and movement are important ways to remove stress out of the body—which is important because stress can get stuck in our system even when the stressor is no longer present.[46] Holding stress or trauma in our bodies can lead to long-term problems that affect us as musicians, teachers, and humans.[47] Therefore, it is important to move and breathe deeply when we feel stress, and to maintain movement and breathwork practices to help us stay resilient from stressors when they arise.

Obviously, music-making involves both breathing and movement. But here I am referring to mindful breathing and movement to reduce stress and expand our sense of possibility. Taking time for *stress-flushing* breathing and movement is not just a luxury for music teachers and learners; it is a necessity. When stress gets "baked in" to our music learning, it can show up as a learned pattern in the music we make.[48] Conversely, habits of relaxation can become automatic when we learn them along with our music. Because breathing and movement are so intricately connected to what we do as music-makers, it is critical to keep those expressive mechanisms open, confident, and at ease.[49]

Breathing is also something that musicians do all the time but often neglect to use for stress reduction. In fact, I have been told by an accomplished brass player that years and years of breathing activities can often work in opposition to uninhibited, easy, relaxed breathing practices. There are countless breathing meditations online and in publications.[50] I encourage you to find some that work for you.

A Mindful Breathing Activity to Try

In addition to being a mindfulness expert, Frank Diaz is also a sought-after guest orchestra conductor—and he has combined these two strengths to publish several mind- and body-centering exercises for orchestras in the *American String Teacher* journal.[51] One of these, "knuckle breathing," is useful for students and teachers in moments of anxiety, hyperactivity, and/or a need to focus (see Box 8d). This

Box 8d Knuckle Breathing Exercise

- Ask students to put their instruments down or away for just a few minutes.
- Have students place the middle knuckle of their right- or left-hand index finger approximately two inches from their lips. Far enough away to see the knuckle but close enough to aim a stream of air at it.
- Ask students breathe in deeply for four counts, hold their breath for four to seven counts, and then exhale for eight counts, aiming squarely at their middle knuckle.
- Remind students to maintain attention on the sensation of breath on the knuckle and to let go of any physical and mental distractions that might arise during this practice.
- After four cycles of inhalation and exhalation, ask student to put their hand back on their lap, allow their breathing to return to normal, and just notice whatever sounds are present in the room.*

*Diaz, "Using Mindfulness as a Strategy," 69–70.

exercise can be adapted to any music learning setting and can also be incorporated into musical performance. Diaz offers one example of inhaling on a down-bow, holding the breath while stopping the bow, and breathing out on an up-bow to become more mindful of musical sensations while invoking a more focused physical and mental state.

Finding Micro-Moments for Wellness

No matter how harried things become, or how quickly a concert or project due date is approaching, there are things we can do to show love to our bodies in every micro-second. For example, I have been inspired by Alexander Technique instruction to invite private students to arrive early to lessons so that they can spend a few minutes in a semi-supine position on the floor to help them center into their bodies.[52] I also like to take just two minutes with students to practice "power poses." Amy Cuddy's research suggests that taking up space with our bodies and making us appear bigger correlates with a change in chemistry to make us feel stronger, more relaxed, and more capable.[53]

Many teachers take just a few minutes in rehearsals for stretching, breathing, and visualization activities. Others play performance repertoire over the speakers as students walk into class while students go immediately into their stretch routine. I'm also a fan of keeping announcements for the middle of a rehearsal, and having students take a stretch, breathing, or movement break while they listen. Let's face it—especially in the afternoon, students are much more likely to listen to us talk when they are tired of playing or singing and are ready for a break, instead of when they first arrive at class and want to move their bodies and make noise!

Other ways to move stress out of the body include belly laughter, positive social interactions, and creative expressions through other art forms.[54] When things get tense during music-making we might insert a joke (I often ask for requests, especially if I'm the one who needs to calm down). We might also do a quick check-in with students about something extra-musical in their lives, such as a community or school event. As described in Chapter 6, we might invite students to internalize the music they are learning or creating through some sort of expressive response with visual art, movement, poetry, rap, clay sculpting, and so forth. Rather than considering such things as distractions from the lesson, we can think of them as an essential seasoning or spice that we "sprinkle" into lessons to maintain freshness. (See Reflection Activities 8.4 and 8.5.)

Seeing Our Limits as Healthy Boundaries, Not Weakness

I began this chapter by lamenting false, empty "self-care" discourse that can do more harm than good to those of us who are already overwhelmed. I return to this idea to close out the chapter, because I do not want these "do-what-you-can-when-you-can" suggestions for self-care to have the final word. The activities presented in this chapter are meant as coping strategies; however, stopping to "strike a pose" every once in a while is not a sustainable long-term solution in a system that will simply continue to perpetuate unhealthy stress. I have many friends and colleagues tell me that they work in a climate that leaves them too often overworked, sick, disconnected from one another and from themselves,[55] and that they are rewarded for working with an oppressive schedule that leaves them simultaneously fantasizing and fearing what would happen if they stepped off the hamster wheel.

In her book *Real Self-Care*,[56] Pooja Lakshmin points out the proverbial elephant in the massage parlor: The concept of self-care has been hijacked by corporations for monetary gain while leaving in place the unrealistic expectations that make us continually in need of more wellness practices. She writes: "Our culture has taken wellness and foisted it on the individual—where it can be bought, measured, and held up as personal success—instead of investing in making our social systems healthy."[57]

Lakshmin explains how the concept of self-care has its roots in psychiatry in the 1950s (where it described patients' ability to act as agents for themselves) and nursing in the 1960s (referring to the need for caregivers to balance care for others with care for self). In the next two decades, self-care became associated with resistance to oppressive systems. As Audre Lorde wrote in 1988, "Caring for myself is not self-indulgence, it is self-preservation."[58] It is in this spirit of self-preservation that Lakshmin offers a kind of self-care that "requires looking deeper, turning inward, and developing a reliable internal method for yourself—not one that has been prescribed for you [. . .] but instead a solution that comes from you."[59] It involves mindful check-ins with ourselves, setting boundaries with others, engaging in nonjudgmental self-compassion, and making choices that align with our own values. (See Reflection Activity 8.6.)

Music teachers are very familiar with setting boundaries in the classroom. However, we are generally not nearly as efficacious at setting boundaries for our own self-care. For me, when it comes to the kind of personal empowerment self-care that Lakshmin advocates, effective boundary-setting is possible only when I know where my limits are in the first place. And I confess that I have a problem recognizing my limits. I absolutely love what I do—but just like when I eat sugar, I tend not to realize when I've had too much until it takes a toll on my body and mind. Sometimes I work myself to the point that I feel completely drained or unable to think clearly or even to put cohesive sentences together. I imagine many of you can relate.

One of the most common soul-crushing moments for me is when I find myself so exhausted that I can't be fully present with my students. At times, I can't even look them in the eyes because my eyes won't focus or even blink. And if I try to power through with a synthetic smile, then my eyes start itching to the point that I want to cry but my eyes won't even do me the service of tearing up . . . and I think to myself, "How do I navigate this moment and be the adult in the room without melting on the floor?"

For me, this is an example of where a mindful moment can come in handy—not as numb-out strategy or escape from present stresses, but instead to look right into the mirror and focus squarely into where something unsustainable needs to change. I have created a list of "Music Teacher Check-In Questions" that I have committed to asking myself from time to time (see Box 8e). Perhaps some of these questions

Box 8e Music Teacher Stress Check-In: Self-Care When Time Is Limited

1. What messages do you say to yourself? Are the messages kind? If not, how might you show more self-gratitude and self-compassion?
2. What goals have you set for yourself that might be adjusted in times of extreme stress?
3. What student words or behaviors have the potential to most easily distract you or get you off course? What have you done (or could you do) to maintain your center and sense of presence at these times?
4. Is there someone in your life for whom you can express gratitude, even in a small way? What might you say to them?

might be useful to you as well, or you might adapt them to suit your own needs and values. (See Reflection Activity 8.7.)

Creating a Culture for Mutual Flourishing

Many music educators live within societies with "never enough" ideologies that create multiple unsustainable ways of being.[60] One of Bridget Sweet's messages to us earlier in the chapter is that pain sends a message that something needs to change. Exhaustion and overwhelm are also signs that something in our life is unsustainable—and having routine check-ins with ourselves can help us know what changes we need to make. In Chapters 2 and 9 I address the importance of interpersonal recalibration to maintain healthy relationships with co-learners. We might also consider using recalibration strategies to maintain mutually flourishing relationships with our work, our colleagues, and ourselves.

OHCME author Estelle Jorgensen writes about the importance of music educators taking care of one another. She implores us—especially in difficult and stressful times—to recalibrate with one another in terms of commitments, noting the unsustainability of adding more and more to our workloads and expectations "without taking others away."[61] She asks us not to forget the humanness in our artwork:

> Ours is a people-centered undertaking, about and for people. [. . .] We might ask: Is it possible to accomplish more with less and remove the clutter of potentially worthwhile activities that together create a perpetual busyness and treadmill existence that prevents us from reflecting on those things of greatest importance and living balanced, happy, and productive lives? [. . .] Caring for people may mean valuing slowness and time for reflection more than we have done in the past and refocusing our efforts on fewer and most important tasks.[62]

Although change is slow, many "adventurous teachers" are starting to band together to move the profession toward more sustainable and life-giving practices.[63]

I am grateful for co-workers who are also committed to the work of health and healing, for students as well as ourselves. Over the past several years at Boston University, my music education colleagues have been working to build a boundary-respecting culture by practicing open communication and making explicit requests for what we need. We encourage one another to take time for rest, stretching, healthful eating, hydration, and family or recreation time. We have also committed to use the "scheduled send" feature for our emails so that we can work at the time that is best for each of us, but so that only time-sensitive or emergency work-related emails arrive in our colleague's inboxes at night or on weekends. I have asked my colleagues to email me (not text) for work-related matters so that my brain and energy aren't spun about like a pinball each time someone reaches out about something. We reserve texts only for time-sensitive situations at work, while still texting about nonwork things such as lovely dinners we are eating, pictures of pets or children, beautiful scenery on hikes, and so forth.

In addition to creating boundaries around time and energy, my colleagues and I have also committed to speaking up about issues of inequity or marginalization when they undoubtedly occur. We are far from perfect in this regard, but we are working together to create a community where people feel free to speak up when they experience or see something that is not right. We have maintained these boundaries with one another to demonstrate our commitment to being both colleagues and friends, and to show that we value preserving these two different aspects of our relationship—each in their own time and space.

Banding Together to Change the Culture: Self-Care as Resistance

As Lakshmin argues, all the scented candles and massages in the world won't bring us inner peace when the rest of the world is working against us.[64] Beyond communicating our personal and professional boundaries with others whom we trust, we need to join together to make systemic change. In the *Trauma and Resilience* chapter mentioned previously, Tawnya Smith speaks to the same kind of self-care-as-resistance that Lakshmin is proposing:

> [M]usic teachers must resist professional discourse that pressures colleagues to "get moving" and shames teachers into taking sole responsibility for their mental wellbeing when faced with external stressors beyond their control. A more effective response may be to unite in support of our collective mental health and to advocate for the external supports that we need to thrive.[65]

We can join together to make change by first resisting the idea that something is wrong with us when our body, mind, or emotions tell us that we need something different from what someone else wants for us. Instead, we can check in with these thoughts and feelings and consider what messages they are telling us about the changes *we* need. Frank Diaz's STOP exercise (Box 8a, above) and Margaret Berg's core reflection activity (Chapter 5) may be helpful for such a discernment process. Then, as we communicate our boundaries and personal and professional needs with trusted others, we can build a coalition for resistance against self-abuse for the sake of keeping up in a society addicted to work.

Of course, I am not suggesting that any of us refuse to do the work that is rightfully ours to do. We have an ethic of responsibility within this caring profession that requires each of us to do our honest best.[66] What I am suggesting is that we remain mindful, moment by moment, day by day, of what our needs, limits, *and* superpowers are—and then communicate to others what we need to function best, thereby ensuring that we (and others) maximize our potential. In Chapter 3 I introduced nonviolent communication strategies, and in Chapter 7 I addressed the power of microinterventions to make change. We might use similar approaches here to question, clarify, and assert boundaries so that we ensure healthful and equitable working conditions for everyone. Open communication and clarification might help others, too, as we can together envision a world where we are each always striving to be the best version of ourselves—no more, no less. (See Reflection Activity 8.8.)

Similarly, we can work together to remove the stigma associated with mental health, and instead seek the supports that we and our students need to thrive. In *Performance Anxiety Strategies* my co-authors and I discuss how mental health is often taboo in our field due to a climate of perfectionism and a belief that only those who are allegedly talented enough, or supposedly work hard enough, can make it to the top.[67] This false "survival of the fittest" narrative perpetuates lies about what success is and how to get it, using very narrowly defined criteria and approaches that were decided by powerful people centuries ago.[68] Such thinking completely disregards the richness and diversity of musical expressions and approaches for getting wherever we each want to be. I hope that we can, instead, advocate for open conversations about mental health supports, while also replacing practices and pedagogies that privilege conformity to one set of standards with those that promote growth, creativity, and individual and collective expression. (See Reflection Activity 8.9.)

Conclusion

Our society is so caught up in a "higher, faster, stronger, better" ideology that we have been conditioned to despise our limits rather than learn from them, and to break boundaries rather than set and communicate them. Even the notion of self-care has become another thing that people are shamed for not doing right, rather than a mechanism for knowing ourselves better and advocating for what we need to thrive. My intent with this chapter is to straddle two worlds: the one we currently live and work within, and one we can envision to be more sustainable. In so doing, I have offered some quick and simple strategies for coping with current stressors, while also encouraging us with ways to use our inner awareness to create boundaries that lead to healthful and sustainable careers for ourselves and others. In this midst of this "race to the top" world I hope we can band together and find ways to be more present with ourselves, our needs, and our values; recognize what is not sustainable; and work with trusted others toward creating systems that work toward mutual flourishing.

Reflection Activities

8.1. Consider the six kinds of music teacher stress listed in the "Understanding Work-Related Stress" section of this chapter. What are specific examples of each that you have seen in music education contexts?

8.2. Which of the supports recommended for work-related stress do you already have? Of those that you don't have, which might be manageable in your music teaching setting? How might you go about advocating for, or implementing, these supports?

8.3. Which of the four types of self-care do you consider the best starting place for you? Why? How might you go about it?

8.4. Which of the box activities in this chapter was easiest for you to do? Which was the most difficult? Why do you think so?

8.5. Which of the box activities would you like to pursue further? What steps can you take to do so?

8.6. What are your own superpowers when it comes to self-care? What are self-care practices that others have, which you might emulate?

8.7. Create your own list of "Music Teacher Check-In Questions" to suit your own needs and values, using the example in Box 8e as a starting point.

8.8. What are some ways that you can use nonviolent communication practices (see Chapter 3) or microintervention approaches (see Chapter 7) to communicate what you and your students need to thrive?

8.9. In what ways might you band together with others to advocate for more normalized self-care practices?

Notes

1. Nel Noddings, *Caring* (Berkeley: University of California Press, 1984), 51.
2. Tawnya D. Smith, *Healing the Fragmentation of Psyche, Society, and Nature within Music Education: A Radical Ecopsychological Approach* (Routledge, contracted).
3. Bridget Sweet, "Self-Care and the Music Educator," in *The Oxford Handbook of Care in Music Education*, ed. Karin S. Hendricks (New York: Oxford University Press, 2023), 339.
4. Jessica Nápoles, "Burnout: A Review of the Literature," *Update: Applications of Research in Music Education* 40, no. 2 (2022): 24, quoted in Sweet, "Self-Care and the Music Educator," 340.
5. Deborah Bradley and Juliet Hess, *Trauma and Resilience in Music Education: Haunted Melodies* (New York: Routledge, 2022).
6. Tawnya D. Smith, "Teaching through Trauma: Compassion Fatigue, Burnout, or Secondary Traumatic Stress?," in *Trauma and Resilience in Music Education: Haunted Melodies*, ed. Deborah Bradley and Juliet Hess (New York: Routledge, 2022), 49–63.
7. Smith, "Teaching through Trauma," 50.
8. Smith, "Teaching through Trauma," 51.
9. Smith, "Teaching through Trauma," 49.
10. See also Sweet, "Self-Care and the Music Educator."
11. Patricia A. Jennings and Mark T. Greenberg, "The Prosocial Classroom: Teacher Social and Emotional Competence in Relation to Student and Classroom Outcomes," *Review of Educational Research* 79, no. 1 (2009): 491–525, https://doi.org/10.3102/0034654308325693; Christina Maslach, Susan E. Jackson, and Richard L. Schwab, "Maslach Burnout Inventory-Educators Survey (MBI-ES)." *MBI Manual* 3 (1996): 27–32.
12. Smith, "Teaching through Trauma," 51; Patricia A. Jennings, *The Trauma-Sensitive Classroom: Building Resilience with Compassionate Teaching* (New York: WW Norton, 2019).
13. Secondary Traumatic Stress Consortium, "What Is STS?," https://www.stsconsortium.com/what-is-sts; Ginny Sprang, Adrienne Whitt-Woosley, and Jessica Eslinger, "Diagnostic and Translational Utility of

the Secondary Traumatic Stress Clinical Algorithm (STS-CA)," *Journal of Interpersonal Violence* 37, nos. 21–22 (2022): NP19811-NP19826, https://doi.org/10.1177/08862605211044961.
14. Smith, "Teaching through Trauma," 55.
15. Arthur C. Brooks, "The Hidden Link between Workaholism and Mental Health," *The Atlantic*, February 2, 2023, para. 9, https://www.theatlantic.com/family/archive/2023/02/workaholism-addiction-anxiety-depression-practical-solutions/672917/.
16. Sweet, "Self-Care and the Music Educator," 340.
17. Sweet, "Self-Care and the Music Educator," 341.
18. Sweet, "Self-Care and the Music Educator," 340.
19. Sweet, "Self-Care and the Music Educator," 341–346.
20. Sweet, "Self-Care and the Music Educator," 342.
21. Sweet, "Self-Care and the Music Educator," 343.
22. Sweet, "Self-Care and the Music Educator," 344.
23. Laura M. Kok, Bionka M. A. Huisstede, Veronique M. A. Voorn, Jan W. Schoones, and Rob G. H. H. Nelissen, "The Occurrence of Musculoskeletal Complaints among Professional Musicians: A Systematic Review," *International Archives of Occupational and Environmental Health* 89 no. 3 (2016): 373–396, https://doi.org.10.1007/s00420-015-1090-6; Noelle Rader, "Body Mapping Informed Pedagogy in the Beginning String Classroom: A Quantitative Investigation" (DMA diss., Boston University Theses and Dissertations, 2023).
24. Sweet, "Self-Care and the Music Educator," 344.
25. Rader, "Body Mapping"; Allison Ross, "Utilizing Body Mapping Principles in the Beginning String Classroom" (DMA diss., Boston University ProQuest Dissertations Publishing, 2022).
26. Pedro de Alcantara, *Indirect Procedures: A Musician's Guide to the Alexander Technique*, 2nd ed. (New York: Oxford University Press, 2013); Barbara Conable, *How to Learn the Alexander Technique*, 3rd ed. (Chicago: GIA Publications 1995).
27. Barbara Conable, *What Every Musician Needs to Know about the Body: The Practical Application of Body Mapping to Making Music*, rev. ed. (Chicago: GIA Publications, 2000); Rader, "Body Mapping"; Ross, "Utilizing Body Mapping Principles."
28. The following are service or certification marks of the Feldenkrais Guild® of North America in the United States: Feldenkrais®, Feldenkrais Method®, Functional Integration®, Awareness Through Movement®, and Guild Certified Feldenkrais Practitioner(CM).
29. Stephen Paparo, "Somatic Self-Care for Music Educators," in *The Oxford Handbook of Care in Music Education*, ed. Karin S. Hendricks (New York: Oxford University Press, 2023), 350–360.
30. Sweet, "Self-Care and the Music Educator," 344.
31. Casey McGrath, Karin Hendricks, and Tawnya Smith, *Performance Anxiety Strategies* (Lanham, MD: Rowman & Littlefield, 2017).
32. Sweet, "Self-Care and the Music Educator," 347.
33. de Alcantara, *Indirect Procedures*; Conable, *How to Learn the Alexander Technique*; Paparo, "Somatic Self-Care for Music Educators," 350–360; Rader, "Body Mapping"; Ross, "Utilizing Body Mapping Principles."
34. See C. Victor Fung, "Ways of Caring in Music Education through the Lens of Classic Confucianism and Classic Daoism," in *The Oxford Handbook of Care in Music Education*, ed. Karin S. Hendricks (New York: Oxford University Press, 2023), 136–137.
35. Antoine Lutz, Amishi P. Jha, John D. Dunne, and Clifford D. Saron, "Investigating the Phenomenological Matrix of Mindfulness-Related Practices from a Neurocognitive Perspective," *American Psychologist* 70, no. 7 (2015): 632, https://doi.org/10.1037/a0039585, as cited in Frank. M. Diaz, Jason M. Silveira, and Katherine Strand, "A Neurophenomenological Investigation of Mindfulness among Collegiate Musicians," *Journal of Research in Music Education* 68, no. 3 (2020): 351–374, https://doi.org/10.1177/0022429420921184.
36. Frank M. Diaz, "Mindfulness, Self-Compassion, and Gratitude in Music Teaching and Learning," in *The Oxford Handbook of Care in Music Education*, ed. Karin S. Hendricks (New York: Oxford University Press, 2023), 329.
37. Karin S. Hendricks, *Compassionate Music Teaching* (Lanham, MD: Rowman and Littlefield, 2018), 143–163.
38. Diaz, "Mindfulness, Self-Compassion, and Gratitude," 330.
39. The STOP exercise is also described in Frank Diaz, "Using Mindfulness as a Strategy to Improve Wellbeing and Self-Regulation within Orchestras," *American String Teacher* 70, no. 3 (2020): 69–71, https://doi.org/10.1177/0003131320940687.
40. Hendricks, *Compassionate Music Teaching*, 47–48.
41. Paparo, "Somatic Self-Care for Music Educators," 350.
42. Somatic education is defined as learning about the "process of the living body (the 'soma') as it acquires awareness through movement within the environment." Yvan Joly, "The Experience of Being Embodied: Qualitative Research and Somatic Education: A Perspective Based on the Feldenkrais Method," *Feldenkrais Research Journal* 1 (2000): 5, http://iffresearchjournal.org/volume/1/joly.
43. Hendricks, *Compassionate Music Teaching*; Paparo, "Somatic Self-Care for Music Educators," 356–358.
44. Paparo, "Somatic Self-Care for Music Educators," 357.

45. Paparo, "Somatic Self-Care for Music Educators," 357.
46. Margaret H. Berg and Megan L. Lewin, "Idea Bank: Stress-Reduction Activities for Music Educators," *Music Educator's Journal* 110, no. 1 (2023): 13–16, https://doi.org/10.1177/00274321231199; Bessel van der Kolk, *The Body Keeps the Score: Brain, Mind, and Body in the Healing of Trauma* (New York: Penguin Books, 2015).
47. Van der Kolk, 2015
48. McGrath, Hendricks, and Smith, *Performance Anxiety Strategies.*
49. McGrath, Hendricks, and Smith, *Performance Anxiety Strategies.*
50. See Chapter 9 of *Performance Anxiety Strategies* for some ideas.
51. Diaz, "Using Mindfulness as a Strategy," 69–71.
52. See de Alcantara, *Indirect Procedures*, and Conable, *How to Learn the Alexander Technique*, for more ideas, but I highly recommend finding an Alexander Technique instructor for the most effective training in this approach.
53. Dana R. Carney, Amy J. C. Cuddy, and Andy J. Yap, "Power Posing: Brief Nonverbal Displays Affect Neuroendocrine Levels and Risk Tolerance," *Psychological Science* 21, no. 10 (2010): 1363–1368, https://doi.org/10.1177/0956797610383437; Amy J. C. Cuddy, Jack Schultz, and Nathan E. Fosse, "P-Curving a More Comprehensive Body of Research on Postural Feedback Reveals Clear Evidential Value for Power-Posing Effects: Reply to Simmons and Simonsohn (2017)." *Psychological Science* 29, no. 4 (2018): 656–666, https://doi.org/10.1177/0956797617746749.
54. Berg and Lewin, "Idea Bank"; Tawnya D. Smith, "Building a Bridge between the Improvisational Expressive Arts and Music Education," in *Applied Arts and Health: Building Bridges across Arts, Therapy, Health, Education, and Community*, ed. Ross W. Prior, Mitchell Mossak, and Teresa A. Fisher (Chicago: University of Chicago Press, 2022), 119–132.
55. See Chapter 2, as well as Tawnya D. Smith, *Healing the Fragmentation of Psyche, Society, and Nature within Music Education: A Radical Ecopsychological Approach* (Routledge, under contract).
56. Pooja Lakshmin, *Real Self-Care* (London: Penguin Life, 2023).
57. Lakshmin, *Real Self-Care.*
58. Audre Lorde, *A Burst of Light* (New York: Dover, 1988), as cited in Lakshmin, *Real Self-Care.*
59. Lakshmin, *Real Self-Care.*
60. Smith, *Healing the Fragmentation.*
61. Estelle Jorgensen, "Caring for Music Education in Troubled Times," in *The Oxford Handbook of Care in Music Education*, ed. Karin S. Hendricks (New York: Oxford University Press, 2023), 27.
62. Estelle Jorgensen, "Caring for Music Education in Troubled Times," 26–27.
63. Estelle Jorgensen, "Caring for Music Education in Troubled Times," 27.
64. Lakshmin, *Real Self-Care.*
65. Smith, "Teaching through Trauma," 60.
66. Brent C. Talbot and Cara Faith Bernard, "An Ethic of Expectation surrounding the Virtual Performance," in *The Oxford Handbook of Care in Music Education*, ed. Karin S. Hendricks (New York: Oxford University Press, 2023), 44–55.
67. McGrath, Hendricks, and Smith, *Performance Anxiety Strategies*, 133.
68. See Tawnya D. Smith and Karin S. Hendricks, "Diversity, Inclusion, and Access," in *Oxford Handbook of Musical Performance*, ed. Gary E. McPherson (New York: Oxford University Press), 528–549.

9

Caring to Change the World(?!)

Chapter Overview

This chapter expands on ideas presented previously, to consider more fully how caring for, about, and with students might lead to positive changes in the classroom and beyond. It addresses actions music teachers can take within themselves, with co-learners, within the field of music education, and within societal contexts to make small and incremental changes to the spaces in which they work and live. The chapter opens with a discussion of how self-compassion and self-grounding, in alternation with an openness to vulnerability and improvisation, are critical steps toward transformation. The chapter next addresses ways to effect change alongside co-learners, and then within the field of music education more broadly.

Specific examples of change in music education include replacing competitive climates, fear-based approaches, and punishment with more care-filled, life-giving pedagogies. Readers are encouraged to interrogate their own practices and create new, more student- and self-affirming approaches that apply to their own contexts. Several examples are provided of music teachers who have cared with co-learners to transform their own music teaching and learning spaces. The chapter concludes with descriptions of what "daring to care" might mean within music education, and how caring *with* might lead to transformations toward collective thriving.

Introduction

Decades ago, when I was an undergraduate student at the Oberlin Conservatory, the admissions office had a marketing campaign that included a poster showing the Earth with the black universe surrounding it. At the top of the poster were words printed in capital letters, using a thin sans-serif font: "Think one person can change the world?" Then, printed in light blue below were the words "So do we." The poster is still easy to find with an internet search if you'd like a visual.[1]

The "one person change the world" recruiting campaign was received by Oberlin students with about a 50/50 level of appreciation versus criticism. On one side, some students believed in the possibility that just one person could somehow make an impact that would improve our social circumstances, even if just through some tiny ripple that might make waves. On the other hand, some students shook their

Daring to Care with Music Education. Karin S. Hendricks, Oxford University Press. © Oxford University Press 2025.
DOI: 10.1093/9780197777589.003.0009

heads and criticized the simplicity of the message, or suggested that it is asking too much for one person to fight against structures far too powerful for one person.[2] In true "Obie" spirit, many students felt both of these feelings simultaneously—including a kind of dread and despair for the state of the world while also sensing a fire inside that propelled them forward to make whatever impact they could.

Oberlin recruiters knew what they were doing. The campaign was meant to attract the kind of socially minded students that Oberlin College (across the street from the conservatory) is well known for enrolling—students who consider a good protest more important to their education than attending class, *and* students who expend great efforts to make themselves look as different from everyone else as they possibly can. Obies are, ironically, quite homogeneous in their efforts to be one of a kind, while also invested in communal efforts to improve the world around them. Herein lies the subtle persuasion of the message to a prospective Obie: the ". . . so do we" in the second line. The admissions folks appear to have been reaching out to people across the world who felt lonely, isolated, and desirous to make change, allowing them space for their sense of individualism while inviting them to be a part of a collective change-making organization—a "one" supported by a larger community of "we."

I imagine that readers of this book will be similarly split in their reception of this chapter title. I, too, am divided; hence my use of a question mark. Most music educators are likely in agreement that there is much in the world that needs to change, although we might disagree about what exactly that is. Some folks might ask: What can a music teacher possibly do to change the state of the world? Some would agree with the Obies who suggest that the fight is too hard and impossible to win. Some would suggest that it is best to keep focused on content and not get distracted by the issues of the day. Some might suggest that it's hard enough to keep up with lesson plans and grading let alone using time and energy to tackle systems that are far too powerful for one person.

Yet others would suggest—as does *Oxford Handbook of Care in Music Education* (OHCME) author Graça Mota—that our lesson plans, grading, and everything else we do in music education should be directed toward the concerns of the world. Quoting Gert Biesta, Mota argues: "if education takes its existential orientation seriously, it has to center on the world—rather than on the curriculum or the child—because it is only there, in the world, with others, that we can actually live our lives."[3] Mota views art as an especially powerful catalyst for change, given how it has the potential to: (a) interrupt habits of thinking and being by reminding us of our humanness; (b) slow us down to make time and space for more creative imaginings; and (c) sustain us emotionally as we do difficult work.[4] The kind of creativity involved in music, she argues, needs to be at the heart of the changes we make.[5]

OHCME author Patrick Schmidt shares Mota's belief in the need for change, as well as the potential of music educators and their students to be change-makers. For Schmidt, the power lies in the "we" surrounding the "one," as he encourages music teachers to join together in solidarity to make policy changes at the personal and local level. Rather than relying on administrators or politicians to decide our operating structures and thus our fate, Schmidt encourages us to engage in a hands-on, "grassroots, systematic, and well-informed policy practice—by music educators, for music educators, and their communities of care."[6]

Schmidt encourages music educators to engage in change-making with a full awareness the costs, which might include: (a) working through our own sense of identity and feelings of imposter syndrome; (b) the possibility of failing in front of students, colleagues, or administrators as we advocate for what we need; (c) letting go of old beliefs and practices; (d) the time and privacy that policy engagement might take from our personal life; and (e) the way our own thinking, seeing, and being in the world might be changed as we engage critically with the world around us.[7] (See Reflection Activity 9.1.)

I considered these and many other viewpoints when I wrote this chapter, and I wondered whether I should soften the title. However, the Obie in me won out. I believe that the Earth, and the social world happening on it, are currently in such a state of dis-care that much—something—anything—needs to change. I do not believe that one person can "save" the world alone—an idea that recalls the myriad troubles inherent in the hero narrative (as discussed in Chapter 1). Yet I am compelled, as are many music educators, to band with others to do what I can to make any change possible. Although I lack the answers and solutions to change the world, I offer this chapter as a space for us (myself included) to think about how music teaching and learning might be a space for visualizing and acting to make the world a better place, in any way that we can.

Caring to Change: The One within the We

Caring—a deep form of authentic connection—is necessary to impact the quality of people's lives.[8] OHCME author Kari Holdhus points to caring for change-making as a fundamental role of music education: "To be truly meaningful, music must be part of and interwoven in societal situations and challenges; and a relationally-oriented, caring teacher will aim at providing possibilities where pupils can experience music as connective in these ways."[9] Although music teachers might agree that change is somehow needed, and that caring through music can be a catalyst for change, we might disagree about the details. For that reason, this chapter takes an individual-to-collective, or a "one" within a "we" approach to care-filled change.

As shown in Figure 9.1, we might start with our immediate surroundings and make changes to our own individual worlds. Each of us knows our unique circumstances better than anyone else. As we feel and sense the changes that are needed, we can determine for ourselves what risks are appropriate and right for us, and what changes we feel ready to make. No one should feel shamed, guilted, or coerced to move in a direction that feels like too much. As I mention later in this chapter, any change (even small) can give us a sense of vulnerability and the feeling that the ground is shifting under our feet. However, we should always feel like we have agency about the changes we make and that we can always come back to a sense of groundedness within ourselves.

Continuing with Figure 9.1, our individual actions might ripple out to make changes with others (co-learners) in ways that are meaningful and important to our respective communities. From there, we can engage in collective change in the field of music education. Finally, it is unknown whether our efforts toward change might extend beyond our field to the larger world. However, given the ways that education orients us to the world, and the world to education, it makes sense for us to try. As OHCME author Estelle Jorgensen explains,

> Change occurs when people show examples of its operation in practice, and ideas and practices catch fire [. . .] as others seek to adopt them. In this way, what happens musically spills out into the school, the community, and wider cultural and political life as people sing and play their way into different beliefs and practices.[10]

Jorgensen honors the limits of music educators to change their own predicaments, let alone change all the problems in the world. However, as the quote above suggests, music teachers have the power to create a ripple effect in the world toward change, simply by the power of our example.

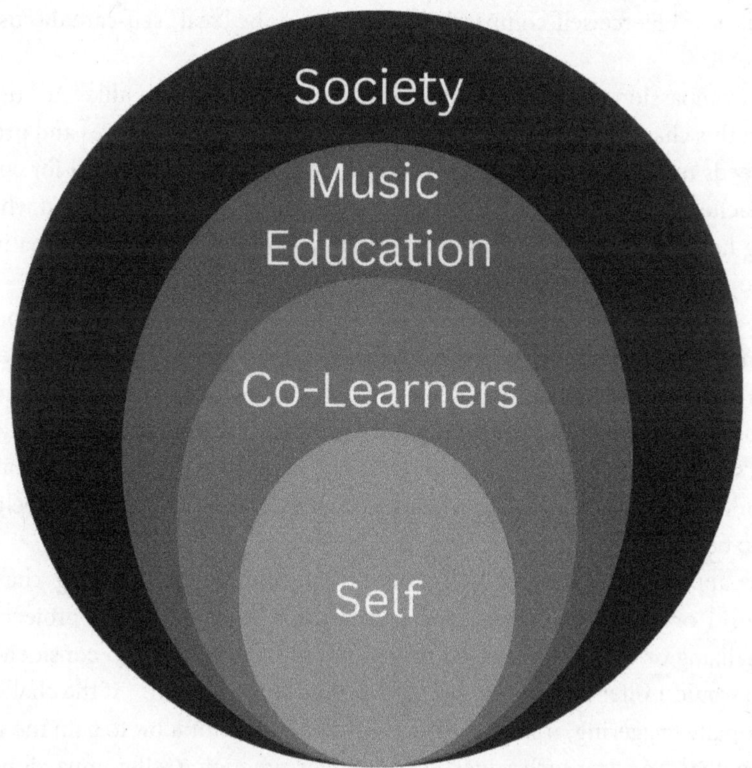

Figure 9.1 Levels of Change. (Design credit: Adam Symborski)

Changing the Self

The title of this book, *Daring to Care with Music Education*, emphasizes how it takes courage, curiosity, creativity, and vulnerability to reach beyond the protective barriers of a "content only" approach into the unpredictable and nuanced space of knowing our students. Daring to care might also mean that we have the courage to see the intersectional complexity of these co-learners as a mirror to ourselves, to consider the ways that we may need to change. Reflection activities throughout this book are a first step toward helping us consider tangible steps toward transformation.

The work of self-transformation also involves self-compassion. According to OHCME authors Rebecca D. Swanson and Mary L. Cohen, a requisite step for caring for self and others is knowing and embracing our own dignity, so that we can see the dignity in others while working toward change together.[11] We can develop inner strength and autonomy and realistic self-awareness through self-compassion, as we (a) offer ourselves nonjudgmental kindness; (b) see our experiences as connected to the whole of human relations; and (c) balance difficult and painful thoughts and feelings with an honest awareness of our whole self, rather than identifying *as* those thoughts and feelings.[12] Swanson and Cohen note that self-compassion involves a balance of "tender" self-compassion, or self-care and self-nurturance; with "fierce" self-compassion, or standing up for oneself and asserting boundaries.[13] Fierce self-compassion is similar to the "real" self-care discussed in Chapter 8.

Self-compassion is important for music teachers and learners alike. As I describe later in this chapter, there is much about music education structures and practices that needs to become more compassionate. Meanwhile, it is critical for students and teachers to practice self-compassion to become resilient and poised when enduring harsh or uncaring climates; maintaining boundaries; and advocating for, and working toward, better ways of learning.

Self-compassion is also fundamental to musical creativity. As composition scholar Michele Kaschub suggests: "Acting with kindness towards oneself and remembering that imperfection is part of the journey is a critical skill equivalent in value to mastering any compositional technique."[14] When composing or writing songs, self-compassion can enable students to see moments of creative inhibition as temporary and help them have the courage to try out new ideas without feeling the need to be perfect.[15]

One approach to learning self-compassion, whether in effecting change in the world or working on the latest composition or songwriting project, is by externalizing or distancing oneself from a particular challenge to consider, "what advice would I offer a friend or peer if they had this problem?" If the challenge is emotionally triggering, it might require stepping away for a bit to gain the mental wherewithal to answer such a question. However, practicing self-compassion, along with learning the ability to help oneself work through temporary setbacks, can help students (and teachers) trust in the ability to succeed in other similar challenges when they arise.[16] We might also model and teach students the "Yes, And . . ." approach described in Chapter 5.

Compassion-Based Activism

Compassion-based activism (CBA) is a concept devised by Frank Rogers, co-director of the Center for Engaged Compassion.[17] CBA is centered in knowing and honoring the self, and then extending outward to catalyze change in the world. CBA begins with self-grounding and self-compassion, then fostering compassion for and with others, and then envisioning appropriate ways to engage in compassionate action. As shown in Figure 9.2, having a core sense of self can help us navigate through other moral imperatives and help us maintain and sustain appropriate caring relations as we continually reach out, reground, and recalibrate relationships. (See Reflection Activity 9.2.)

As we work toward change in the world, Swanson and Cohen remind us that "our core self is wise and compassionate but can be disrupted by violence and violation. Until restored and regrounded, the self cannot respond with compassion and love."[18] CBA focuses on self-compassion and self-grounding to help us interrupt harmful behavior against us or others. It also focuses on transforming destructive

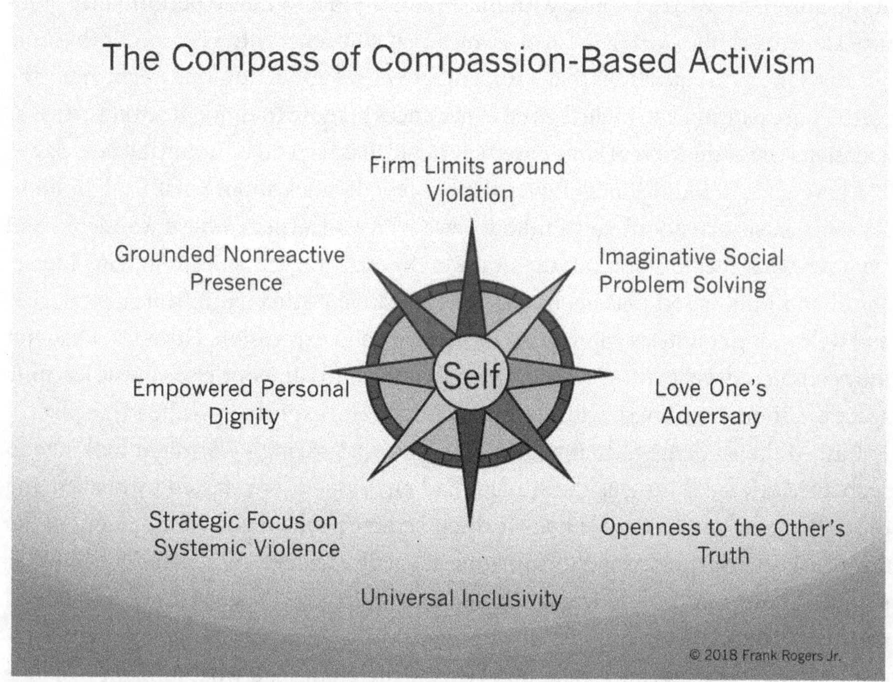

Figure 9.2 Compass of Compassion-Based Activism, copyright 2018, Frank Rogers Jr., Center for Engaged Compassion. Used with permission.

relationships into life-giving and self- and other-affirming connections through practices of authentic listening and recognition of our shared humanity.[19] Swanson and Cohen draw on CBA to envision how music's potential for social connection, coupled with compassion and self-compassion, can help music co-learners develop a sense of care for one another. I draw on their ideas and findings about change through co-learning later in this chapter.

Other than emphasizing the importance of self-compassion and self-grounding, I don't believe it would be appropriate for me to offer specific suggestions for how you, the reader, might want or need to change your own self. This is such a personal and individual question, and it depends on your context, your students, your career, your goals, and your dreams. Instead, I offer a personal reflection of my own, followed by a reflection activity from OHCME author Emily-Good Perkins. After that, I invite you to consider creating your own set of questions that are appropriate and helpful for you on an individual level.

What I Learned This Week from *Daring to Care*, and Students Who Cared with Me

As I was finishing up this book, I had a wonderful opportunity to travel to the University of Illinois at Urbana-Champaign as an invited clinician for a noncompetitive high school orchestra event. The day before the event I gave a guest lecture at the university, where I spoke with music education and music performance graduate students about *Daring to Care*—which had all been written except for this final chapter. One of the questions that a student raised was about how one might apply the concept of caring *with* to invited guest experiences in more traditional settings, such as a masterclass, or the kind of large ensemble clinic that I would be doing the next day.

I have given a lot of thought over the last few decades about what I might do in my own music classroom and studio to care with co-learners. I have wondered and explored what that kind of care might mean for engaging students, removing hierarchical and rank-based placements, facilitating student-directed rehearsal strategies, and welcoming countless approaches to creativity and expression. However, I had not fully considered what it might mean when walking into someone else's music learning space as a short-term guest, with certain traditions and expectations already in place.

I asked the students to brainstorm with me what caring *with* might look like in such a traditional setting as the student had envisioned. We started by challenging the notion of a "masterclass." First, we discussed the problematic connotations of the term "master," often ascribed to someone allegedly deemed to be superior to other people, or even to have power or dominance over others. Second, we questioned that someone had truly "mastered" or perfected anything, or if people are continually learning, growing, and changing. We considered instead what it might look like for the guest speaker to continue learning by engaging in activities and experiences that the people in any particular community wanted. We wondered: What might it be like to ask the people in that community what they hoped for, what they hoped to gain? We agreed that it would likely be different for every community based on their interests, needs, and values. Rather than expecting or assuming that what worked for one outsider (the "guest") might be best for that community, there would be a lot more questions and openness to everyone learning and growing.

The students were exquisite coaches for my activities the following day, as I had an opportunity to practice these ideas as a guest clinician at the orchestra event. Although I have learned quite a bit about pedagogy and technique over the years—and although there are always things that can be said to support and help students perform—I realized that my hearing of one performance cannot encompass all the hopes, struggles, goals, and journeys the students and their teacher took to get to that place in time. So, before beginning each clinic, I asked their teacher, and then the students, what they hoped to gain and learn from the experience. Further, I realized that the "hold my beer while I conduct your ensemble" approach did not align with caring-*with* music education. Instead, I asked each teacher if they would be interested in trying different approaches at (or near) the podium, including them conducting, me conducting, students leading themselves, and so forth.

With each clinic group, we discussed ideas, characters, goals, techniques to try. We traded off with different viewpoints, focusing on expressive goals, and how to get there, rather than what I thought about them after just one listening. The greatest joys of the day came when I heard and felt the students attune to one another, focused on expressive goals. It was also thrilling to watch conductors lead their own ensembles with brightened spirits and high energy, with confidence that this work could and would continue under their own leadership when they returned home.

How grateful I am that I had a chance to brainstorm the day prior about what it meant to care *with* as an invited clinician. If I had focused only on my past training as a conductor and what I had been taught to believe was right or true, I could not have possibly reached the depth of connection with these co-learners. They sounded amazing, and I can thank the Illinois graduate student who dared to ask the question and challenge something I would have otherwise taken for granted.

Yet I also realize that these micro-changes in my own teaching and clinician approaches can go much deeper and further. For example, when my friend and colleague Tammy Yi is invited as a guest conductor or clinician, she takes extra time out of an already busy event schedule to connect with the community she visits, beyond the event locale. For example, she travels early in the morning before the event starts to visit other schools in the area that are not on the event roster, where students might not be able to afford the event in the first place. She visits each community with a caring-*with* approach, getting to know the people in the area prior to her visit and staying in contact with them afterward. This is something that I had never even considered from my place of financial privilege. It causes me to wonder: What will I learn next from thoughtful and creative friends and colleagues about how to care *with*?

Inquiry and Analysis of Current Practices

OHCME author Emily Good-Perkins offers a series of steps for self-reflection about music teacher identities, assumptions, and practices, and how they might affect our interactions with co-learners. In Box 9a, she invites us to evaluate our beliefs about music teaching and learning. What aspects of music education have you come to assume are universal? I invite you to take time to write out responses to each of the questions in Box 9a, making sure to circle back to the steps of self-compassion (addressed earlier in this chapter and in Chapter 8) with each prompt.

In Box 9b, Good-Perkins encourages us to reflect on the ways that our beliefs might impact our teaching. These teaching beliefs influence the learners in our care. How have you developed the beliefs that you have? I invite you to use these prompts to maintain self-compassion as you interrogate your beliefs, especially those beliefs that you considered to be irrefutable.

Box 9c provides a space for us to consider alternative beliefs to the ones that we have held. Good-Perkins invites us to rethink our values and practices to consider what a more multi-centric approach might look like. Please circle back to self-compassion and self-grounding with each prompt.

Now that you have thought deeply and honestly about the beliefs you have about teaching and learning, I invite you to construct your own set of reflection questions. They might center around things you'd like to change, what you might need to do so, or what information you need to better understand your goals, and so forth. The questions are up to you, depending on what you'd like to learn or change about yourself and your world. (See Reflection Activity 9.3.)

Changing with Co-Learners

From a space and practice of self-grounding and self-awareness, we are better able to change with others. A caring-*with* approach to change is reciprocal and responsive. Similar to the caring-*with* pedagogies described throughout this book, such change with others involves attention to relational trust, mature empathy, unselved and ecological humility, authenticity, and an openness to vulnerability. I invite you to contemplate each of these terms, using the book index to revisit each of them as they occur throughout the book. (See Reflection Activity 9.4.)

Vulnerability, Power, and Change

Vulnerability requires additional attention when working toward change. One aspect of vulnerability that is important to consider is the relationship between vulnerability and power. Historically, the term "vulnerable" has been associated with

Box 9a Music Teacher's Credo—What Are My Beliefs and Assumptions?

Consider your beliefs about music teaching and learning—that which you have come to believe as universally applicable. Use the following guiding questions to devise statements about your beliefs.

Overarching

- What methods and beliefs inform my teaching?
- How do students respond to my teaching?

Discipline/Classroom Management

- What do I believe is appropriate or inappropriate behavior in the music classroom?
- How do students respond to my classroom rules?

Vocality (Singing and Speaking)

- What singing styles have I been taught to "correct"?
- How do students respond to my singing and speaking voice?
- Do my students sing freely in the classroom or do they feel inhibited or nervous about singing?

Movement

- What body movements have I been taught to "correct"?
- What do I believe is appropriate musical embodiment in the music classroom?

Methods

- What do I believe about musical standards and musical literacy?

Listening/Music Engagement

- What do I believe is appropriate music listening behavior in the music classroom?
- What musical forms or ways of making and experiencing music do I discourage?

Repertoire

- What do I believe is appropriate repertoire for music teaching?
- How do students respond to the repertoire I choose?

Caring/Knowing My Students

- What are my assumptions about my students and their musical backgrounds?
- How do I get to know my students?

Interactions/Engaging My Students

- How do students respond to my body language?
- How do I interact with my students?
- How do I know if my students are engaged?*

*Emily Good-Perkins, "The Sounds of Hope: Music Homeplaces and Compassionate, Abolitionist Music Teaching," in *The Oxford Handbook of Care in Music Education*, ed. Karin S. Hendricks (New York: Oxford University Press, 2023), 449–462.

Box 9b Music Teacher's Workshop—How Might I Interrogate That Which I Believe?

Now, consider the ways in which your beliefs impact your teaching and students. How do we come to believe what we believe? Use the following questions to guide your inquiry and interrogation of that which you had assumed to be irrefutable.

Overarching

- What will happen if I allow musical sounds, musical movement, and musical behavior that I believe are incorrect or inappropriate to take place in the classroom?
- In what ways might my teaching be alienating students?
- In what ways is my teaching impacted by my definition of musical success?
- Do I employ methods without careful consideration of their impact?

Vocality (Singing and Speaking)

- Do I believe that I must achieve a unified vocal sound? If so, why?
- Do I discourage certain ways of speaking and singing? If so, why?

Methods

- Why do I value certain music teaching methods?
- In what ways do my teaching methods inform my beliefs about teaching and music-making?
- How do my students respond to my methods?
- Do I discourage certain musical activities and behaviors? If so, why?

Repertoire

- Do I believe that certain repertoire is more appropriate than other repertoire? If so, why?

Caring/Knowing My Students

- Do I feel cautious about getting to know my students? If so, why?
- Is it hard for me to understand my students and their behavior?*

*Good-Perkins, "The Sounds of Hope."

Box 9c Music Teacher's Expansion—How Might I Rethink My Practice and Assumptions?

With the following guiding questions, consider the ways in which you might expand your practice to incorporate a multi-centric approach to music teaching.

Overarching

- How might I re-think my beliefs about what is musically incorrect or correct?
- How might I approach all aspects of my music teaching from multiple musical vantage points?
- How might I discover new ways of making and *knowing* music?
- How might I incorporate a wide range of musical ways of knowing into my teaching?

Discipline/Classroom Management

- How might I rethink the ways in which I consider discipline?
- How might I discover the underlying reasons of student disengagement?

Vocality (Singing and Speaking)

- In what ways can I make my singing and speaking in the classroom be familiar for students?

Movement

- In what ways can I allow my students to have freedom of movement and expression in the classroom?

Methods

- How do I find ways to implement my students' musical cultures into my teaching?
- How might I broaden my understanding of the elements of music and musical literacy?
- How might I demonstrate the value of oral musical traditions?

Listening

- How can I challenge Western classical assumptions about music listening?
- Can I allow my students to freely dance while listening? Make sound? Sing along?

Repertoire

- How might my repertoire choices reflect the cultures of my students?
- In what ways can the repertoire I choose deepen my students' understanding of diverse musical ways of knowing?

Caring/Knowing My Students

- How do I get to know my students?
- How do I care for my students?
- How do I create a musical homeplace in which my students feel able to express themselves freely?

Interactions/Engaging My students

- How might I interact with my students in meaningful ways?
- How might I incorporate their ways of communication into my teaching?

Student Empowerment

- How do I empower and motivate my students?
- How can I celebrate my students' musical-cultural identities in the classroom?

Student Choice/Agency

- How do my students experience music outside of school?
- How would my students like to experience music in the classroom?
- In what ways can I allow my students to make curricular and musical choices in the classroom?

Creativity

- How might I incorporate more opportunities for my students to create and be creative agents of their own musical expression and entrainment?
- How might I incorporate musical creativity and composition in ways that differ from the way they are conceived within a Western classical way of knowing?*

*Good-Perkins, "The Sounds of Hope."

weakness or with a risk of being hurt or taken advantage of.[20] Yet vulnerability can also translate to adaptability and a high creative potential for making change.[21]

Both students and teachers enter music learning settings with a sense of vulnerability, often for very different reasons.[22] However, traditional music education structures give music teachers inherent power over students, meaning that co-learning and co-constructed change likely requires that we, as music teachers, may need to risk vulnerability to the extent that we no longer feel fully grounded or clear about the direction the change might take.[23] Risking vulnerability may be necessary to equalize conditions for co-learning and authentic transformation; otherwise, we may keep doing what we have always done without fully honoring the contributions of students in our care. Returning to the notion of Compassion-Based Activism in the previous section, it is imperative that we remain grounded in our own self. From that space of knowing our self, we can entertain a willingness to change along with co-learners, by continually circling inward for self-assessment and self-awareness while remaining open to new ideas and new opportunities.

Risking vulnerability is key to trust, and the first step toward change. Yet the experience of vulnerability is very personal and context-specific.[24] It is inappropriate for anyone else to decide for you what should or shouldn't make you feel vulnerable. Likewise, we cannot decide this for co-learners in our care. Even our best attempts at reaching out with empathy cannot help us truly understand the kinds of change that are too risky or challenging to another.[25] Continued dialogue and consent are critical when working toward change. Now might be a good moment to revisit the costs of change noted by Patrick Schmidt earlier in this chapter. How might each of these play a role in terms of our willingness to risk vulnerability with co-learners? (See Reflection Activity 9.5.)

Changing Elitist Structures and Practices to Address Real-World Concerns

In Chapter 7 I described wonder, curiosity, improvisation, and accompaniment as aspects of identity-affirming pedagogy. I argued there that any kind of caring-*with* approach to music teaching requires pedagogical improvisation, no matter the genre. OHCME author Panagiotis A. Kanellopoulos notes that, in improvisation, vulnerability emerges not as a weakness but "as a strength, for it creates space for caring with the other, not merely about the other."[26] Below, I offer two examples of how music teachers leaned into their own vulnerability in a spirit of improvisation and accompaniment, to co-construct new approaches to music teaching and learning with their students.

Mental Health Activism

In Chapter 3, I introduced strategies for supporting students with mental health provided by OHCME author Rachel Dirks. Her research on mental health has had a substantial impact on the way she engages with students in her own orchestra program at Kansas State University. She has re-envisioned the top-down, elitist structure of orchestral performance to a caring-*with* model, where she interacts with students as co-learners to address concerns that impact their adolescent lives. As described in Box 9d, she and the ensemble members worked together to design a series of performances and engagements "to encourage conversation, engagement, and activism within the ensemble as well as with the orchestra's larger audience community"[27] around the topic of mental health and suicide prevention.

Rachel Dirks's changes to her program and programming did not require her to completely disrupt or do away with approaches that had been working for her and her students. Instead, she kept parts of her program that were enjoyed by students,

Box 9d Changing an Elitist Tradition to a Space for Mental Health Activism

Global warming. Gun violence. Loneliness. Today's adolescents and young adults are experiencing a combination of societal stressors that have led to a generational mental health epidemic. By learning to identify and label the complex emotions we all feel, we are better prepared to forge meaningful connections with those around us. Empowering students to become more proactive in their education may help establish a stronger sense of mental wellness. During the 2022–23 concert season, the students of the Kansas State University Symphony Orchestra took on the challenge to create meaningful connections as they embarked on a performance season intentionally designed to encourage conversation, engagement, and activism within the ensemble as well as with the orchestra's larger audience community.

Each concert of the season was centered around the juxtaposition of two emotions: mourn and dance, love and hate, hope and despair, and lost and found. The group performed selected repertoire that highlighted these emotion pairs. The orchestra's leadership team led discussions with the ensemble regarding specific societal concerns they wanted to explore with each other and their audience. Throughout each concert cycle, the students discussed a unique topic, leading the orchestra to embrace increasing numbers of solution-seeking strategies and activities throughout the season. Team members held brave conversations as an ensemble and discussed topics that are often considered taboo, such as mental health and suicide. The end product revealed an intentional and meaningful season featuring performances like *Love and Hate*—a focus on mental health awareness that included a performance of Tchaikovsky's Romeo and Juliet Overture paired with Green Bandana suicide awareness training for the orchestra members.*

*This language is taken from the advertisement for Dirks's (and her students') 2024 Texas Music Educators Association conference presentation, shared through personal communication on February 14, 2024.

while increasing opportunities for student involvement and dialogue about issues that deeply mattered to them. Furthermore, concerts and other outreach opportunities provided a means for them to inform the public about pressing social concerns such as mental health. (See Reflection Activity 9.6.)

Authentic Connections across Prison Walls

For over a decade prior to the pandemic, Mary Cohen practiced caring-*with* and co-learning in the context of the Oakdale Prison, a medium security men's prison in Iowa. Here, she facilitated community choir performances—with an equal number of incarcerated individuals and people outside the prison in the choir—that involved singing together, reflective writing, songwriting, and creating "communities of caring" inside and outside the prison walls. Performance audiences included hundreds of people from both inside and outside the prison. Mary explains that singing together as choir members brought people together, irrespective of their backgrounds or incarcerated status:

> Listening to the group blindfolded, one could not distinguish which voices would leave the facility at rehearsal's end and which would stay. In this way, the communal voice created in choral singing was both an embodiment and a symbol of universal inclusivity.[28]

Choir activities also involved songwriting as an avenue for authentic connection, especially as choir members sang original songs by members of the group and helped outsiders attune to the pain and difficulty of imprisonment. Mary approached outsider-insider encounters with deep care, including beginning each rehearsal and some concerts with a meditation where people could relax into their breath and release unnecessary tension and settle into a state of openness with one another. Mary has done a substantial amount of training in peacebuilding and self-care practices to do this work—something that is important prior to engaging with trauma-affected individuals such as those who have been imprisoned.[29]

The connections forged in the choir encouraged Mary to design a peacebuilding class where students could engage together in problem-solving related to restorative justice. Students in the class designed two peacebuilding projects. The first project was to help students foster personal inner peace, and the second was for peacebuilding with another person.

Songwriting workshops also helped Oakdale participants practice self-compassion. Mary used a four-step critical response process[30] to encourage participants to practice self-compassion and compassion for others. First, songwriters shared original songs or lyrics, to which listeners responded with affirmations and acknowledgments of meanings conveyed through the song or lyrics. Second, the songwriter asked the other participants questions about their song. Third, respondents offered ideas mindfully, in the form of neutral questions that did not impose a value judgment or suggested direction. Finally, the songwriter had an option to invite other participants' opinions—a step that allowed the songwriter to maintain their own sense of self-grounding and dignity.

Lessons Learned

Mary Cohen and her OHCME co-author Rebecca Swanson, who taught piano classes in the Oakdale prison, each describe how they were in a perpetual space of co-learning and transformation with members of the Oakdale community. For Mary, such learning and change included coming to understand how some of the practices she had engaged in with the singers did not honor the full history and practice behind the Navajo song "May You Walk in Beauty," which she had used to encourage the singers to offer love and care to one another in a circle. Rather, she learned that the song was intended to honor travels through life by living in alignment with each of the four cardinal directions (North, South, East, and West).[31] She apologized to the singers about this oversight, explaining how her intent to foster community among the ensemble had not reached to the point of full connection with building caring communities beyond that group. Mary reflected on this experience in an email to me:

> Not realizing the deeper meanings of the "beauty way path" or "hozho naasha" was a huge oversight because we sang "May You Walk in Beauty" at the end of EVERY choir rehearsal, every concert, the end of every songwriting workshop session (in the summer months), and the end of each informal songwriting workshop performance. Do you know the song by Laurence Cole with lyrics by Maya Angelou, "Do the Best You Can?"[32]

In typical Mary Cohen fashion, Mary offered her deepest reflection on this experience through song. The lyrics of "Do the Best You Can" embody Mary's work in the world, and her continued desire toward co-learning and transformation: "Do the best you can until you know better and when you know better, do better."[33]

Rebecca Swanson's co-learning-turned-transformation involved an increased understanding of the ways that the songs she taught in piano class centered in European classical music and American folk songs. She noticed that the students in her class were reluctant to engage in the songs. She dared to care as she asked the students for honest answers about their disengagement, and she embodied a genuine willingness to change her own practices as a result. The students responded that they would rather learn songs from more popular music genres such as pop and Hip-Hop. Swanson writes: "I admitted my mistake of assuming only Eurocentric music was appropriate for a piano class and changed our repertoire to songs that more closely aligned with students' musical interests and experiences."[34] She reports that class attendance "nearly tripled" after she included songs that the students cared about.

From their experiences and their research, Rebecca Swanson and Mary Cohen suggest that change can occur in ways both small and great when co-learners practice self-compassion and compassion toward others. From a place of self-grounding and self-awareness, we may be better able to recognize, celebrate, and encourage others' strengths. From there, co-learners can work together to discuss societal concerns and envision together how we can engage in music-making to respond and engage with some of the pressing issues of our time.

Changing Music Education

Two major pushbacks that I often receive about my publications related to care and compassion have to do with philosophies related to competition and punishment. In almost every talk I give, I expect that at least one person will raise their hand and tell me (and all the people in the audience who are listening out of care and respect) that (a) competition is natural in society, and/or (b) that consequences happen when people don't do their work; therefore, they assert that it is best to prepare students for such "life realities" through music education. In other words, these critics suggest that competition and punishment must stay in our field because they prepare students for a competitive and punishing livelihood.

I wholeheartedly agree that our job as educators is to help students navigate through life. However, I believe that our job is to teach for a well-lived life, not to reinforce its harshness. Whatever we teach, we perpetuate. If students learn harshness from their interactions with us, they will perpetuate harshness. On the other hand, if they learn care from their interactions with us, it is more likely that they will extend care in and beyond our circle of influence.[35] Further, what students learn about the workings of care in caring-*with* environments may help them refuse to tolerate, and become resilient to, any harm done by others—which may help them work toward a more caring and loving world.[36]

More than ever, practices and habits in music education (as well as the broader world) that were acceptable and even revered in the past are starting to be recognized as harmful.[37] To me, daring to care means having the courage to see that many of the ways we have taught music in the past may have been ineffective at best or abusive at worst, to name them as such, and to find a better way. Even in instances where there is little we can change about the culture in which we work, replacing approaches of harsh control with gentle flexibility—as we are able—may lead to massive changes in the future. OHCME author C. Victor Fung uses water as an analogy for the way that gentle flexibility can lead to lasting change:

> Only by being flexible and soft can human beings respond to the constant changes [. . .]. Water is identified as the most flexible of all the elements because it can be in any shape or state; it can penetrate and erode the hardest of stones through long periods of drips [. . .]. Being flexible is the key to adapting to constant changes in the way to *care* and being *cared for*.[38]

This water analogy can also be applied to the ways that change ripples outward, as illustrated in the circles of change in Figure 9.1. Care involves changing harmful structures at the places where we stand, and putting energy forward to allow those changes to ripple outward beyond where we are.

In this section I offer some ideas about how the field of music education might change. These examples center around ways to replace competitive climates and the use of fear or punishment, with approaches that are more mutually beneficial and life-giving. Beyond the ideas I give, I invite you to consider other ways that you believe change is warranted in our field.

Competitive Climates

In Chapter 5, I addressed the ways in which competitive events might interfere with a student's sense of competence, autonomy, and relatedness. I offered three recommendations for working within competitive *structures* to support student growth and intrinsic motivation. These include: focusing on goals toward competence development, co-creating expressive goals, and learning from others (emphasizing tangible skills that students are capable of emulating)—rather than focusing on beating out others or using fear of failure to motivate students to practice or finish assignments. In this chapter I write more directly about the detriment of competitive *climates* and how we might change them.

Over the past two decades I have committed a great deal of my scholarly work to studying the troubled and complex relationship between music education and competitive climates.[39] From that research, I can offer with conviction that caring-*with* approaches work in opposition to competitive cultures (and vice-versa), whereas collaboration and cooperation are embodiments of caring-*with.* Because I have observed competitive climates mostly from the perspective of instrumental performance, the examples in this section lean heavily toward that area of music teaching and learning. However, the principles are applicable to other contexts as well.

While studying competitive events, I have witnessed countless students displaying physical and emotional manifestations of stress so high that they matched the same extent displayed by people in danger of losing their life due to some sort of physical threat. Although most in our field would call for emergency support if these symptoms were displayed in a different context, many have come to accept them as normal in music education competitions—even routinely supposing that the problem belonged to the person rather than with the system. "Survival of the fittest" is a term often used to suggest that competition is a necessary part of weeding out those who just aren't "good enough" to "make it" in the field.[40] Considered differently, however, it is more likely that these competitive structures just continue to reinforce actions and behaviors of the powerful few who set up the system of rewards and punishments in the first place.[41] Further, they celebrate the people who had the financial and other support mechanisms to make it where they are.[42]

As people care *with* one another in music education, they are open to vulnerability, to learning new things, and to recognizing that there are multiple paths toward musicianship. However, competitive climates allow for only one "right" approach, judged within a hierarchy of superiority according to standardized rubrics.[43] As long as someone or something must be deemed "superior" to another, there must be disconnection between them.[44] And as I discussed in Chapter 2, a lack of connection with others is literally lethal.

Separation from others through rank-based competition has an even more direct connection to anti-care. Tawnya Smith has compared the "invented hierarchy" of musical competitions with the society's hierarchical system in economics, where certain people "rise to the top" financially and then hire or force others (who are deemed as having inferior status) to do the "dirty work" of caring for them, thereby absolving themselves of the responsibility of caring:

> [F]ormal education has become a vehicle to help individuals escape from the responsibilities and obligations to care: If one can *elevate* themselves through education, one can enjoy a higher status according to the invented hierarchy, and have enough income or wealth to pay or force others to care—effectively erasing from view the dirt, sweat, blood, and suffering with which marginalized others contend so that one has the luxury not to care.[45]

In this line of thinking, care (including care for oneself) is relegated to others whose time is deemed inferior; therefore, the drive toward "superiority" involves the privilege of having others do one's work for them. And as long as the metrics (whether in music education or in society) are standardized, the people with power can continue to decide what "superiority" looks like within this invented hierarchy.[46]

Authentic connection is lost in a system of rankings where people are deemed superior or inferior through a synthetic measurement of individual human worth, and where care is treated as the work of "inferior" people. As teachers, we need only look at our paychecks and limited autonomy to recognize where educators—we who are expected to care for others—are situated in the social hierarchy. Yet as Patrick Schmidt suggests, now may be the time for music teachers to reimagine our possibilities and make steps toward change: "If the 2020 pandemic has indeed provided lessons about the fragility of institutions, relations, and social norms, it must also have alerted many to the possibilities—awaiting mobilization—of a redirection and amplification of educational aims."[47] The possibilities are endless, as each of us makes even the smallest steps toward change wherever we are. Below I offer two visions, after which I invite you to consider your own.

An Ecological Vision

What would it look like if we took current music education approaches and activities, kept what was care-filled—and repurposed what was not, into something much more life-giving? OHCME author Tawnya Smith, along with OHCME authors Kevin Shorner-Johnson, Martha Gonzalez, and Daniel J. Shevock, extend the work on the work of OHCME author June Boyce-Tillman to propose an ecological vision for music education.[48] In this caring-*with* approach, musical materials and their construction are not separated from, but rather are integrated with, their creative expression and community's values.[49] Here, competition against others is pointless because each community determines what forms of musical expression are most meaningful, relevant, and sustainable to them.

Instead of striving for status or power over others, the goals of an ecological music education include mindful presence with others, the sacredness of shared musical experience, and deep care for the full wellbeing of other people in and beyond the music-making space.[50] Separation and dominance over others is replaced by an understanding of one's own unique niche within the community ecosystem. Caring *with* one another in an ecological space involves honoring and celebrating each person's "unique creative gifts, skills, and purpose in life as well as the ways that one's contributions might simultaneously benefit oneself, others, and the [Earth]."[51] As described in Chapter 2, this ecological vision considers humility not in terms of comparison to anyone else, but instead how one can learn, contribute, and engage in collective thriving with others.

Smith draws on this ecological vision to propose an alternative, caring-*with* approach for one area of music education that is very dear to her own heart: marching band.[52] She draws on her deep love of marching band—a place she felt fully at home and experienced much success in her earlier career—to consider what it might look like if it were based in an ecological worldview. A portion of this vision is presented in Box 9e.

According to this ecological approach to marching band, *rank-based competitions*, which have been shown to privilege and celebrate those who have financial resources over those who do not,[53] would be replaced with *place-based celebrations.* Such an approach maintains the exhilarating and community-supportive elements of marching band such as collaboration, artistry, athleticism, and musical brilliance. Yet rather than pitting communities against one another according to a standardized metric, it creates a space for communities to work together to recognize and celebrate their own unique strengths while also supporting one another with theirs.

One alternative Smith offers in Box 9e is to celebrate what is already working well, whereas the second option involves community-based problem-solving or solution-finding. This second option would likely resonate well with Generation Z students, who appear generally more concerned than previous generations about the state of the world beyond their classroom.[54] Both options allow for a more sustainable and life-giving music education where the goal is not about taking home the trophy, but rather making their home and surrounding communities more vibrant and alive. (See Reflection Activity 9.7.)

Mixing Up Ensemble Seating for Belonging and Holistic Growth

In several of my own studies related to competition, I have observed the effect of competitive climates on student self-beliefs. In one study, I found that students who were auditioning for rank-based seating associated their performance capabilities less with their ability to perform expressively, and more with their ability to impress someone else.[55] As I crunched these data and read this particular statistic on the output grid, I asked myself: "Is it possible that our use of seating auditions as an attempt to motivate students to practice might actually lead to musical inhibition? If so, is this really the approach we want to use?"[56]

Box 9e An Ecological Vision for Marching Band

Instead of competitive festivals, what about collaborative ones where resources and ideas are shared among those living within a bioregion? For example, perhaps students in a cluster of neighboring schools might work together to identify some issue or theme that is important to them. [. . .] In this case, the students could craft a collaborative marching band show with music, movement, and visuals that celebrate something that is treasured about the wider community. Students might partner with area businesses, community interest groups, or government organizations or leaders to fund [and promote] the show. Such a collaboration could provide the opportunity for the students to learn what is valuable about their community—what they can feel proud of or good about. The focus would cease to be upon an invented value hierarchy and the comparison of those with and without resources or opportunities.

Alternatively, the students might identify something about their community that is threatened or is problematic (such as local environmental degradation and unsustainable practices). The students might choose to investigate this issue in partnership with community stakeholders and work to identify and honor various perspectives or solutions. As such, the marching band show might include music and spoken word, visuals, or enactments that depict such perspectives or solutions. [. . .]

Interschool collaborations would be a necessary component to break down value hierarchies and allow for a sharing of resources including instruments, equipment, rehearsal spaces, venues, and teachers. Student representatives from each school could work together to manage organizational tasks. Some might brainstorm, narrow down, and decide upon a theme for the show; others could make connections with community partners; and others could organize equipment and logistics. In this way, all the students in the ensemble could hold a leadership role. They might learn when to lead and when to follow. They might learn more deeply that it takes everyone in the community to contribute to ensure thriving and success—that each person brings something unique and that what one contributes will look different from individual to individual. In this way, each student may learn that they are valued for their contribution and that the size or the type of contribution is not subject to social comparison. The emphasis is less upon individual achievement and more upon group achievement: "Is everyone using their superpower to ensure that we collectively create an amazing show?"*

*Tawnya D. Smith, "An Ecofeminist Vision of Music Education: Resisting the Intertwining Logics of Domination," in *The Oxford Handbook of Feminism in Music Education*, ed. Marissa Silverman and Nasim Niknafs (New York: Oxford University Press, in press). Used with permission.

On the other hand, I have had the pleasure of learning from and with many music educators who have done away with rank-based seating placements in ensembles, instead using systems of rotation and strength-based seating in which students are placed near someone with a complementary skill set. In other words, a person with a resonant tone might be seated next to someone with a strong sense of rhythm, and so forth.[57] Recalling the earlier idea of understanding and occupying one's own unique niche within the musical ecosystem,[58] such seating arrangements emphasize individual strengths while encouraging peer mentoring and support toward growth, rather than pitting students against one another.

In such seating "mixups" there may still be assigned leaders. However, these leaders might rotate throughout the ensemble and be expected to help their peers through a sense of responsibility and care, rather than spending their energy and focus fighting off potential adversaries who might be eyeing their position at the top. I described such systems of caring-*with* student leadership in *Compassionate Music Teaching*, particularly in the leadership and circle-based ensemble approach used by band director Steve Massey.[59] Other examples are described in the writings of Louis Bergonzi,[60] Andrew Goodrich,[61] and Tammy Yi.[62]

In the case of Yi's research, students who were placed in an anti-hierarchical seating system showed increased student collaboration, motivation, and engagement, while also demonstrating dramatic improvement in performance quality, especially among students who did not have prior musical training or could not afford private lessons.[63] This research debunks common myths about using rank-based seating to motivate students to practice. Instead, it shows the importance of encouraging students to support one another in their musical growth.

Lexington High School Orchestra Director Jessica Billings-White (whom I introduced in Chapters 2 and 3) uses a mix-up seating approach similar to those described above, as a means of building community and a sense of belonging. She describes:

> I make sure that class camaraderie is ingrained from day one in every single one of my ensembles. [. . .] I teach from the get-go that it is not your position in the seating that makes you an integral part of this orchestra. Everyone is important. So we have rotational seating where every student sits in the back, middle, and front of the section for every concert. If they want to be pitted against their peers and want to be ranked based on their ability and seating auditions, I give them a list of extracurricular orchestras they can audition for. I am so lucky that my colleagues and I see eye to eye on this and it is the same throughout their middle and high school careers.[64]

As illustrated in the quote above, Jessica is not swayed by a few students in her class (or their parents) who might ask for a more hierarchical ranking system. Instead, she keeps her own self-grounding by maintaining a focus on belonging.

In such cases, with confidence and with the support of her colleagues, she simply suggests other ensembles outside the school where students can have such competitive experiences, while maintaining her value of collaboration and connection.

Punishment and Fear

Even more troubling than the use of competition as a motivator is the use of punishment and fear. Music education has capitalized on anxiety much too often, using fear of lack or attack as a means of getting people to do things they love, in ways that they don't love. In the research I have conducted on competition I have observed music teachers capitalize on students' fears to threaten them with failure at competitive events if they didn't practice, didn't move quickly enough, and so forth.[65]

I am confident that I, too, have fallen into such teacher behavior in the past, especially when I lacked self-grounding and when my own fear of judgment got in the way of me seeing the humanness of the students in front of me. Fortunately, teacher-initiated threats of failure appear to have become less frequent in more recent years. However, students are still routinely subjected to such traumatic experiences without receiving the support they need to survive and thrive.

As I have presented conference sessions and workshops on music performance anxiety over the past decade, I have consistently and persistently hoped that the topic would become irrelevant as the field became more loving and caring, and as students became more resilient and resistant to harmful practices. Unfortunately, the audiences have grown and the need for the topic has become more pressing. Last year, two of my colleagues and I gave several presentations related to care, compassion, anxiety, and mental health at a major state music education conference in the United States. After the sessions finished, people lined up to tell us personal stories of pain, of fear, of frustration, of loneliness and isolation. They told us, over and over, that the approaches they learned are simply not working for them nor for their students, and they are not sure if they can stay in the profession. Many of them mentioned how affirming it was to be at those sessions with hundreds of other teachers and feel—many for the first time— that they were not alone.

In *Performance Anxiety Strategies*, my colleagues and I write about how music educators need to do more than slap a bandage on a problem or give someone the "top 10 list" to quickly overcome stage fright.[66] The problem may extend beyond a person's own dispositions to encompass flaws with the system, including traditions of harm that we have learned from others and perpetuated in our own practices. Tawnya Smith gives one example:

> A wind band is rehearsing and when the ensemble comes upon a difficult technical passage, the music breaks down. This musical collapse has happened in

> previous rehearsals, so the conductor angrily requires that each of the members of the implicated section perform the technical passage independently in front of the other members of the ensemble. This practice is sometimes called "going down the line."
>
> This act of public shaming [. . .] was normalized violence and was commonplace during the time I was enrolled in my pre-service teacher education program. My peers and I accepted this practice and assumed that when it occurred that we "had it coming" because we were ill-prepared for rehearsal, whether that was the case or not. Of course, believing that such treatment was justified is what we had been taught to think, and we even perpetuated this myth by blaming and shaming one another after rehearsal [. . .]. My peers and I were prepared to teach using such techniques, and because they were normalized, it is likely that such techniques have been reproduced as a result of our pre-service teacher education.[67]

This "going down the line" approach was also addressed in Chapter 5, through a vignette from Margaret Berg in which a music teacher wrestles with their decision to use or not use this practice. In the vignette, the music teacher uses core reflection strategies instead, to find ways to help students mentor, support, and help one another practice effectively.

Public shaming is just one example of a fear-based approach used in music education. Of course, there are others. And of course, music education is only a small part of a larger ecosystem where people experience different forms of symbolic violence every day. In Reflection Activity 9.8, I invite you to consider other types of fear-based motivation and what approaches might replace them.

Diffusing Fear through Bespoke Pedagogy in Composition and Songwriting

One approach to replacing fear and punishment is a bespoke pedagogy, where educational activities are customized for each student, with a celebration of their unique contributions and possibilities for learning.[68] Michele Kaschub describes a bespoke pedagogy in composition and songwriting as one that affords music teachers and students the space "to engage in an emergent curriculum and to honor the different ways that students communicate how they think and feel alongside what they know and can do."[69] Similar to caring *with* students through empathy, a bespoke pedagogy involves teachers studying their students to understand the various ways that they communicate and express themselves, and then to nurture the student's creativity in ways that are individually and uniquely meaningful. In a composition or songwriting context, it might mean that teachers:

- Listen perceptively and offer encouraging feedback;
- Offer to perform or play students' compositions to provide an outsider perspective on various challenges that the pieces might introduce;
- Compose or create alongside students to model the ups and downs of the process and how to work through challenges;

- Use a broad range of pedagogical and compositional techniques to meet various learners where they are and to foster student autonomy.[70]

Calling In and Calling On, Not Calling Out

Another form of public shaming is call-out or cancel culture, where people are publicly shamed for saying or doing something hateful. It is disheartening that the music education profession, especially music teacher education, is full of examples of public shaming in this way. For example, much like the students in Smith's "down the line" example above, I have found myself increasingly anxious when any of my deeply respected music education colleagues takes to social media to call out the wrong choices that someone else has made, rather than communicating in private with these individuals.

I often agree with the assertions that my colleagues make about hateful or hurtful behavior. However, when I witness public shaming—even if the person is not named—I feel a sense of separation from the person calling out, no matter how much I might hold them in esteem. I also feel a state of panic as I think: "Am I next? What have I done that is similar, and that someone else will point out to the world?"

The fear is the same as what I felt as a young child, in a music classroom, with heart pounding and mind racing as I witnessed classmates get singled out for disappointing the teacher. Such fear-based approaches did not help any of us in that class feel more creative or expressive, nor did they promote a sense of belonging or trust. I confess that many of these social media instances have similarly caused me to spend less time around those who call out, to not show up at certain events where there was a possibility for such public call-outs, or to even write less about the things I feel passionately about, simply because it felt safer to say nothing than to be publicly shamed for making mistakes while trying. I wonder how many people feel similar to how I do when they see such call-outs.

Black feminist scholar Loretta J. Ross explains that calling people out through social shaming guarantees one thing: "You've just invited them to a fight, not a conversation, because you are publicly humiliating them."[71] Ross further explains that calling people out leads us to "sabotage our own happiness" and make the world crueler than it needs to be."[72] Of course people who hold power should be held accountable for harm done to others. But matching hate with hate does not improve the situation. It is much more likely to perpetuate disconnection, stymie growth, and build resistance to change.[73]

Instead of calling out, we might practice *calling in*, as advocated by Ngọc Loan Trần, a Việt/mixed-race, disabled, queer writer who lives in the Southern United States.[74] Loretta J. Ross describes calling in as "a call out, done with love."[75] Calling in invites an authentic conversation with loving attention—something we all want and need. It provides a space for authentic conversation where micro- or macroaggressions can be discussed, through thoughtful dialogue such as with the nonviolent communication or microintervention strategies addressed in Chapters 3 and 7. Box 9f contains a few phrases Ross offers for starting a call-in conversation.

Box 9f Phrases for Starting a Call-In Conversation

- "I need to stop you there because something you just said is not accurate."
- "I'm having a reaction to that comment. Let's go back for a minute."
- "Do you think you would say that if someone from that group was with us in the room?"
- "There's some history behind that expression you just used that you might not know about."
- "In this class, we hold each other accountable. So we need to talk about why that joke isn't funny."*

*Loretta J. Ross, "Speaking Up without Tearing Down," *Teaching Tolerance* 61 (2019): 19–22, https://static1.squarespace.com/static/5acd28c45417fc580e6016ca/t/5ef66facf78dbd596217c732/1593208749026/Speaking + Up+Without + Tearing+Down + Article+%281%29.pdf.

In contrast to calling *out*, calling *in* on social media might include posts by people who use the space to be instructive, using a caring approach to provide examples of ways to see and honor one another. Calling someone *in* creates an opportunity for respect, love, and growth—something that is the backbone of caring education. Yet calling in requires that we dare to care enough to first assess ourselves, to question our motives. It involves assessing our own mental and emotional state, to determine if we are in a condition to devote time and energy to understanding and caring for someone else's complex emotions.

If we are not in a state to dedicate ourselves to someone else's growth, Ross encourages us to neither call out nor to call in. Instead, she invites us to *call on* someone else by simply inviting them to rephrase something they have said. After a simple question such as "I beg your pardon," followed by a period of waiting for a response, Ross suggests that most people will walk themselves back from hateful speech or behavior as they re-assess what they have said or done.[76]

I see correlations between a call-on approach and what we do as music teachers, such as when we invite students to try a passage or musical expression one more time before offering solutions, trusting that they have it in themselves to work it out on their own. Such call-on approach may afford people the creative space to work through their own growth because they are not in a defensive position such as they would be following a call-out attack. According to Ross, the courage to call in or call on rather than call out is more than worth it: "All we risk losing is our pain [. . .] Fighting hate should be fun. It's being a hater that sucks."[77]

Daring to Care, Daring to Care With, *Daring to Change*

Currently there is a societal debate about what it means to be responsible members of society, especially when it comes to doing one's job at work or at school. Some people suggest that responsible citizenship means putting your head down and doing the work you are asked to do, no matter what it is, whereas others believe that responsible citizenship means naming injustices and demanding better working and living conditions. Many people in the former group assert that life is difficult, and people need to learn to do difficult things. I agree wholeheartedly—yet in the spirit of care, there is a need to revisit many of the *ways* in which work is difficult, and we need to revisit many of the *reasons* work is difficult.

As I reflect on what I have learned from other OHCME authors, I envision that "daring to care" might mean that we don't just ask students to perform at their best—and if it doesn't happen, then simply repeat the same instructions again but louder. It might also mean that we don't threaten students with being inferior to others, assuming that doing so will magically create better results. Instead, I wonder if daring to care might mean that we reach out to those who don't show up or don't fulfill their obligations, find out what is going on in their world, and ask them what supports they need to be successful. As noted in Chapter 4 by Midwest Clinic performer Sundas Mohi-Truong, this kind of caring conversation takes time, but it can reap rewards that are worth far more than the investment.

I wonder if daring to care might mean that we don't simply mark someone as deficient on an assignment because they didn't turn it in—something I have admittedly done at times in my career, but something I am now reconsidering along with many other teachers based on what I am learning about student mental health.[78] Instead, daring to care might mean that we dare to look at ourselves and the contexts in which we work and live, and ask—along with our students—why it is that the students are not showing up, not turning in assignments, not practicing, not playing with more feeling when we invite them to do so, and so forth. During to care might mean that we dare to ask students directly about their behaviors and choices—not in a sarcastic way, but in a genuinely honest and authentic way, expecting that they will give us genuinely honest answers that may require us to do or be differently.

Some critics of this book might say that life does not work this way, and that we need to prepare people for life by showing students the consequences. I agree with the critical importance of teaching students about life's consequences. But from the lens of care, education is an ideal space[79] to support students through navigating those challenges, as well as creating a more sustainable, caring way of living.[80]

Daring to care might mean that we step in between actions and consequences to support students, to help them understand how to get from one step to another. More importantly, however, daring to care might mean that we co-construct a new reality and envision a world where we do not live our lives within logics of punishment, but rather centered in love and freedom.[81] I recall Box 2e in Chapter 2, where New York City music educator Martin Urbach suggests that

> [L]ove is something we can and must learn; after all, we are teachers. The transformative power of education lies in the symbiotic relationship between teacher and learner, and those labels apply to all in the relationship. We are to learn how to love, and we are to teach how to love.[82]

As several OHCME authors have asked: If not in music education, then where will we learn how to care in this way?

I believe it is imperative to change a culture where it is expected for musicians to endure anxiety, fear-based motivation, competitiveness, and even abuse to become experts in an art and craft intended to share, heal, and bring people together in community. Notions of innate talent and motivation are far too often used by teachers as an excuse to celebrate people who happen to learn, create, produce, perform, and engage in the same way that they do, while punishing and disempowering those who do not.[83] These are dangerous assumptions that continue to privilege and empower certain people at the expense of others. OHCME authors Guadalupe López Íñiguez and Heidi Westerlund advocate that we engage in *systems reflexivity*, including a willingness to question and challenge our own values and assumptions and the systems that reinforce them. They argue that "through such reflexivity it is possible to transform the entire education system so that it can recognize its unwanted outcomes—such as ableism, abuse, and elitism—and establish an agenda of care in music education."[84]

Daring to care suggests that we are willing to open ourselves up to how we might need to learn and change and be differently. As Tawnya Smith envisions for ecological music education:

> Practices that isolate must be replaced with practices that re-connect and promote belonging. Practices that reinforce self-interest within a system of invented hierarchies must be replaced with those that situate learners within a web of [. . .] relations. Practices that overshoot the capacity of the learner or harm those involved must be replaced with those that honor the limits of nature, including human nature. Practices that privilege the mind over the body, and at the expense of the body, must be replaced with a holistic approach.[85]

We might need to slow down and do less as an act of care—not as a means of expecting less from students, but expecting *more* in terms of quality, dignity, and authentic connection.

What these changes in practice might look like will be different in every context, with every set of co-learners. As this book illustrates, I do not believe in standardized "best practices" in music education—only fitting ones for different contexts and with different co-learners. As OHCME author Laura Benjamins suggests, we might face discomfort as we face unknown possibilities for music teaching, which will likely be different in every encounter with a co-learner.[86] Daring to care might allow us space to explore possibilities for change and increased connection as it befits each of us, in our unique circumstances.

It can be scary for us as music educators—especially if we have invested our whole lives into succeeding in the current system—to recognize that what we are doing might be harmful. It may even seem unfair to some to have had to endure abuse to "rise to the top," only to be told that rules are changing and the pedestal one worked so hard to climb is now crumbling. But things are indeed changing. Daring to care means recognizing that the path to expertise is a winding and never-ending road, and that the notion of "master" is fundamentally flawed. Daring to care means seeing students as equals who can help us learn how to teach better, live better, and do better.

By daring to care, we dare to transform ourselves. From a place of self-compassion and self-grounding, we can dare to care *with* students, as co-learners, toward change—not to change *them*, but to change *with* them in ways that are mutually healthy and sustainable. As the music teachers featured throughout this book suggest, such collaborative transformation can help us and our students work in whatever ways we can, in ways that befit our specific contexts, to transform the systems in which we work and live. In many ways the odds are against us. However, the efforts of many, when multiplied, can make an impact. As Patrick Schmidt writes, "The jury is out, but the path is promising."[87]

Conclusion

I return to the Oberlin advertisement with which I began this chapter—the audacious claim that one person can change the world. I do not believe that one person can do such work alone. I believe it is the "one" within the "we" where change takes place. The "one" is powerful when self-compassionate and self-grounded, when ready to engage with the "we," to band together—through honest and open dialogue, with a willingness to make tangible actions to transform self and surrounding systems.

In this precarious age of civil unrest, climate catastrophes, and concerns over physical and emotional health, it seems that we need care more fully and deeply than ever before—not just on an individual level from teacher to student, but in ways that extend to collective care for the common good. To rephrase words of climate activist Greta Thunberg, it is time to *care* "as if the house was on fire"[88]—not only to survive, but to thrive as a species. Care ethics offer a vision for individualized yet holistic, relational decision-making and change-making possibilities where we can be fully present with students and meet their needs in ways that matter most to them and to their communities, in music learning spaces and beyond.

Caring for, about, and with students can lead music teachers and learners beyond instances of self-actualization to that of "co-actualization," or collective thriving.[89] Nel Noddings asserts that happiness is the purpose of life, and that education should be a preparation for such a well-lived life.[90] The OHCME authors offer a further argument: Education is both a preparation for a well-lived life, and a distinctive and critical element of students' lived experiences in the present moment. "Real life" is already occurring all around music learners of all ages. If music is a reflection of life, then music education should not only prepare students for vocational success but support them—in the present—to experience collective thriving.

A Personal Reflection

It is impossible to articulate just how much I have learned about teaching, music, and care from this project, and from the OHCME authors and other teachers who have contributed ideas and practices to this book. As I close the final chapter it feels daunting to consider all the ways that my own teaching must change. I feel as though I know less about the details than I did when I started this project; at least I know now what I didn't know then. As I wrote earlier in this chapter about co-learning and co-constructed change, I feel that sense of vulnerability inside myself, to the extent that I no longer feel fully grounded or clear about the direction the changes in my own life and career might take. As I go back to my inner core and reground, I am satisfied that leaning into this feeling is my own version of daring to care. (See Reflection Activity 9.9.)

I am simultaneously thrilled and terrified as I consider what *Daring to Care* means for me as a teacher and co-learner, but I am excited to find out where the path might go. I hope that this book might offer a few ideas for other music teachers too, in your efforts to not only practice care with your students, but to similarly care for yourselves. In this space of caring, perhaps we may all be better positioned to continually revisit our pedagogical practices and priorities toward co-actualization, and to foster meaningful, authentic connections in all the ways that music makes possible.

Reflection Activities

9.1. Consider each of the costs associated with change-making, as described by Patrick Schmidt. Which of these do you resonate with? How might you go about working through those costs in your own life and work?

9.2. As you study the Compass of Compassion-Based Activism, allow yourself the space to envision the importance of returning within yourself and regrounding as you engage in each of these steps.

9.3. After completing the reflection activities provided by Emily Good-Perkins, construct your own set of reflection questions. What do you need to learn to improve yourself and your practice?

9.4. Using this book's index, revisit the following terms as they appear throughout the book: trust, mature empathy, unselved and ecological humility, authenticity, and vulnerability. How might each of these qualities help you engage in change with other co-learners?

9.5. Revisit each of the costs associated with change-making, as described by Patrick Schmidt. How might each of these play a role in terms of your willingness to risk vulnerability with co-learners?

9.6. What are specific concerns that your students care about? How might you work with your students to engage in conversation and action related to these concerns?

9.7. Consider your most beloved form of music-making. How might you envision it as even more ecological and life-giving?

9.8. What are commonly used forms of fear-based motivation in music education? What are some practices that might replace them?

9.9. What is your own version of "daring to care"? What terrifies and excites you about your future as a music teacher?

9.10. Create a playlist that reflects your experiences while reading each chapter of this book. If you are reading this book in a group, share your playlists with one another and explain your reasons for choosing the songs you did. After you have shared these with others, I invite you to take a look at mine, which is available using the QR code in Figure 9.3.

Figure 9.3 QR Code for Karin's *Daring to Care* Playlist.

Notes

1. Kameron Dunbar, "In Praise of One Person," Oberlin Blogs, January 19, 2018, https://www.oberlin.edu/blogs/praise-one-person.
2. Dunbar, "In Praise of One Person."
3. Gert J. J. Biesta, "Trying to Be at Home in the World: New Parameters for Art Education," *Artlink* 39, no. 3 (2019): 17; As cited in Graça Mota, "In Search of Meaning, Joy, and Justice in Music Education: Teachers Matter," in *The Oxford Handbook of Care in Music Education*, ed. Karin S. Hendricks (New York: Oxford University Press, 2023), 558.
4. Biesta, "Trying to Be at Home in the World."
5. Mota, "In Search of Meaning," 559; see also Ed Sarath, *Black Music Matters: Jazz and the Transformation of Music Studies* (Lanham, MD: Rowman & Littlefield, 2018).
6. Patrick Schmidt, "Policy Practice as Citizenship Building: From Duty to Care to Solidarity in Music Education," in *The Oxford Handbook of Care in Music Education*, ed. Karin S. Hendricks (New York: Oxford University Press, 2023), 583.
7. Schmidt, "Policy Practice as Citizenship Building."
8. Susan O'Neill, "Foreword to Section 3: Caring for Wellbeing and Human Flourishing," in *The Oxford Handbook of Care in Music Education*, ed. Karin S. Hendricks (New York: Oxford University Press, 2023), 304.
9. Kari Holdhus, "Conveying Pupil Access to Wellbeing through Relational Care in Music Education," in *The Oxford Handbook of Care in Music Education*, ed. Karin S. Hendricks (New York: Oxford University Press, 2023), 426.
10. Jorgensen, "Caring for Music Education in Troubled Times," 28.
11. Rebecca D. Swanson and Mary L. Cohen, "Music-Making in Prisons and Schools: Dismantling Carceral Logics," in *The Oxford Handbook of Care in Music Education*, ed. Karin S. Hendricks (New York: Oxford University Press, 2023), 517–529; see also Frank Rogers, *Practicing Compassion* (Washington, DC: Fresh Air Books, 2015); Frank Rogers, "Warriors of Compassion: Coordinates on the Compass of Compassion-Based Activism," in *Taking It to the Streets: Public Theologies of Activism and Resistance*, ed. Jennifer Baldwin (Lanham, MD: Rowman & Littlefield, 2018), 25–42.
12. Swanson and Cohen, "Music-Making in Prisons and Schools," 519; see also Kristin Neff, "Self-Compassion: An Alternative Conceptualization of a Healthy Attitude toward Oneself," *Self and Identity* 2, no. 2 (2003): 85–101,

https://doi.org/10.1080/15298860309032; Kristin Neff, *Fierce Self-Compassion: How Women Can Harness Kindness to Speak Up, Claim Their Power, and Thrive* (New York: HarperCollins Publishers, 2021).
13. Swanson and Cohen, "Music-Making in Prisons and Schools," 519; see also Neff, "Self-Compassion," Neff, *Fierce Self-Compassion*.
14. Michele Kaschub, "Marginalized No More: Composition in Music Education," in *The Oxford Handbook of Music Composition Pedagogy*, ed. Michele Kaschub (New York: Oxford University Press, 2024), 19.
15. Kaschub, 'Marginalized No More," 3–24.
16. Kaschub, 'Marginalized No More."
17. https://www.centerforengagedcompassion.com/rogers.html. See also Rogers, *Practicing Compassion*; Rogers, "Warriors of Compassion."
18. Swanson and Cohen, "Music-Making in Prisons and Schools," 520; see also Rogers, "Warriors of Compassion."
19. Swanson and Cohen, "Music-Making in Prisons and Schools."
20. Lauren Kapalka Richerme, "Vulnerable Experiences in Music Education: Possibilities and Problems for Growth and Connectivity," *Bulletin of the Council for Research in Music Education* 209 (2016): 27–42; see also Brené Brown, *Daring Greatly: How the Courage to Be Vulnerable Transforms the Way We Live, Love, Parent, and Lead* (New York: Gotham Books, 2012).
21. Schmidt, "Policy Practice as Citizenship Building."
22. Karin S. Hendricks, *Compassionate Music Teaching: A Framework for Motivation and Engagement in the 21st Century* (Lanham, MD: Rowman & Littlefield, 2018); Parker J. Palmer, *The Courage to Teach* (Hoboken, NJ: Jossey-Bass, 2007).
23. Richerme, "Vulnerable Experiences in Music Education."
24. Richerme, "Vulnerable Experiences in Music Education."
25. See Kelly Bylica, "Critical Listening and Authorial Agency as Radical Practices of Care," in *The Oxford Handbook of Care in Music Education*, ed. Karin S. Hendricks (New York: Oxford University Press, 2023), 482–493; Karin S. Hendricks and Juliet Hess, "Troubling Empathy in Music Education: Pathways and Pitfalls," *Bulletin of the Council for Research in Music Education* 239 (2024): 7–25, https://doi.org/10.5406/21627223.239.01.
26. Panagiotis A. Kanellopoulos, "Care-ing in the Musical Pedagogical Moment: Navigating Challenges," in *The Oxford Handbook of Care in Music Education*, ed. Karin S. Hendricks (New York: Oxford University Press, 2023), 3.
27. Rachel Dirks, personal communication, February 14, 2024.
28. Swanson and Cohen, "Music-Making in Prisons and Schools," 524.
29. See Mitchell, "Music's Relational Imperative: Wellbeing, Music-Making, and the Interconnections between Music Therapy and Music Education," in *The Oxford Handbook of Care in Music Education*, ed. Karin S. Hendricks (New York: Oxford University Press, 2023), 361–372.
30. Liz Lerman and John Borstel, *Liz Lerman's Critical Response Process: A Method for Getting Useful Feedback on Anything You Make, from Dance to Dessert* (Tacoma Park, MD: Dance Exchange, 2003), as cited in Swanson and Cohen, "Music-Making in Prisons and Schools."
31. See https://nativeamericanconcepts.wordpress.com/walking-in-beauty/.
32. Personal communication, March 7, 2024.
33. https://www.laurencecole.com/album/do-the-best-you-can/, accessed March 7, 2024.
34. Swanson and Cohen, "Music-Making in Prisons and Schools," 526.
35. Nel Noddings, *Caring: A Feminine Approach to Ethics and Moral Education* (Berkeley: University of California Press, 1984).
36. Tawnya D. Smith, *Healing the Fragmentation of Psyche, Society, and Nature within Music Education: A Radical Ecopsychological Approach* (Routledge, under contract).
37. Randall Everett Allsup and Cathy Benedict. "The Problems of Band: An Inquiry into the Future of Instrumental Music Education," *Philosophy of Music Education Review* 16, no. 2 (2008): 156–173; Karin S. Hendricks, Tawnya D. Smith, and Jennifer Stanuch, "Creating Safe Spaces for Music Learning," *Music Educators Journal* 101, no. 1 (2014): 35–40; Tawnya D. Smith, *Healing the Fragmentation*.
38. C. Victor Fung, "Ways of Caring in Music Education through the Lens of Classic Confucianism and Classic Daoism," in *The Oxford Handbook of Care in Music Education*, ed. Karin S. Hendricks (New York: Oxford University Press, 2023), 136–137.
39. For example, see Karin S. Hendricks, *Relationships between the Sources of Self-Efficacy and Changes in Competence Perceptions of Music Students during an All-State Orchestra Event* (PhD diss., University of Illinois, 2009); Karin S. Hendricks, "The Philosophy of Shinichi Suzuki: 'Music Education as Love Education,'" *Philosophy of Music Education Review* 19, no. 2 (2011): 136–154; Karin S. Hendricks, "Changes in Self-Efficacy Beliefs over Time: Contextual Influences of Gender, Rank-Based Placement, and Social Support in a Competitive Orchestra Environment," *Psychology of Music* 42, no. 3 (2014), 347–365, https://doi.org/10.1177/0305735612471238; Hendricks, Smith, and Stanuch, "Creating Safe Spaces for Music Learning"; Karin S. Hendricks, Tawnya D. Smith, and Allen R. Legutki, "Competitive Comparison in Music: Influences upon Self-Efficacy Belief by Gender," *Gender and Education* 28, no. 7 (2016): 918–934, https://doi.org/10.1080/09540253.2015.1107032;Hendricks, *Compassionate Music Teaching*.

40. Casey McGrath, Karin S. Hendricks, and Tawnya D. Smith, *Performance Anxiety Strategies* (Lanham, MD: Rowman & Littlefield, 2016).
41. Sean Robert Powell, "Competition, Ideology, and the One-Dimensional Music Program," *Action, Criticism and Theory for Music Education* 20, no. 3 (2021): 19–43.
42. Hendricks, *Compassionate Music Teaching;* Jordan Stern, "Marching on an Uneven Field," in *Sociological Thinking in Music Education: International Intersections*, ed. Carol Frierson-Campbell, Clare Hall, Sean Robert Powell, and Guillermo Rosabal-Coto (New York: Oxford University Press, 2022), 117; Jordan Stern "Correlations between Socioeconomic Status and Scores at a Marching Band Contest," *Journal of Band Research* 56, no. 2 (2021): 1–75.
43. Powell, "Competition, Ideology, and the One-Dimensional Music Program."
44. Karin S. Hendricks, "Authentic Connection in Music Education: A Chiastic Essay," in *Authentic Connection: Music, Spirituality, and Wellbeing*, ed. Karin S. Hendricks and Joyce Boyce-Tillman (New York: Peter Lang, 2021), 237–253.
45. Tawnya D. Smith, *Healing the Fragmentation*.
46. June Boyce-Tillman, "Towards an Ecology of Music Education," *Philosophy of Music Education Review* 12, no. 2 (2004): 102–125; Tawnya D. Smith, *Healing the Fragmentation*.
47. Schmidt, "Policy Practice as Citizenship Building," 581.
48. Boyce-Tillman, "The Hospitality of Wonder and Its Relation to Care and Compassion in Music Education," in *The Oxford Handbook of Care in Music Education*, ed. Karin S. Hendricks (New York: Oxford University Press, 2023), 79–90; Kevin Shorner-Johnson, Martha Gonzalez, and Daniel J. Shevock, "*Convivencias* and a Web of Care," in *The Oxford Handbook of Care in Music Education*, ed. Karin S. Hendricks (New York: Oxford University Press, 2023), 69–78; Tawnya D. Smith, "Caring with the Earth, Community, and Co-Learners for the Health of Biological, Social, and Musical Ecosystems," in *The Oxford Handbook of Care in Music Education*, ed. Karin S. Hendricks (New York: Oxford University Press, 2023), 141–152.
49. Boyce-Tillman, "Towards an Ecology of Music Education."
50. Boyce-Tillman, "Towards an Ecology of Music Education"; Shorner-Johnson et al., "*Convivencias* and a Web of Care," 69; Tawnya D. Smith, "Caring with the Earth."
51. Tawnya D. Smith, "Caring with the Earth," 145.
52. Tawnya D. Smith, "An Ecofeminist Vision of Music Education: Resisting the Intertwining Logics of Domination," in *The Oxford Handbook of Feminism in Music Education*, ed. Marissa Silverman and Nasim Niknafs (New York: Oxford University Press, in press).
53. Stern, "Marching on an Uneven Field"; Stern, "Correlations between Socioeconomic Status and Scores at a Marching Band Contest."
54. Corey Seemiller and Meghan Grace, *Generation Z: A Century in the Making* (New York, NY: Routledge, 2018).
55. Hendricks, "Relationships between the Sources of Self-Efficacy and Changes in Competence Perceptions."
56. John Findlay and Karin S. Hendricks, "Seating Assignments: Are They Necessary?" *Utah Music Educators Journal* 57, no. 1 (Fall 2011): 30–32.
57. For additional ideas, see Louis S. Bergonzi, "'Whadya Get?': Evaluation, Recognition, Motivation, Competition, and School Orchestra Programs," in *Teaching Music through Performance in Orchestra*, ed. David Littrell (Chicago: GIA, 2003), 15–39.
58. Tawnya D. Smith, "Caring with the Earth."
59. Hendricks, *Compassionate Music Teaching*.
60. Bergonzi, "Whadya Get?"
61. Andrew Goodrich, *Peer Mentoring in Music Education: Developing Effective Student Leadership* (Oxfordshire: Taylor & Francis, 2022).
62. Tammy S. Yi, "Alternative Seating Practices: Pedagogy of the Back of the Orchestra," *Music Education Research*, 25, no. 2 (2023): 190–204, https://doi.org/10.1080/14613808.2023.2187042.
63. Yi, "Alternative Seating Practices."
64. Jessica Billings-White, personal communication, February 24, 2024.
65. For example, see Karin S. Hendricks, "Relationships between the Sources of Self-Efficacy and Changes in Competence."
66. McGrath, Hendricks, and Smith, *Performance Anxiety Strategies*.
67. Tawnya D. Smith, *Healing the Fragmentation*.
68. Robyn Thomas Pitts, "Bespoke Learning," *Curriculum and Teaching Dialogue* 25, nos. 1–2 (2023): 217.
69. Kaschub, "Marginalized No More," 10.
70. Michele Kaschub and Janice P. Smith, *Experiencing Music Composition in Grades K-2* (Lanham MD: Rowman & Littlefield, 2022).
71. Loretta J. Ross, "Don't Call People Out—Call Them In," August 2021, Monterey, TED Talk, 14:05, https://www.ted.com/talks/loretta_j_ross_don_t_call_people_out_call_them_in.
72. Jessica Bennett, "What if Instead of Calling People Out, We Called Them In?" *New York Times* (New York), November 19, 2020.
73. Bennett, "What if Instead of Calling People Out, We Called Them In?"

74. Ngoc Loan Tran, "Callin IN: A Less Disposable Way of Holding Each Other Accountable," *BGD* (Blog), December 18, 2013, https://www.bgdblog.org/2013/12/calling-less-disposable-way-holding-accountable/.
75. Ross, "Don't Call People Out—Call Them In," 5:56.
76. Ross, "Don't Call People Out—Call Them In," 9:10.
77. Ross, "Don't Call People Out—Call Them In," 14:05.
78. Juliet Hess, "Madness and Distress in Music Education: A Mad-Affirming Approach," in *Madness and Distress in Music Education*, ed. Juliet Hess (New York: Routledge, 2024), 1–23.
79. Noddings, *Caring*.
80. Swanson and Cohen, "Music-Making in Prisons and Schools."
81. Swanson and Cohen, "Music-Making in Prisons and Schools."
82. Gareth Dylan Smith, Brandi Waller-Pace, Martin Urbach, and Bryan Powell, "Love, Care, Revolution, and Justice: Loving Oneself and Loving One's Students," in *The Oxford Handbook of Care in Music Education*, ed. Karin S. Hendricks (New York: Oxford University Press, 2023), 501.
83. Karin S. Hendricks and Gary E. McPherson, "Reconsidering Musical Ability Development through the Lens of Diversity and Bias," in *The Oxford Handbook of Care in Music Education*, ed. Karin S. Hendricks (New York: Oxford University Press, 2023), 408–420; Guadalupe López Íñiguez and Heidi Westerlund, "The Politics of Care in the Education of Children Gifted for Music: A Systems View," in The Oxford Handbook of Care in Music Education, ed. Karin S. Hendricks (New York: Oxford University Press, 2023), 115–129.
84. López Íñiguez and Westerlund, "The Politics of Care," 117–118.
85. Tawnya D. Smith, "Intersections of EcoJustice Education, Radical Ecopsychology, and Music Education: A Framework toward Justice, Wellbeing, and Resilience," *Diskussion Musikpädagogik* 102 (2024), Article 2. https://www.junker-verlag.com/dmp-102-o-b.
86. Laura Benjamins, "Caring through Dialogical Relations in Community Music Settings," in *The Oxford Handbook of Care in Music Education*, ed. Karin S. Hendricks (New York: Oxford University Press, 2023), 103–114.
87. Schmidt, "Policy Practice as Citizenship Building," 590.
88. Greta Thunberg, "'I Want You to Panic': 16-Year Old Issues Climate Warning at Davos," *Guardian News*, January 25, 2019, YouTube Video, 2:53, https://www.youtube.com/watch?v=RjsLm5PCdVQ.
89. Mitchell, "Music's Relational Imperative"; see also Renate Motschnig-Pitrik and Godfrey Barrett-Lennard, "Co-Actualization: A New Construct in Understanding Well-Functioning Relationships," *Journal of Humanistic Psychology* 50, no. 3 (2010): 374–398, https://doi.org/10.1177/0022167809348017.
90. Noddings, *Caring*.

Afterword

We have reached the end of the *Daring to Care* journey. I have had the honor of accompanying you while sharing a small fraction of what I have learned from *Oxford Handbook of Care in Music Education* (OHCME) authors along the way. In the spirit of caring *with*, it seems appropriate to end this book with a few general ideas that I have learned while collaborating with OHCME authors and other music teachers who were spotlighted throughout this book.

Here are 20 notable ideas that I have learned about care through this project:

1. Caring takes time and energy. But it may create more of both than it ever required.
2. One of the best ways to overcome loneliness is to reach out to others.
3. Empathy is neither good nor bad. It's how we use it that makes the difference.
4. Empathy can help us connect with others, although we will never fully understand someone else's experience.
5. The path to musical development changes before you get where you are going.
6. Identity is multifarious, multifaceted, and ever changing—yet identity responsiveness is the key to care. Therefore, care must also be continually flexible and emergent.
7. Trauma-informed approaches can be helpful for all music students and teachers, and they do not require teachers to know students' individual trauma histories or to cross professional boundaries by taking on therapy roles that teachers are not trained for.
8. Apologies make us feel vulnerable, but they are the cornerstone of lasting relationships.
9. Humans share a common trait of having bias against people who are different.
10. Letting go of being the authority can elicit deeper and more authentic respect.
11. People trust you more when you are honest about what you don't know.
12. Unselved or ecological humility isn't about comparison to others. It's about understanding how we fit.
13. Trust is rarely noticed until it is lost. Yet when caring *with*, it is critical to start with trust, build trust, maintain trust, and work at the speed of trust.

Daring to Care with Music Education. Karin S. Hendricks, Oxford University Press. © Oxford University Press 2025.
DOI: 10.1093/9780197777589.003.0010

14. Conduct less, and students watch more.
15. Direct less, and students will likely do more.
16. Musicians and music teachers embody caring through creativity, improvisation, and accompaniment.
17. In music technique as well as life, intense gripping leads to weakness; yet it doesn't take strength to let go of control. Balancing flexibility and authority brings resonance and connection.
18. Microaffirmations have a macro effect.
19. Those who care, care. But most of us have to learn how.
20. Just as many drops of water can erode rock over time, acts of flexible and gentle care from many of us—through individual and collective efforts—can lead to powerful and lasting change in our field and perhaps even in our world.

I finished these final words at the beach on Cape Cod bay, as the sun set on a clear, cold, winter day. I thought of you while walking along the shore. I imagined that you might want a picture of the scene I had while reflecting on how much I have learned from the process of editing the OHCME and writing *Daring to Care*. Figure 10.1 is for you.

This picture illustrates the power of many collective drops of water, making waves and channels through the sand. After I took the picture, I stayed at the ocean and watched as the waves rippled in and out, consistently and persistently yet never

Figure 10.1 The sun sets on this book project, but our collective work continues.

the same. It reminded me of how caring evokes a constant process of reciprocity, responsiveness, and continual evolution.

I am a different person than when I began this book, with deeper expectations for myself about caring for, about, and with others. At the same time, I must heed the advice of OHCME authors and remember to practice self-compassion while changing those things that are within my control and advocating for a better world. I hope the same for you.

After writing about reciprocal and responsive caring *with*, I recognize even more fully how much each of us learns from one another: book editor and contributors, book author and readers, colleagues, students, administrators, members of our broader music learning communities—all as co-learners. In that spirit of reciprocity and responsiveness, I invite your thoughts about the takeaways you had from this experience. Which OHCME chapters did you seek out for a deeper dive? What questions do you have about care and music education after this experience? What further ideas do you have to share? I hope for a continued dialogue where we can learn with one another in the future. Thank you for coming on this journey with me.

As always, take care.

Index

For the benefit of digital users, indexed terms that span two pages (e.g., 52–53) may, on occasion, appear on only one of those pages.

Boxes are indicated by an italic *b* following the page number.